TARADIDDLE

CHARLES H. TRAUB

essay by
DAVID CAMPANY

Charles H. Traub
Taradiddle

Designed by David Schorr

Published by Damiani srl
info@damianieditore.com
www.damianieditore.com

Printed in May 2018 by Grafiche Damiani – Faenza Group SpA, Italy.

ISBN 978-88-6208-621-9

tar′a•did•dle (tă rĕ dĭ dl) ***n.*** 1.petty lie 2.pretentious nonsense

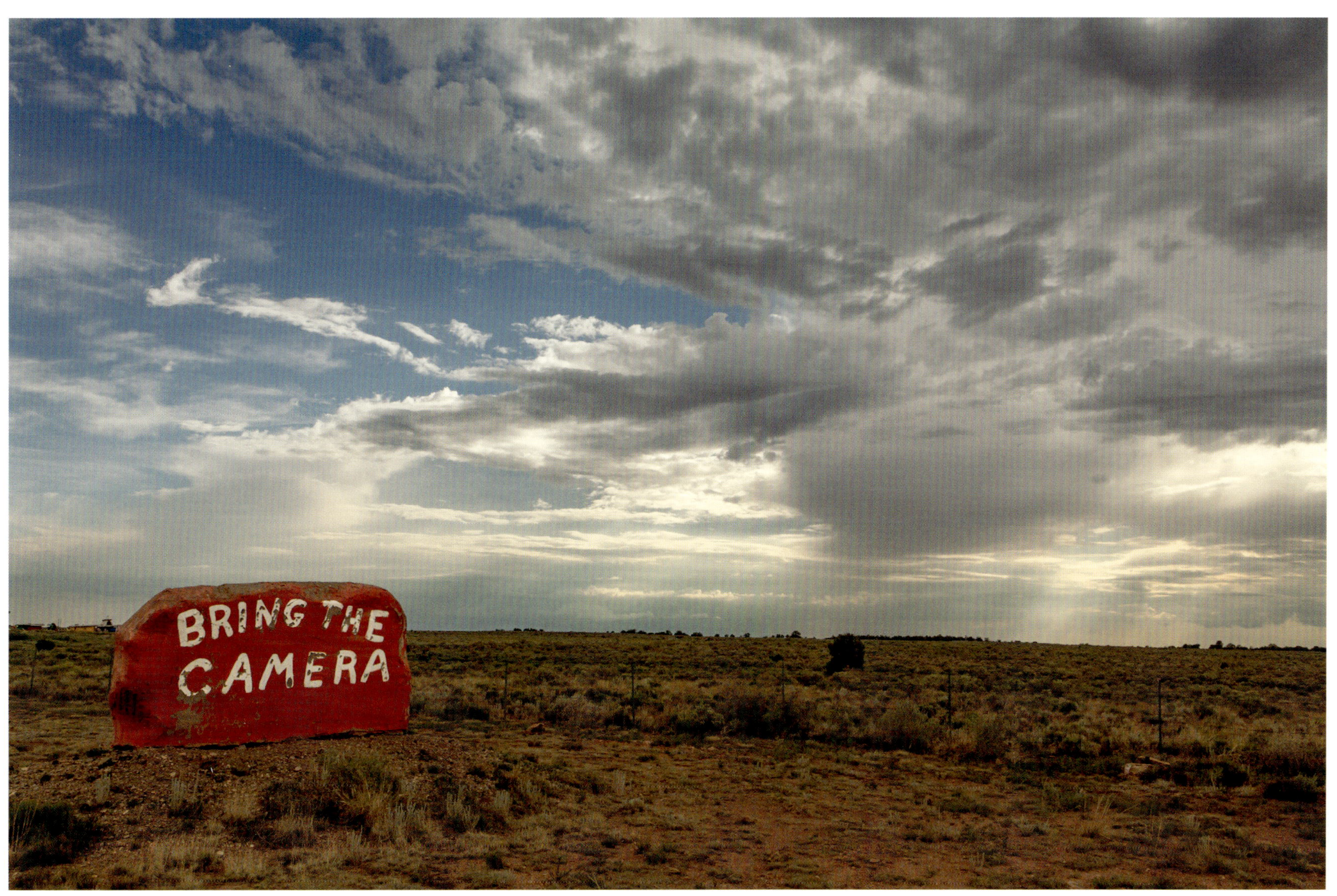
BRING THE
CAMERA

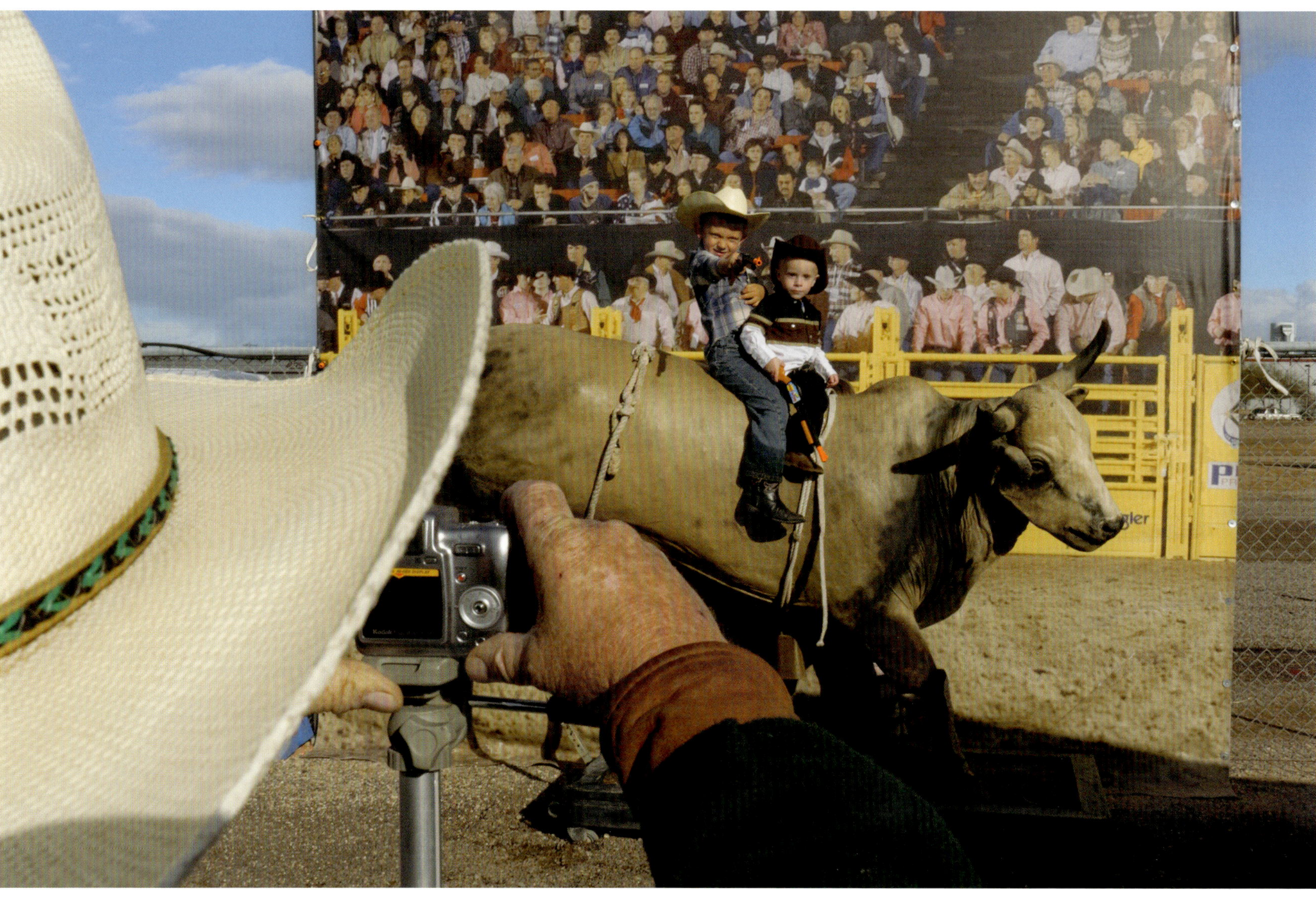

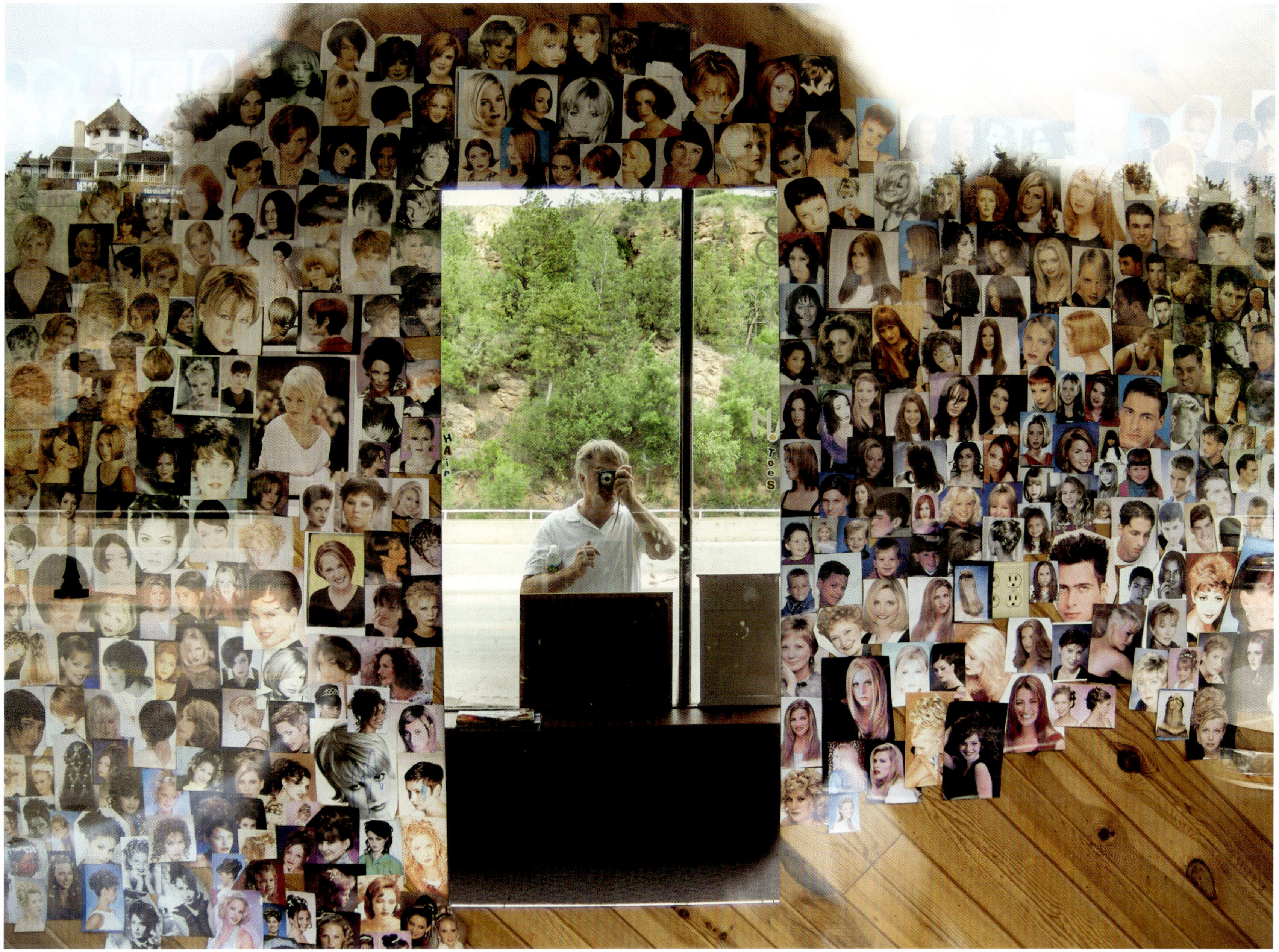

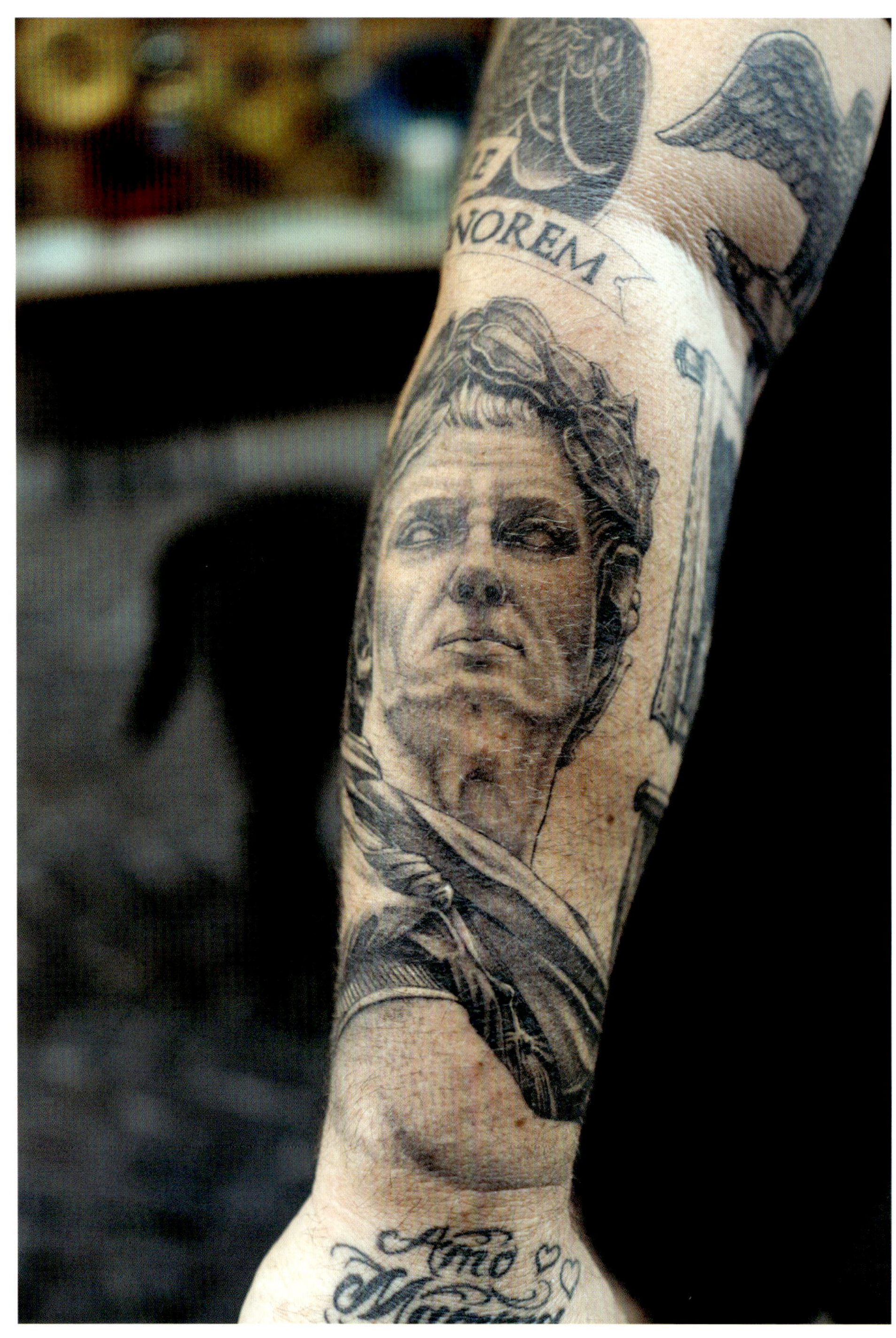
NOREM
Amo

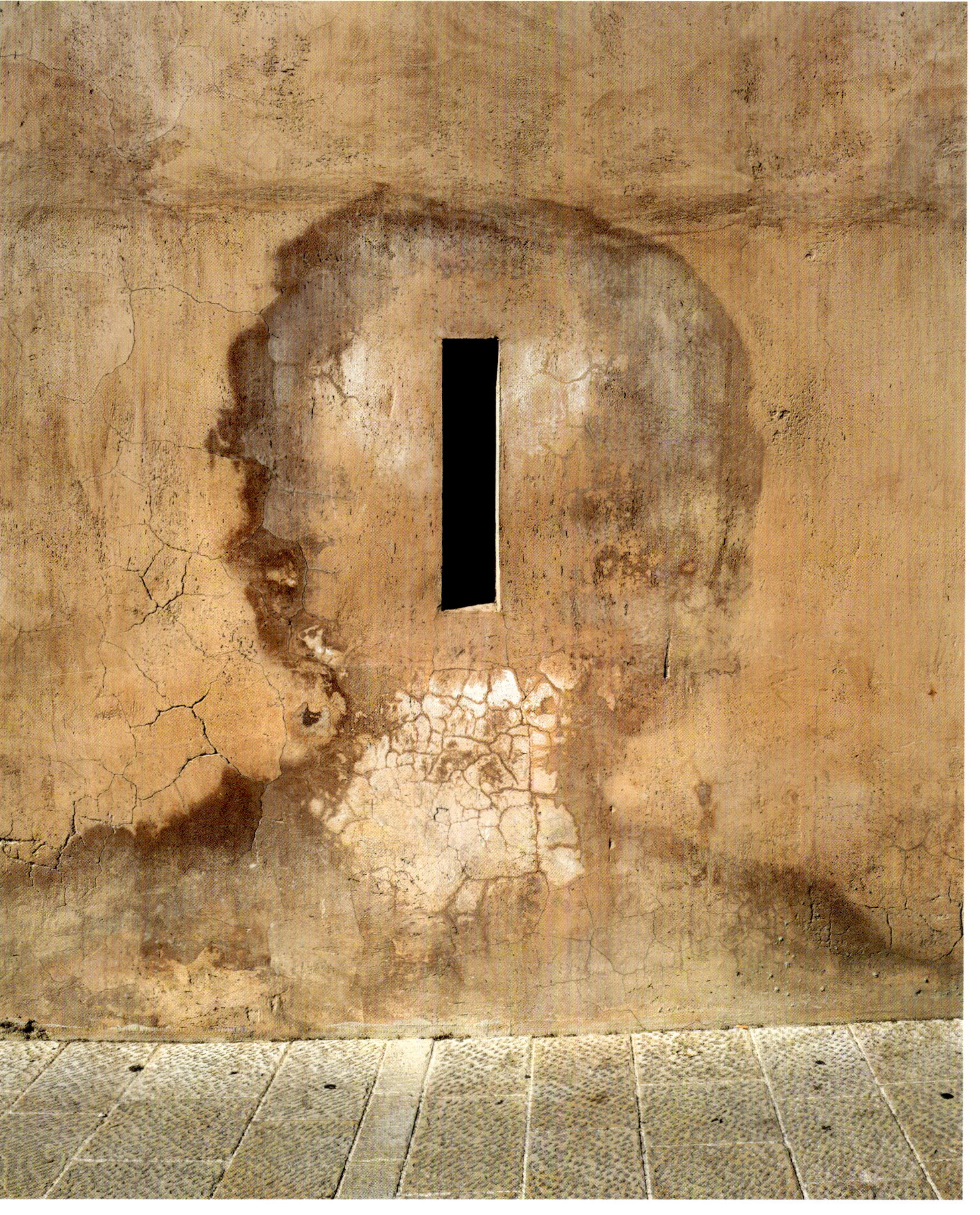

6

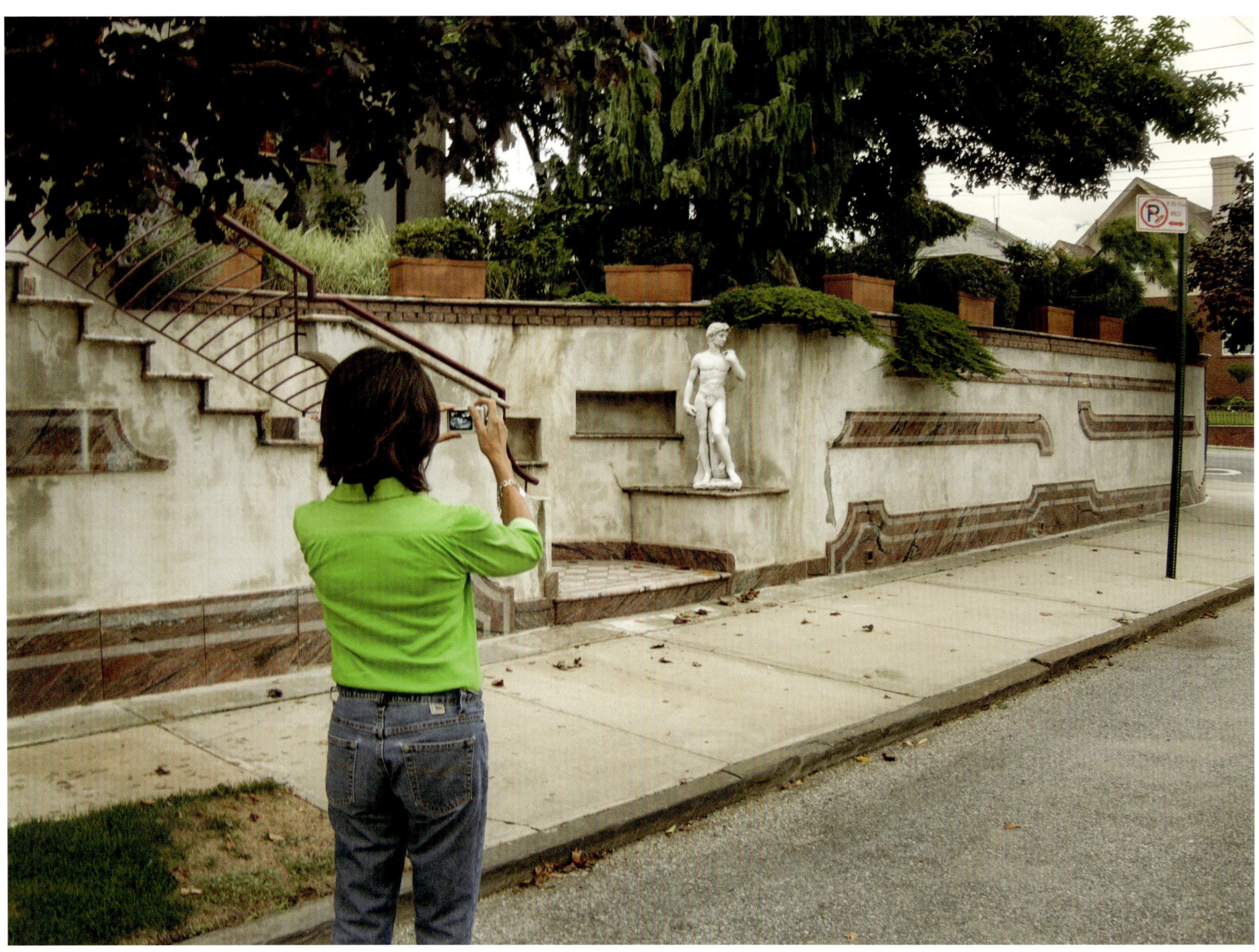

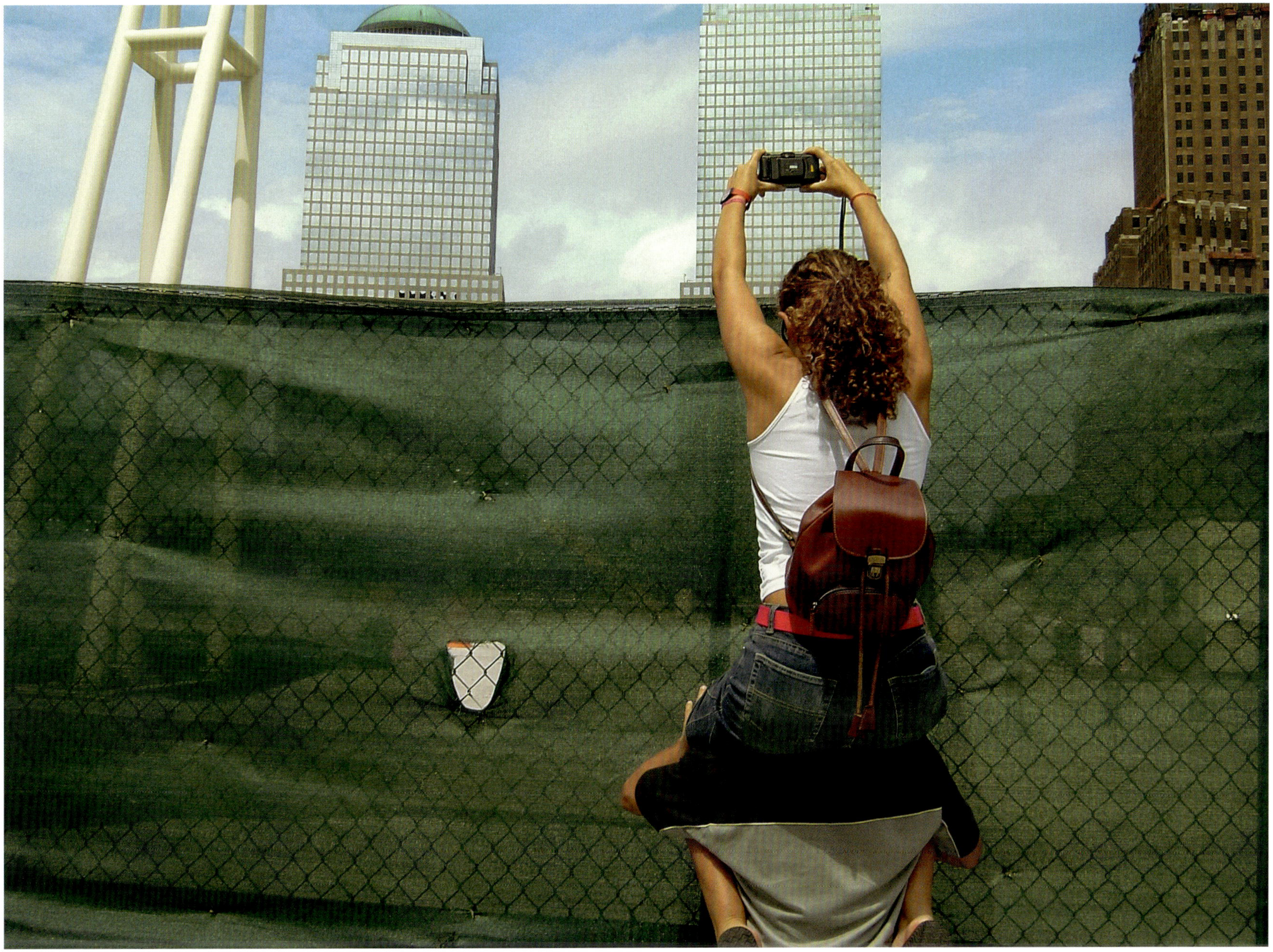

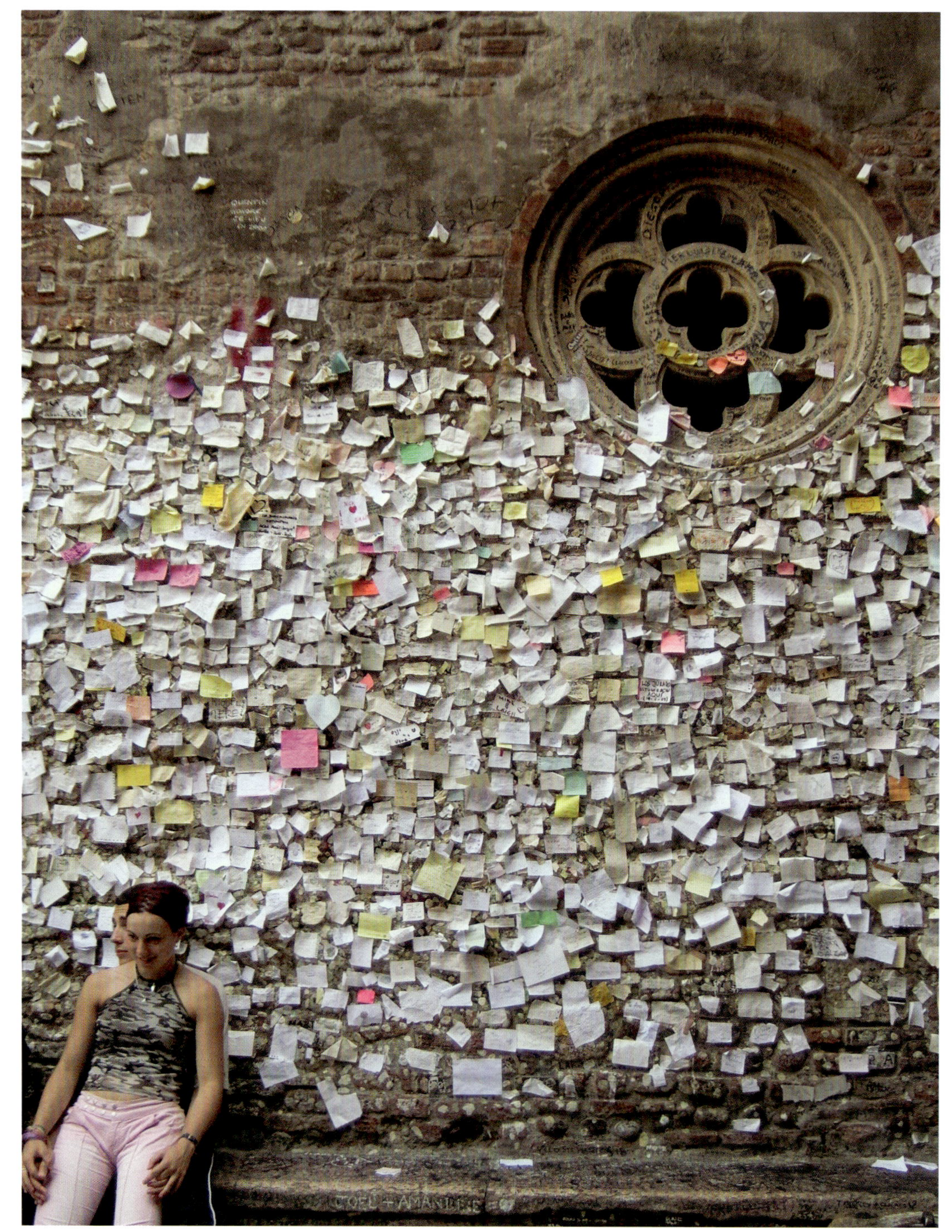

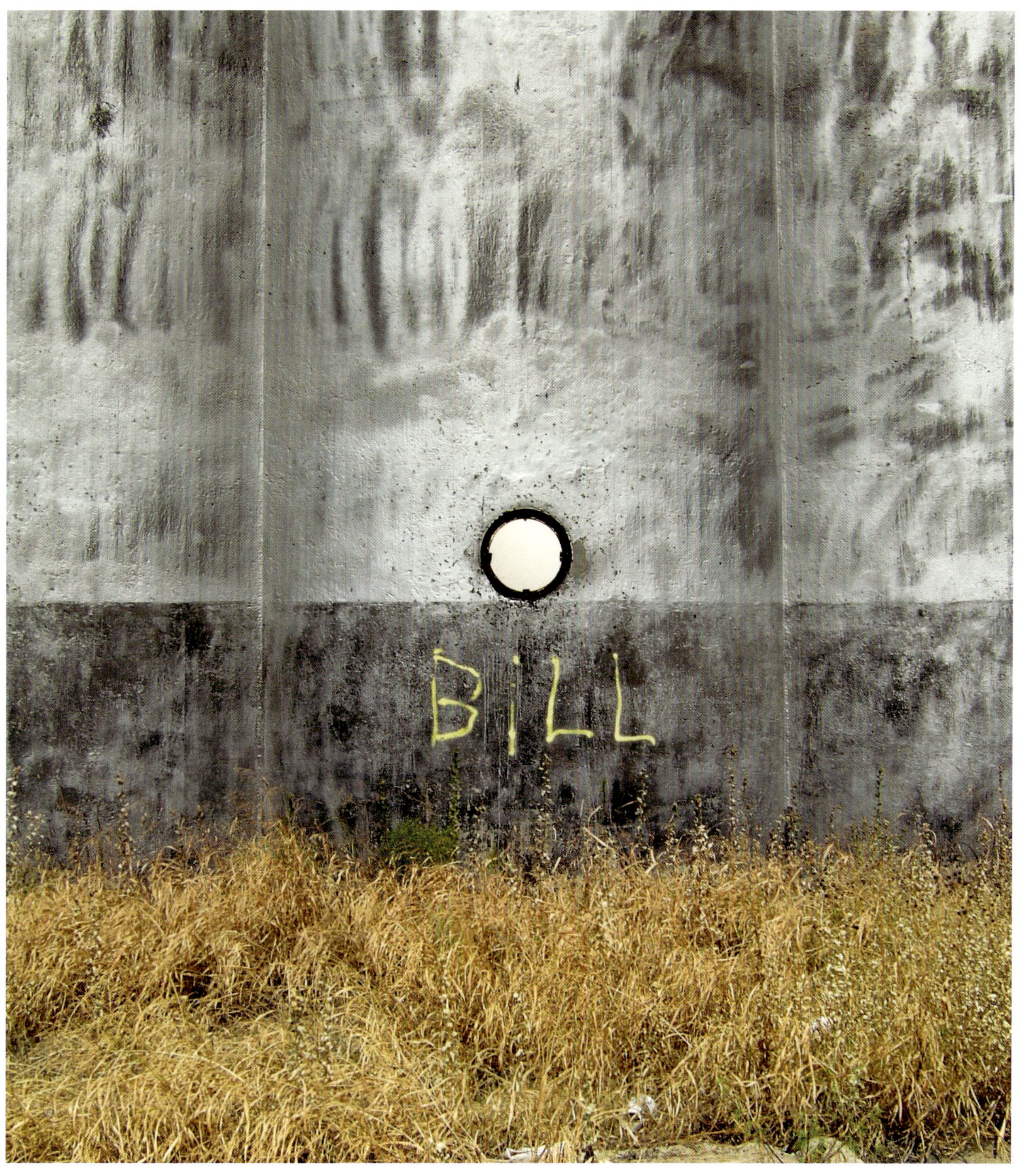
BiLL

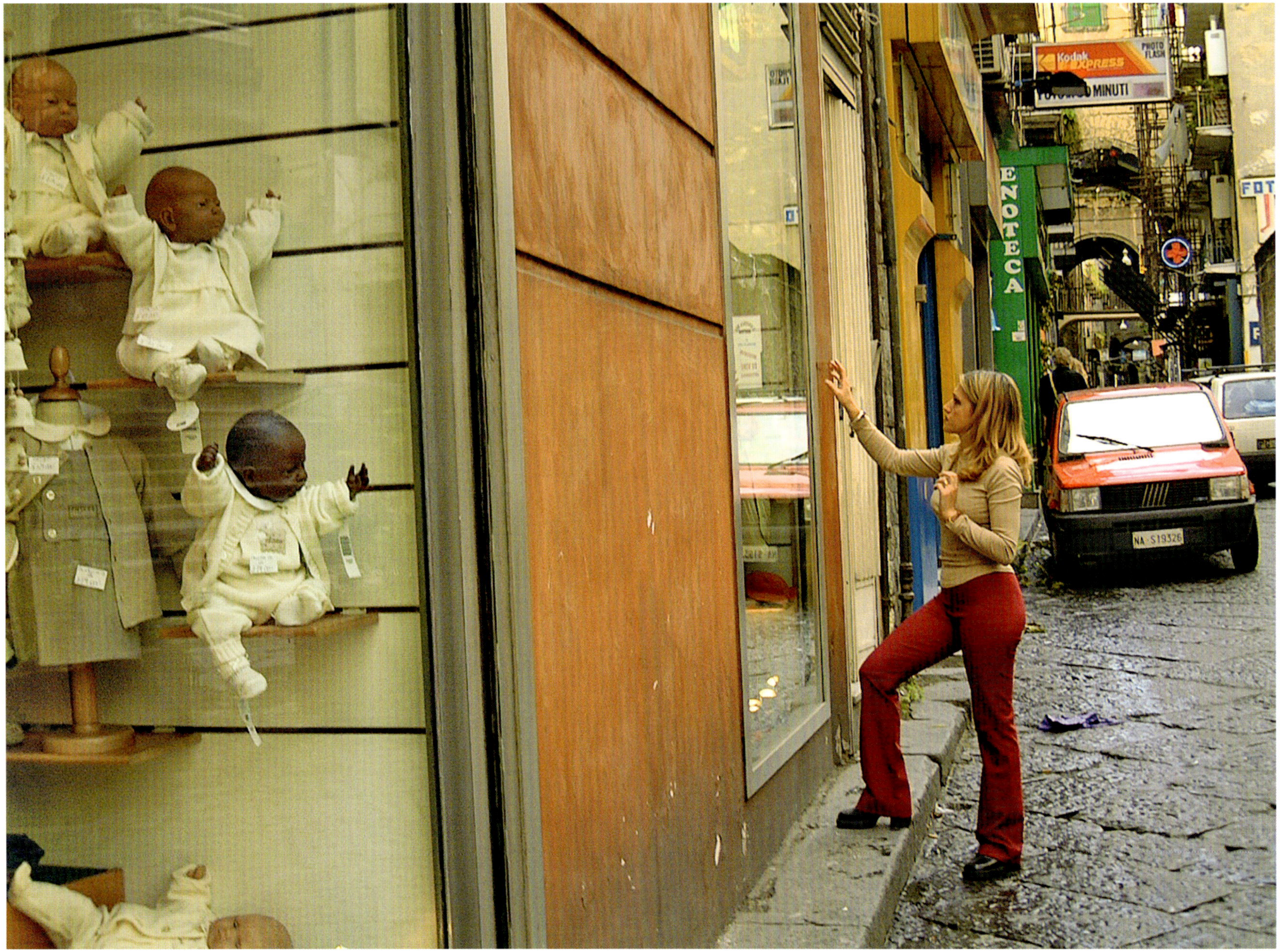

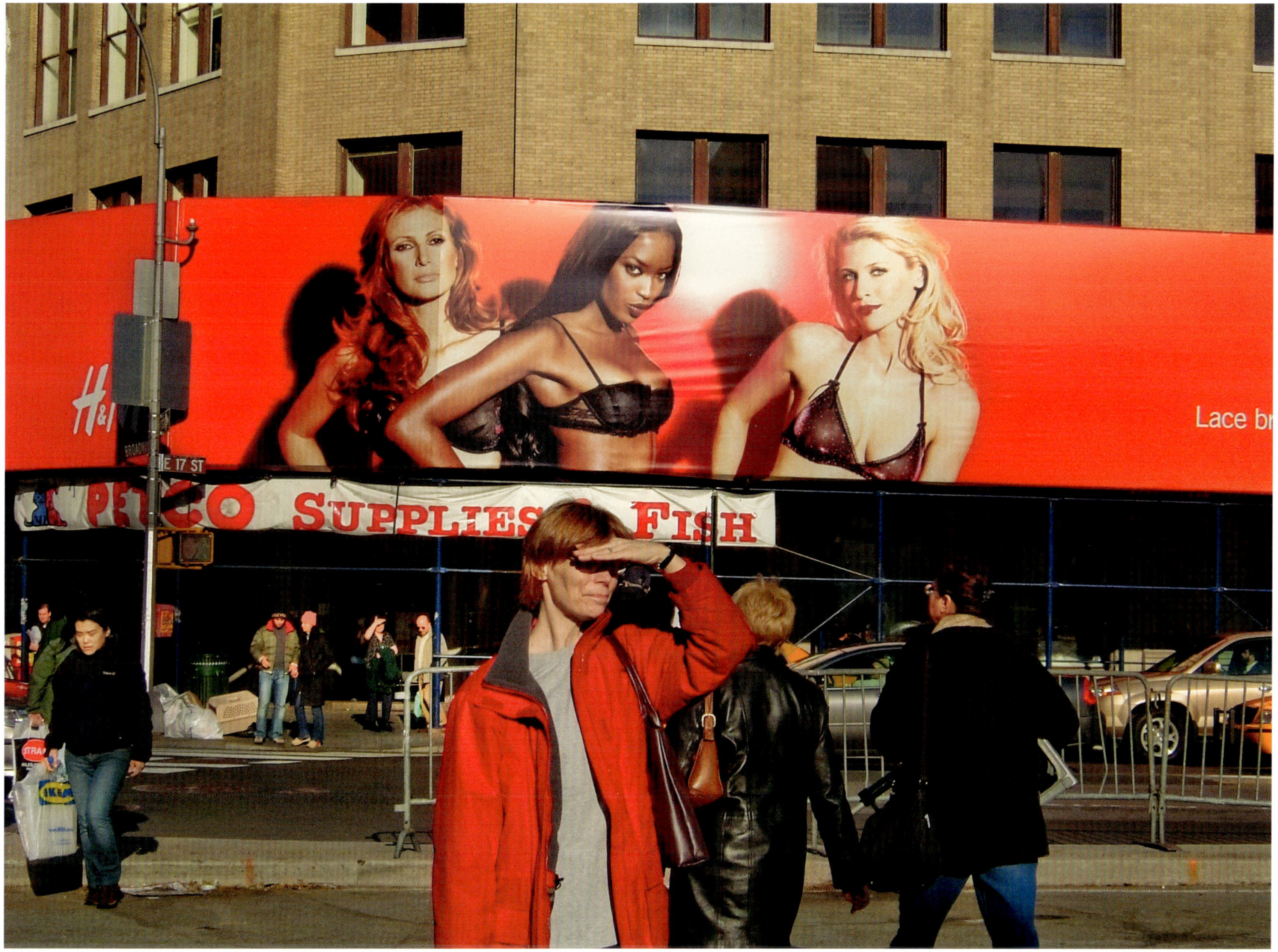

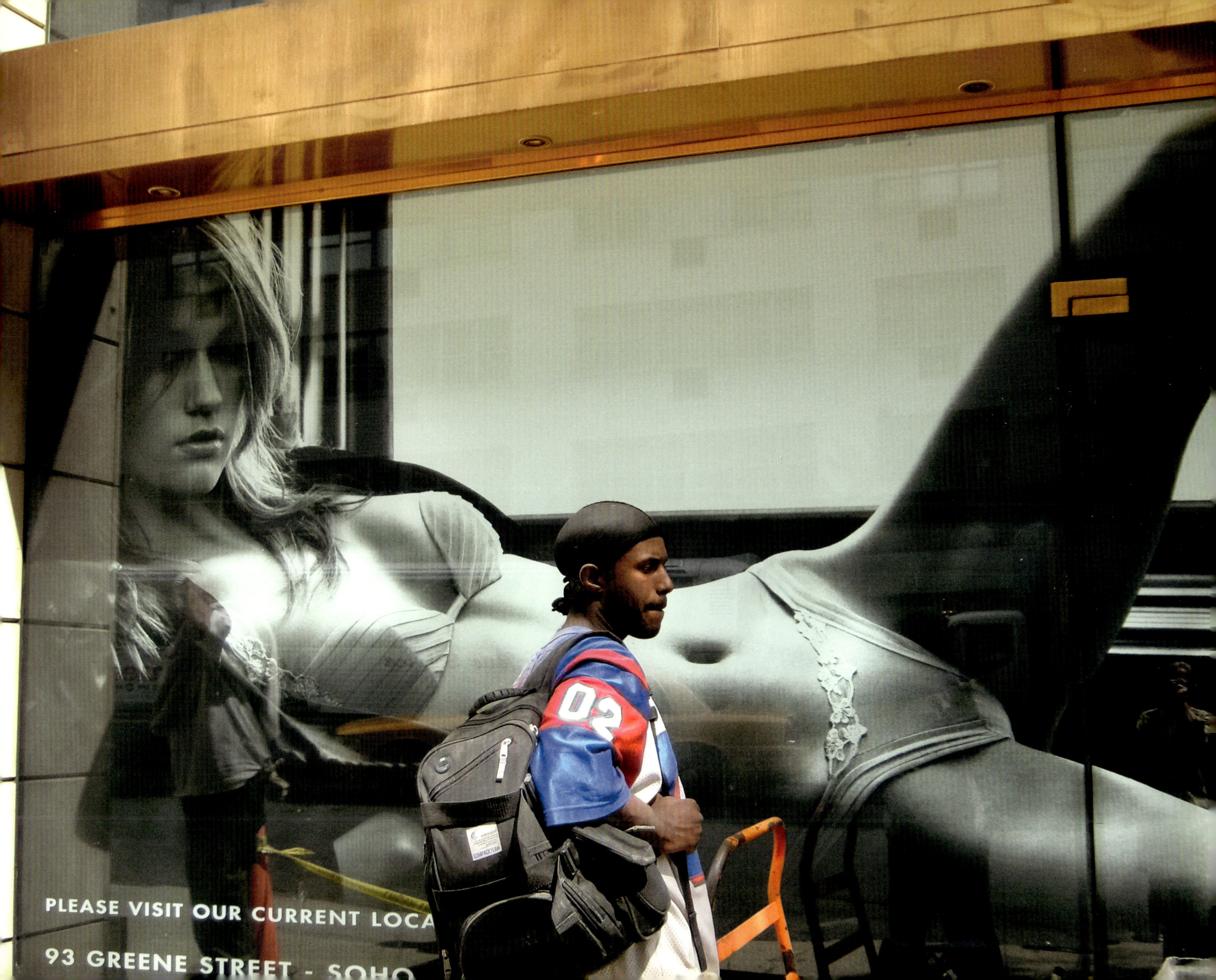
02
PLEASE VISIT OUR CURRENT LOCA
93 GREENE STREET - SOHO

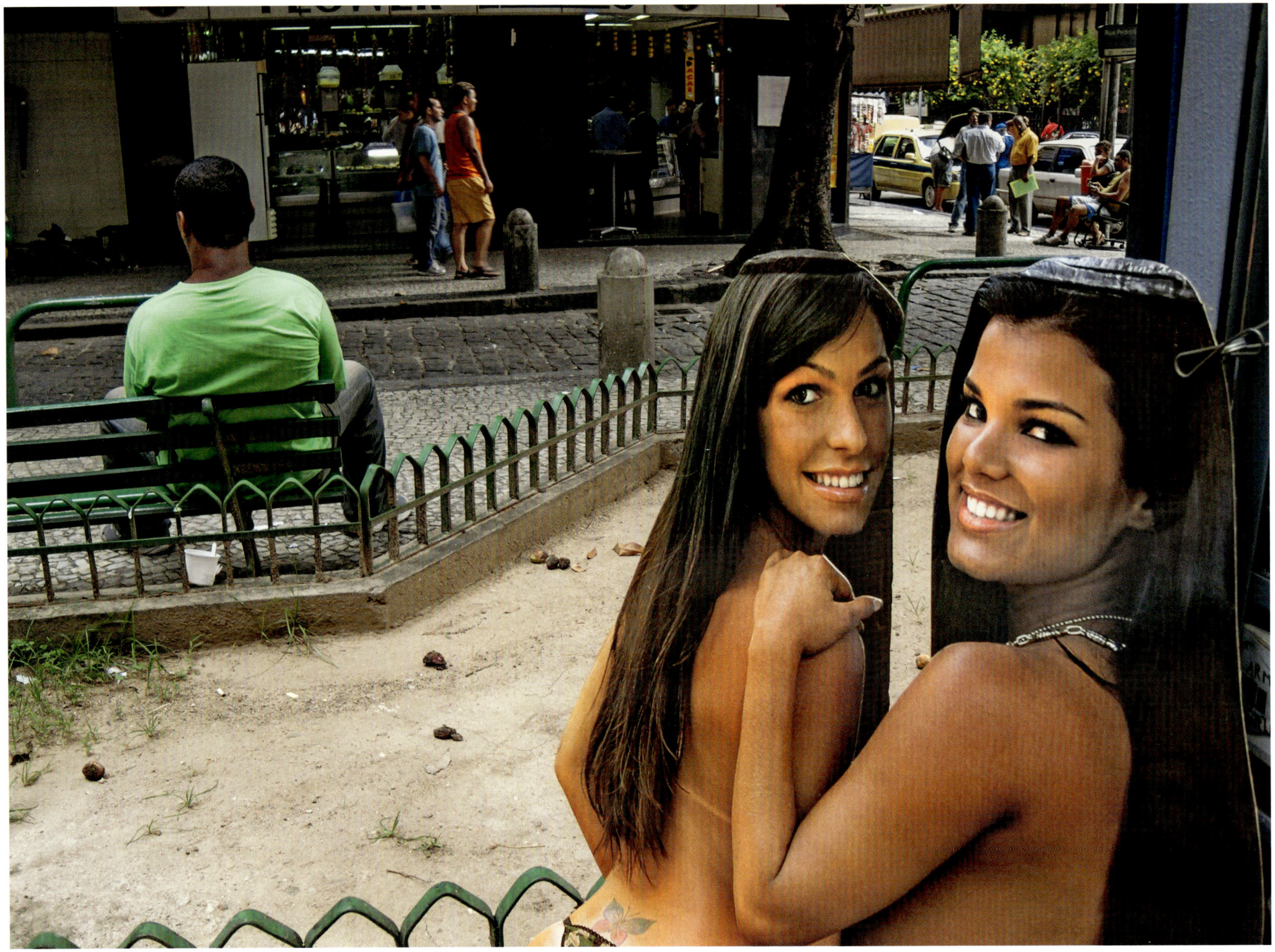

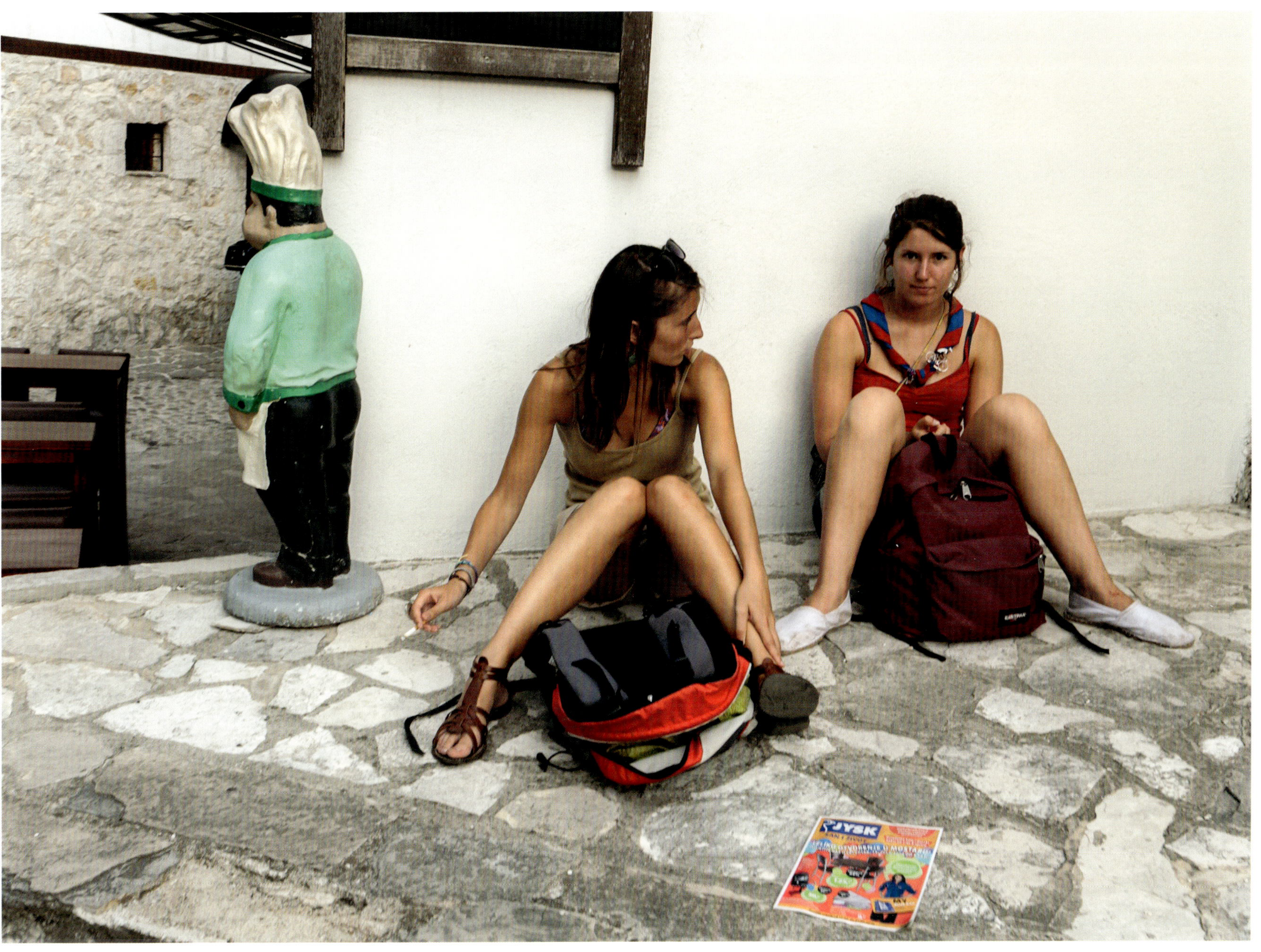
JYSK

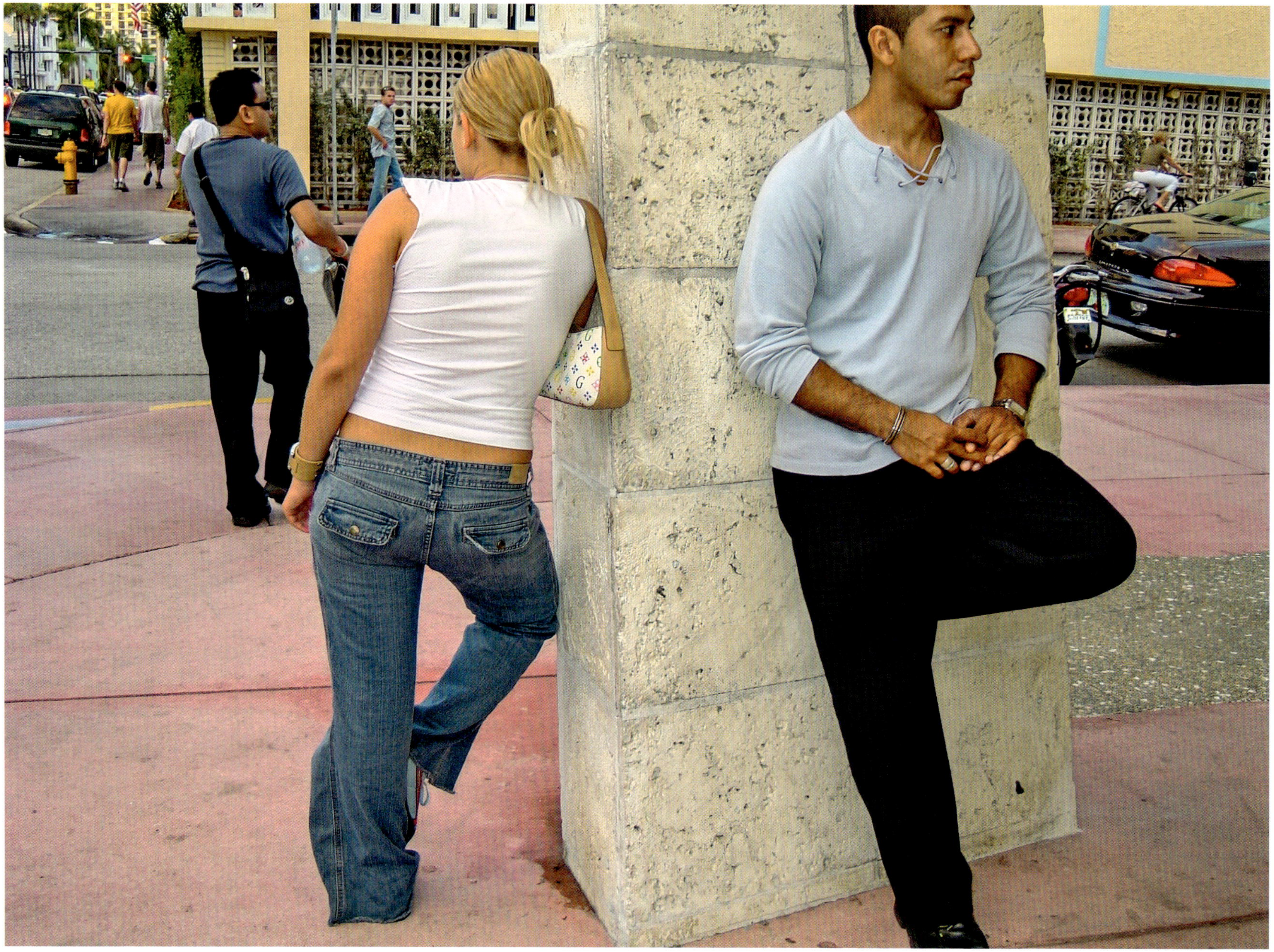

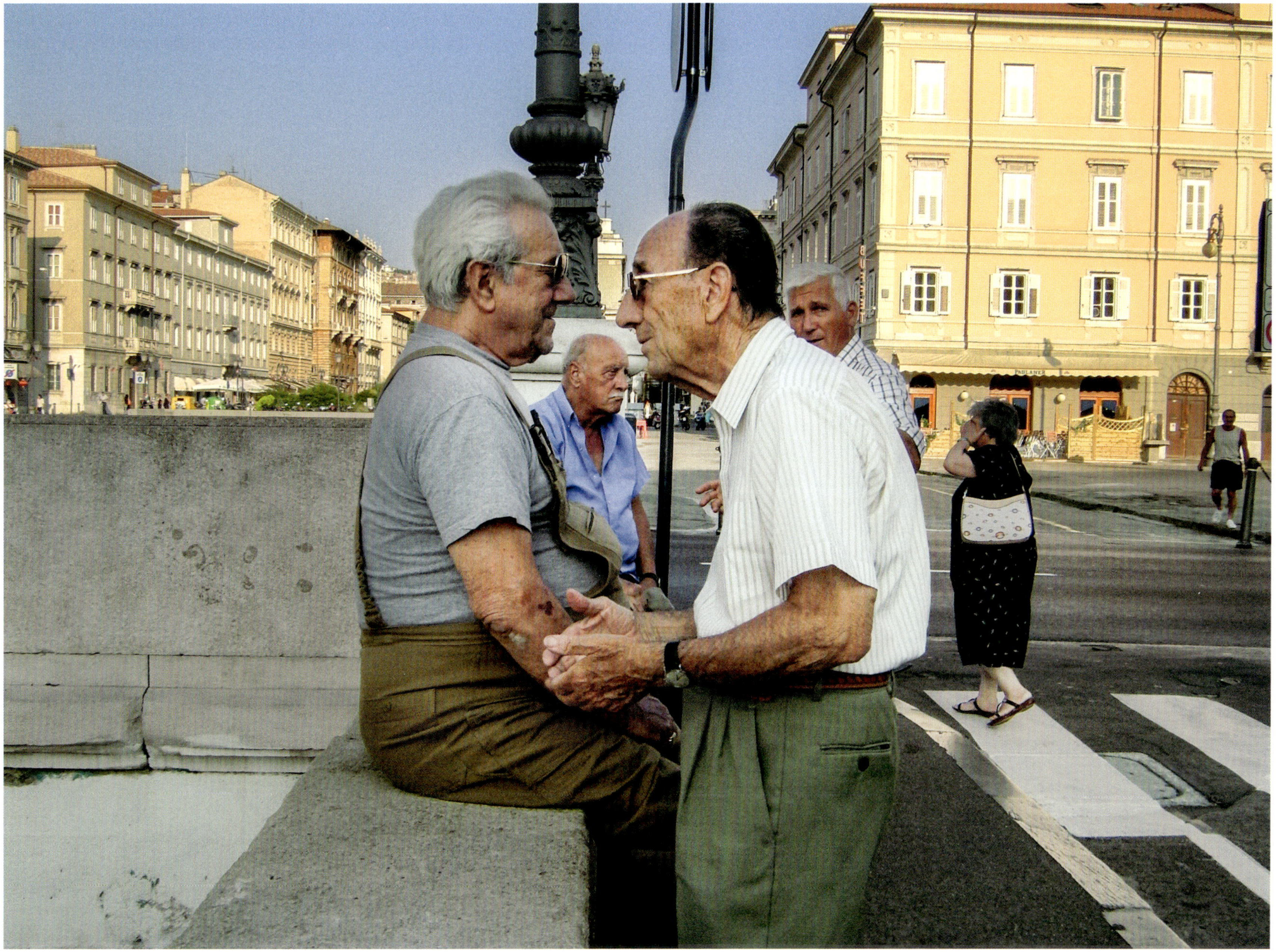

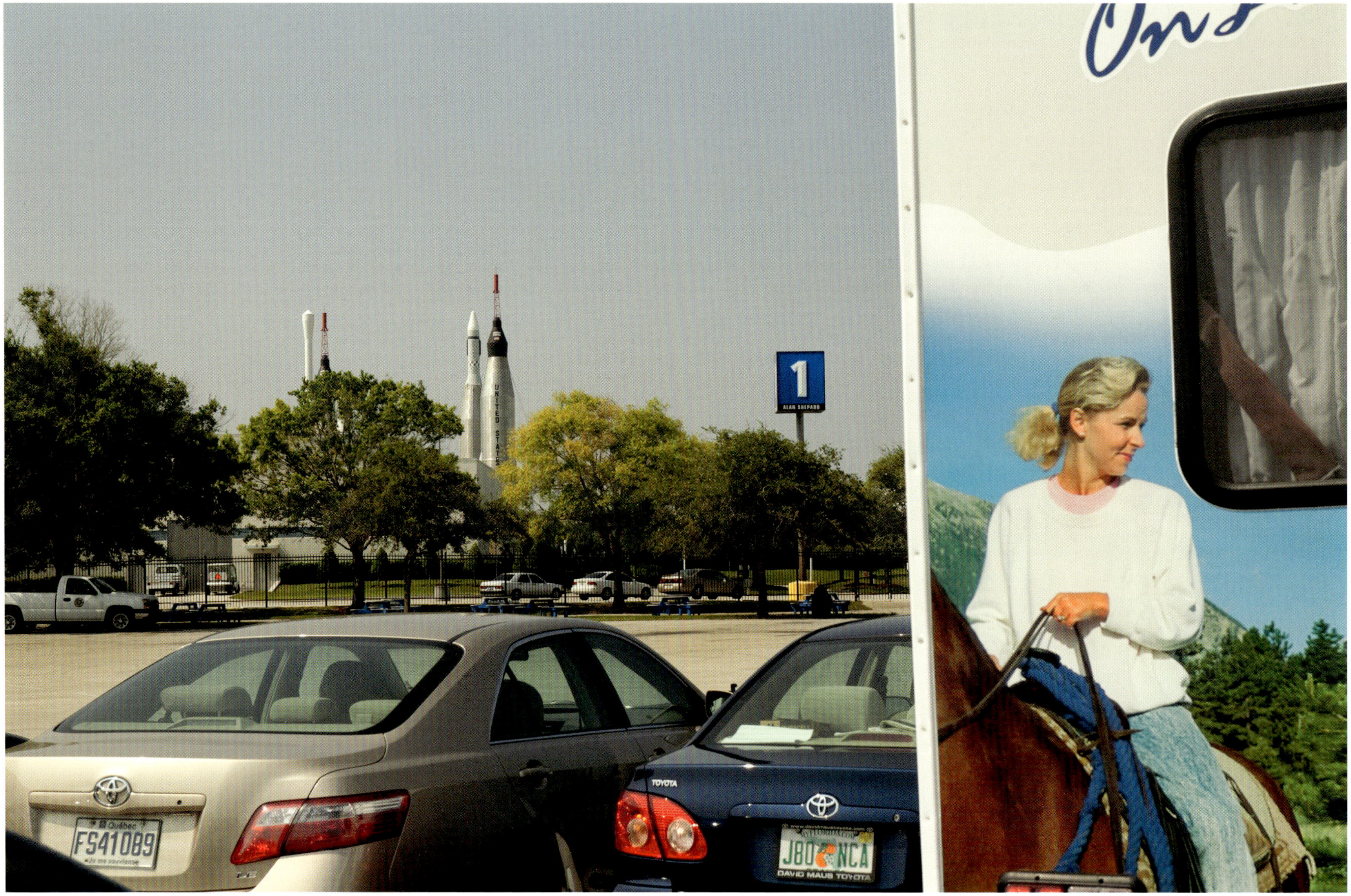

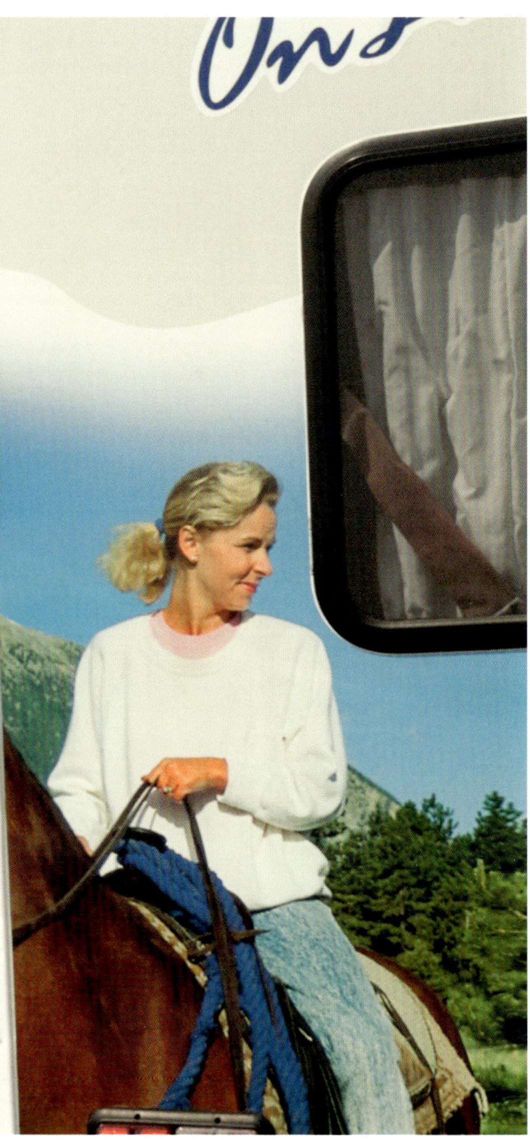

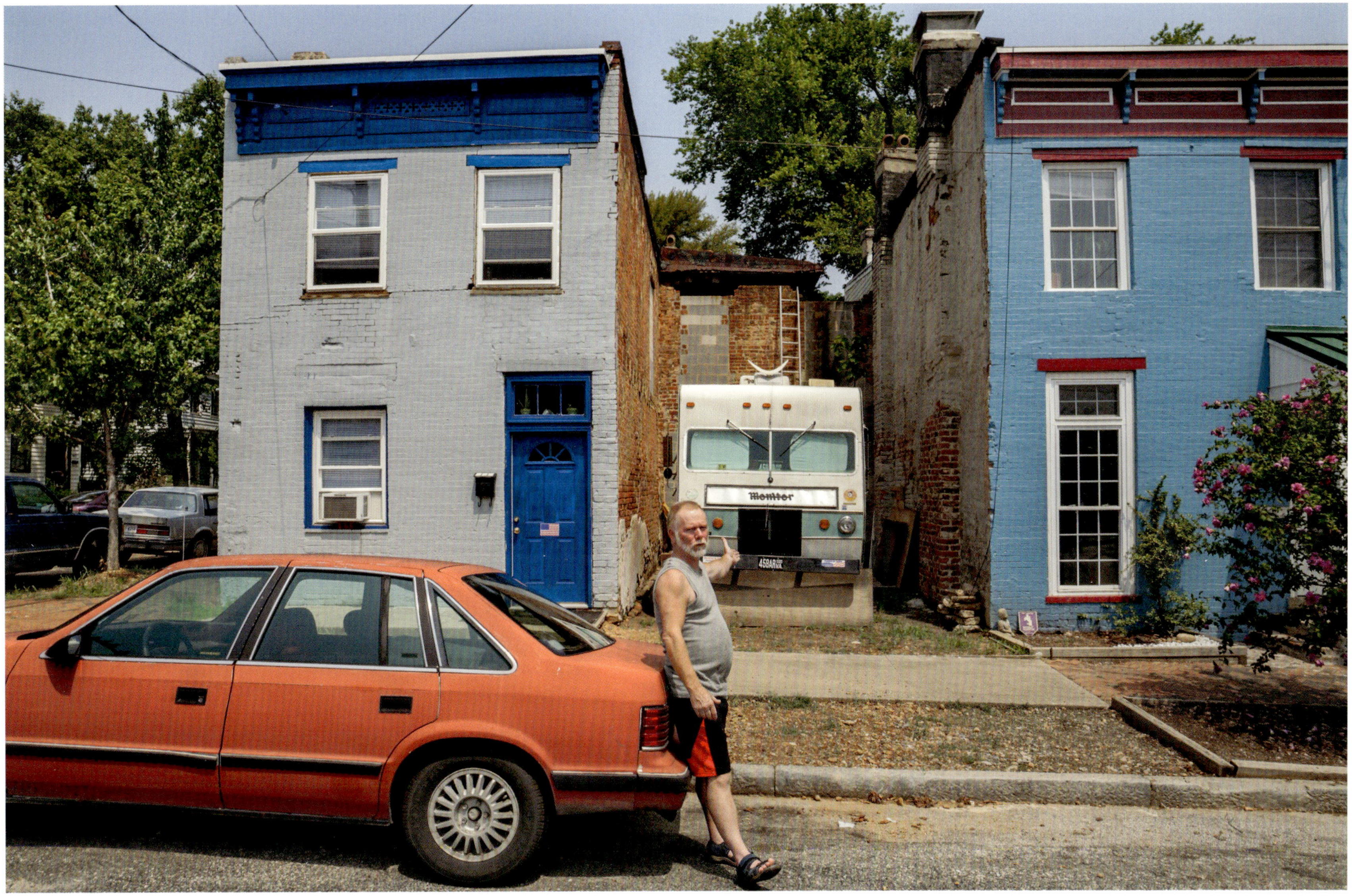

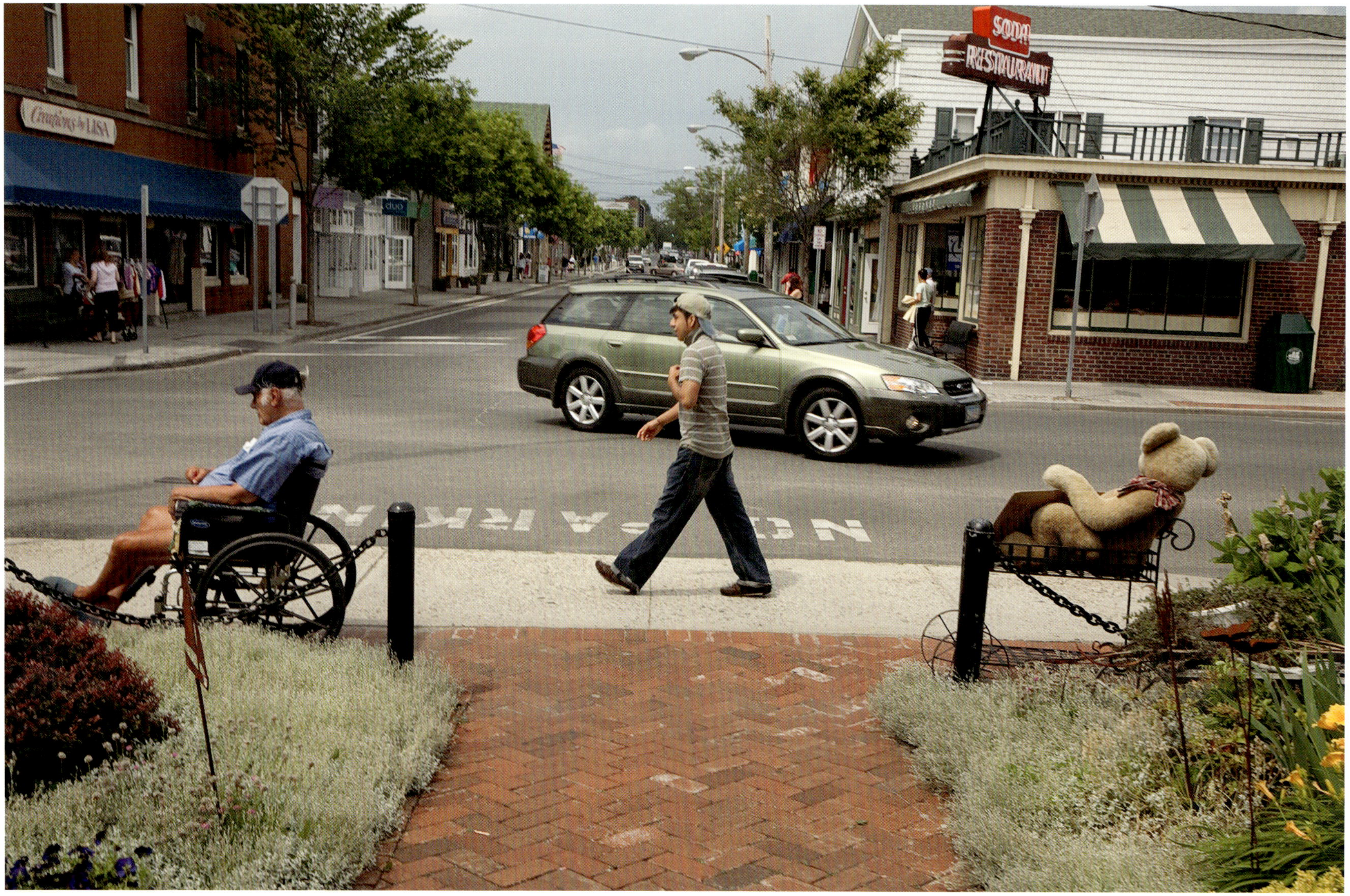

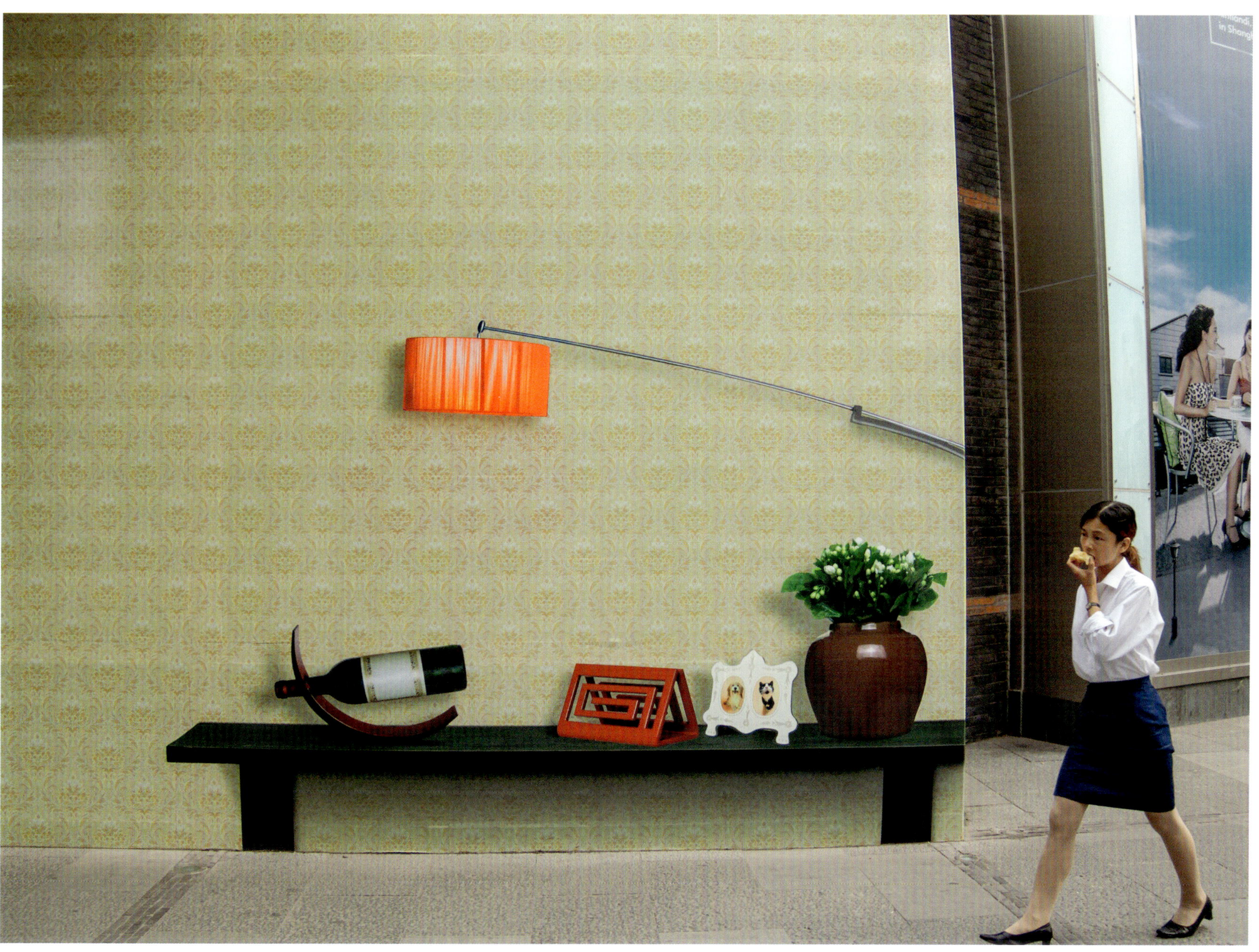

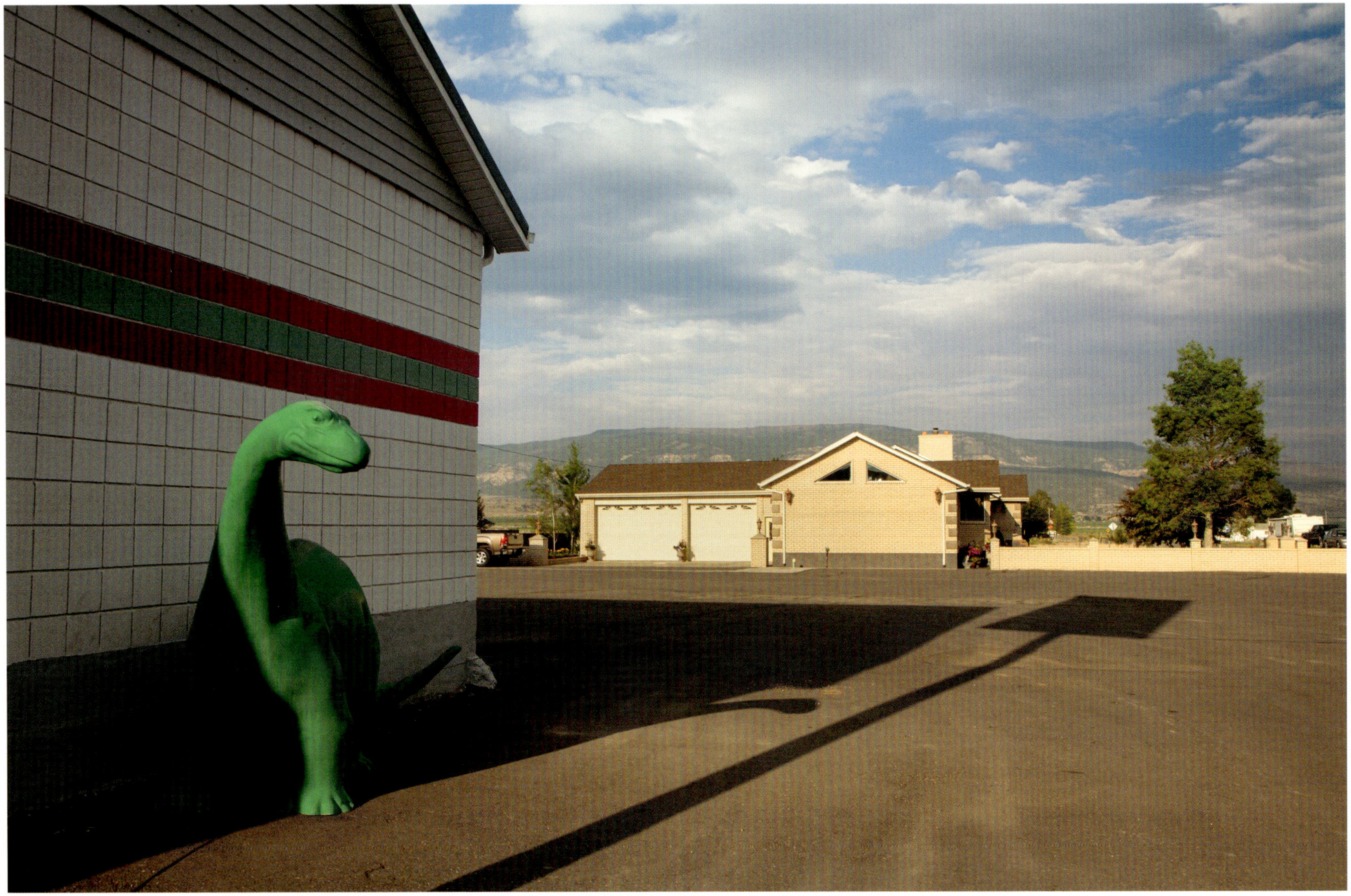

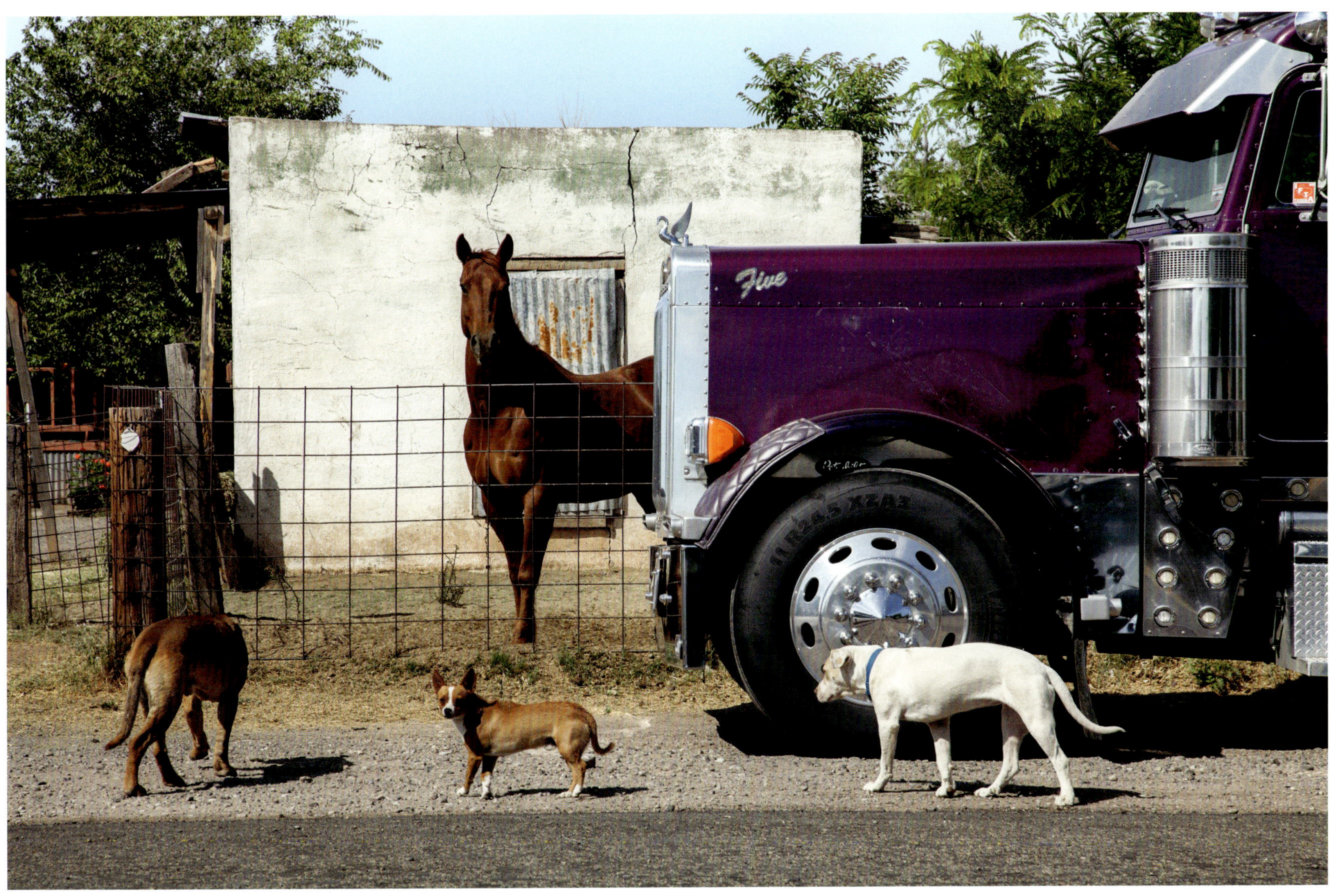
Five

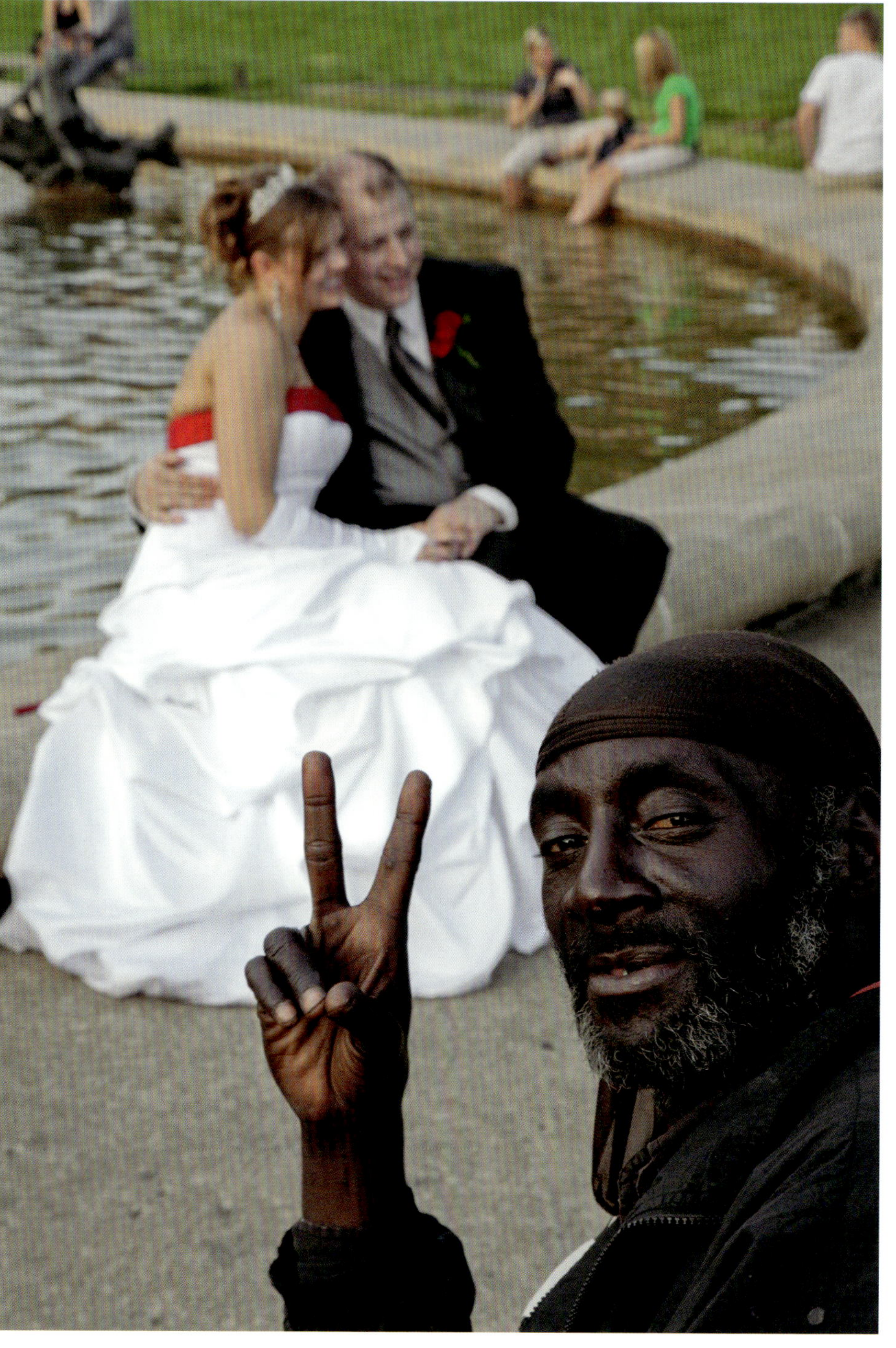

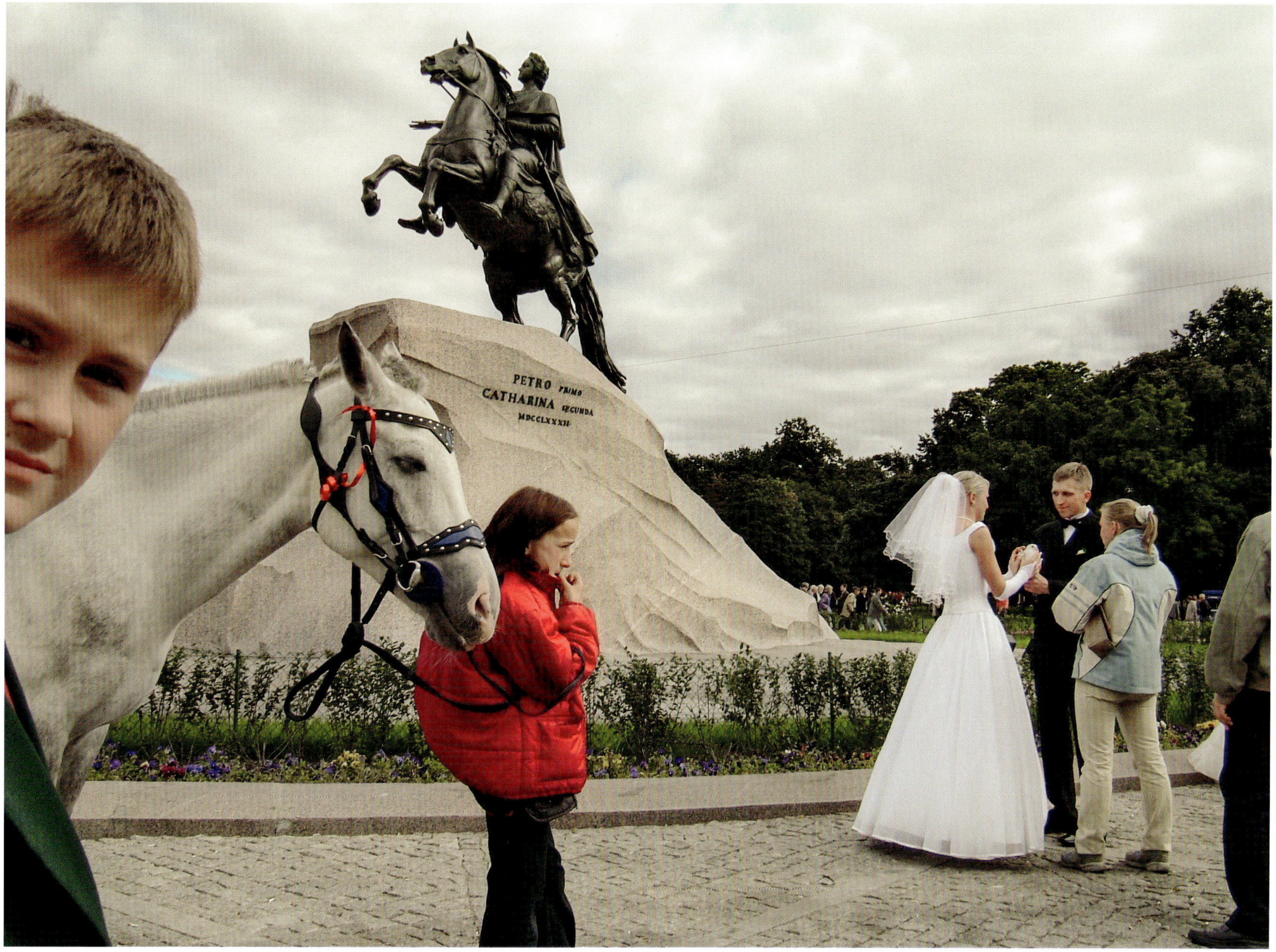

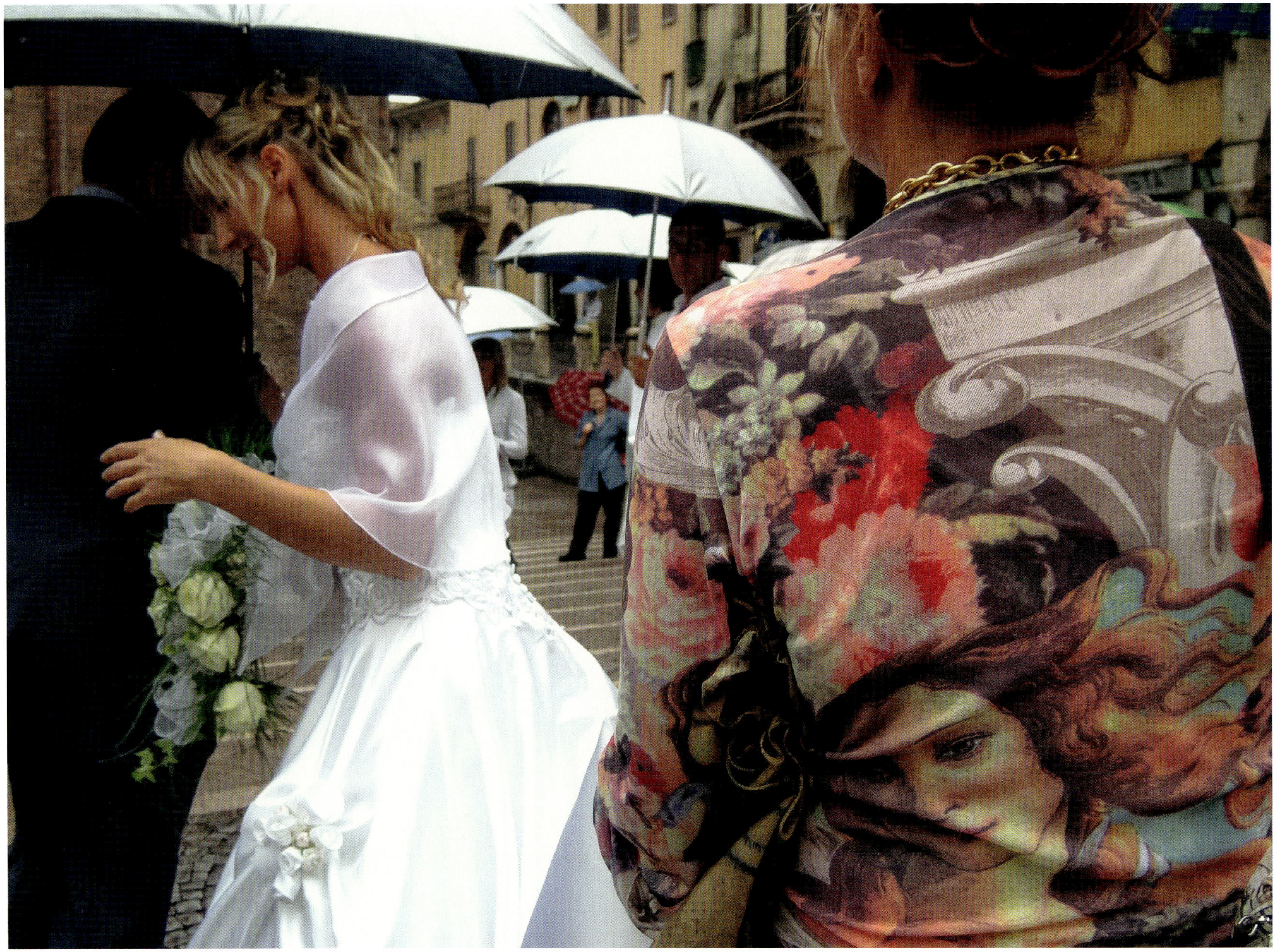

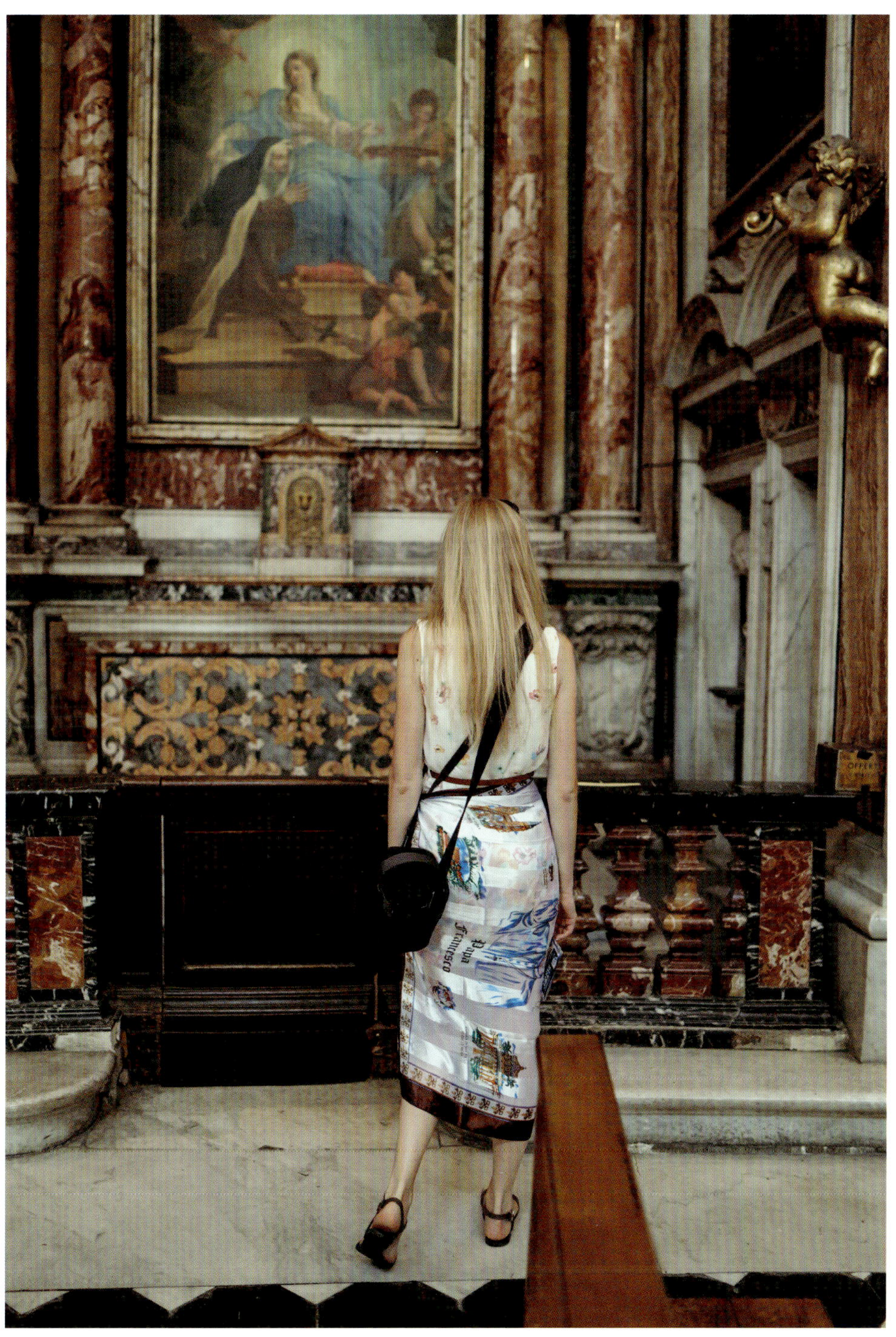
Papa Francesco

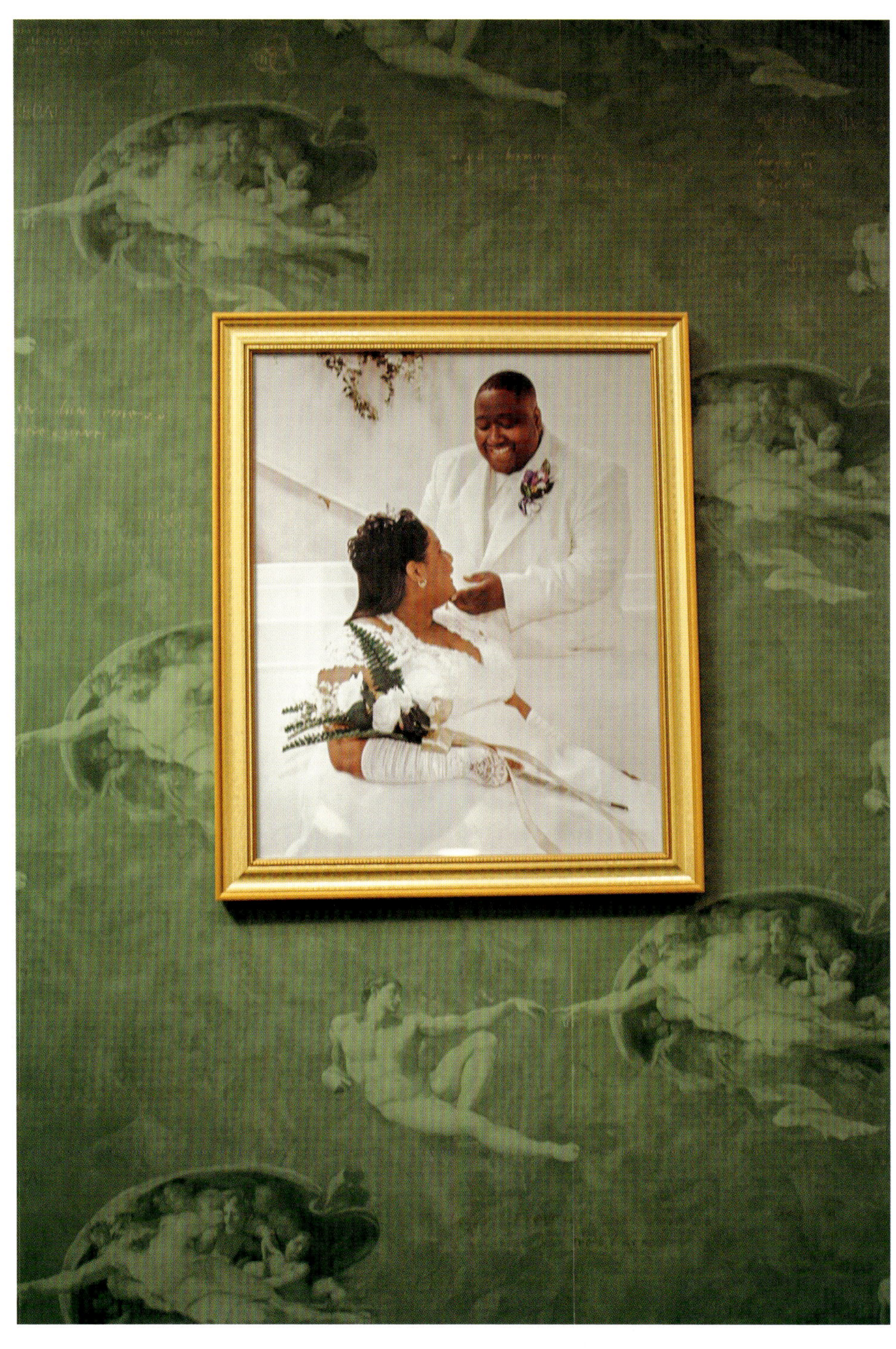

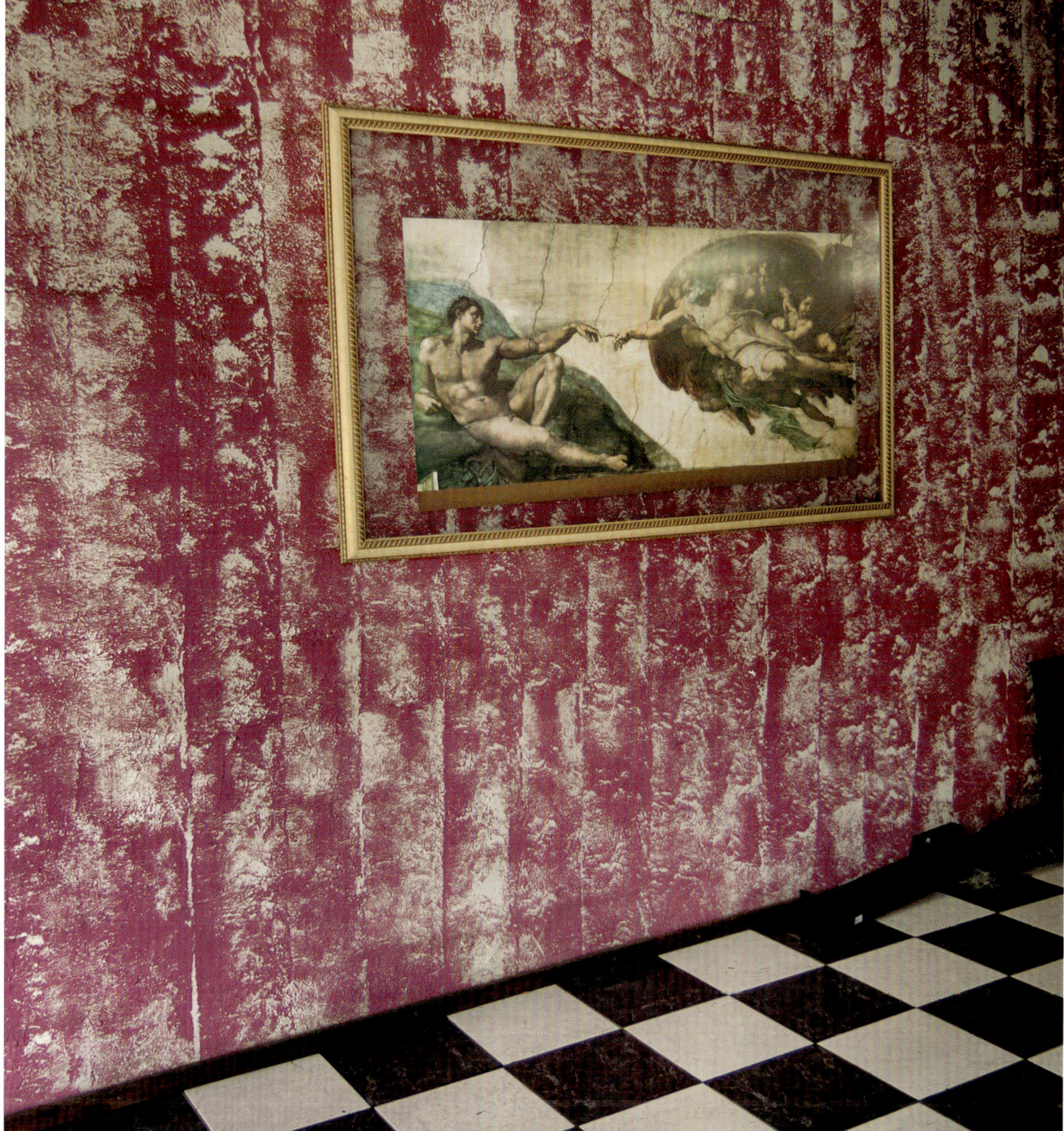

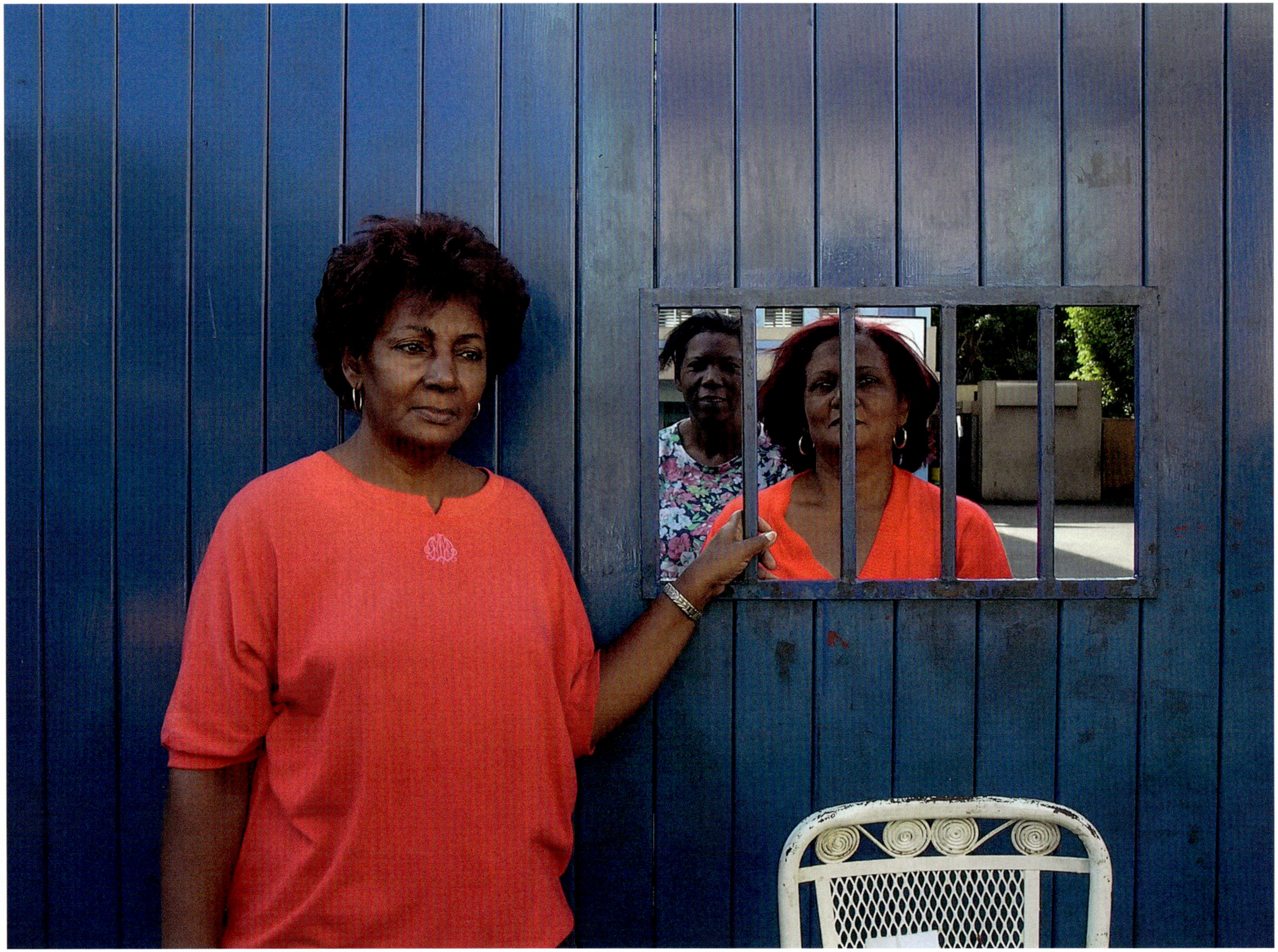

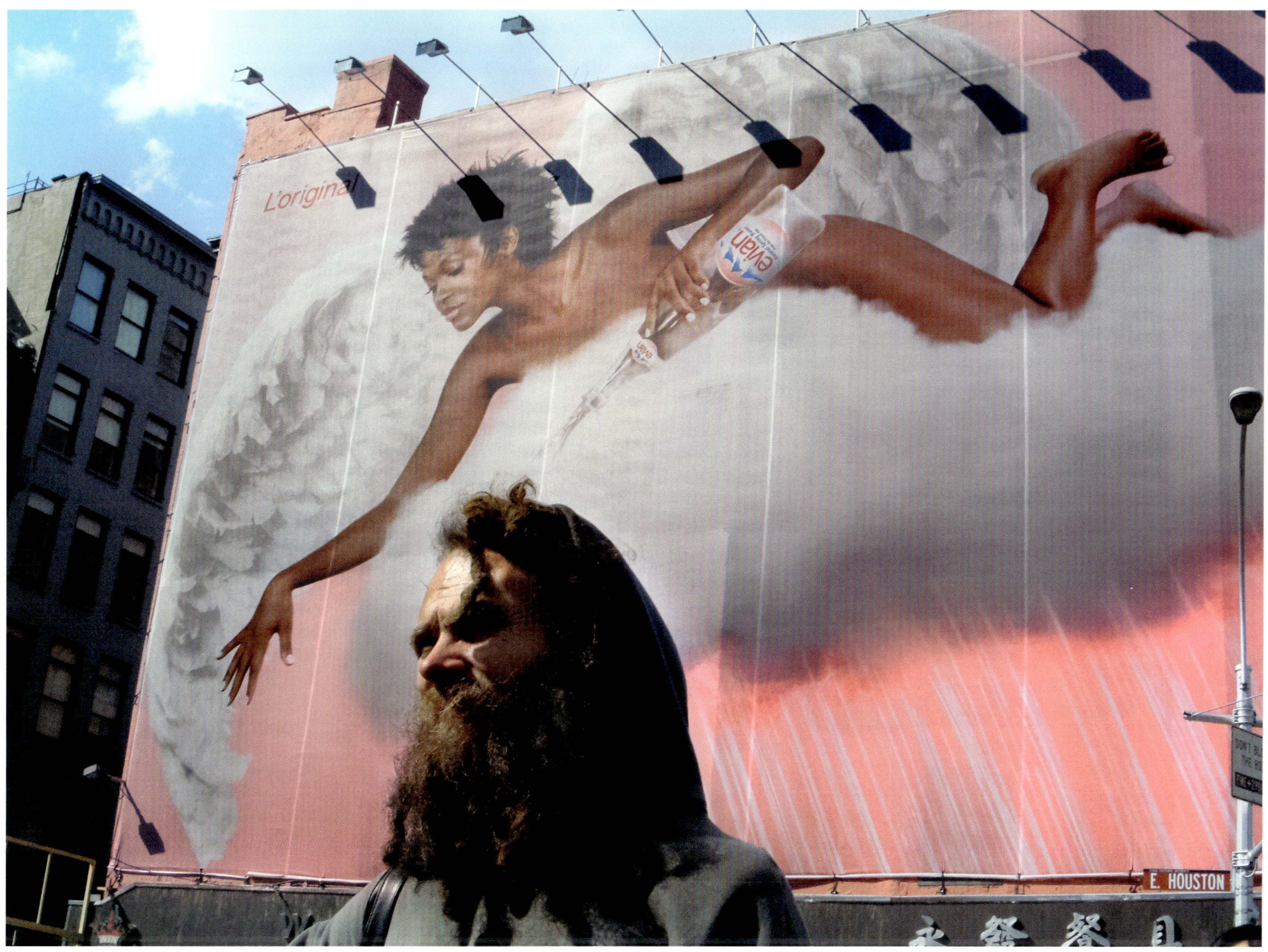
L'original
evian
E. HOUSTON

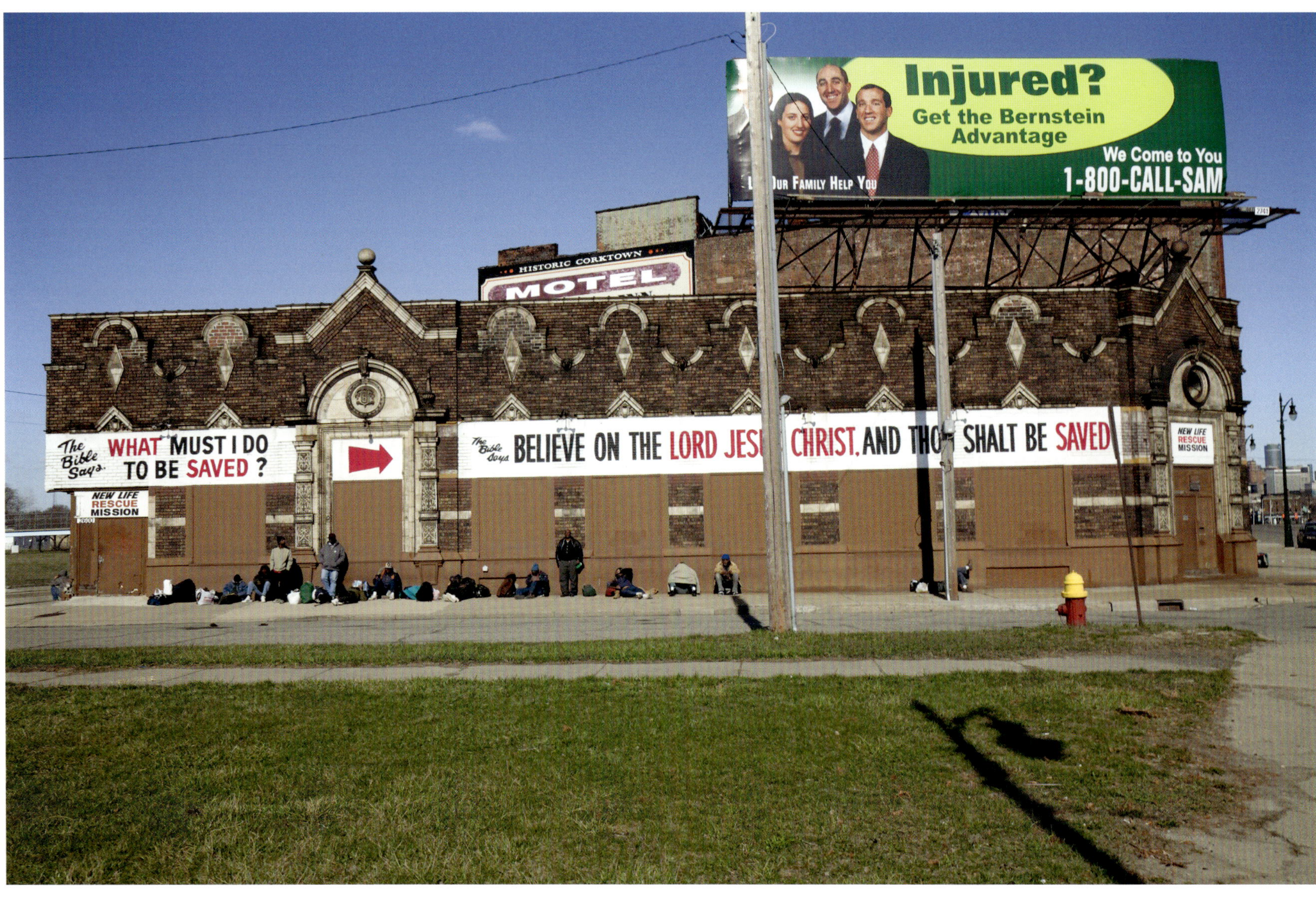

Injured?
Get the Bernstein Advantage
We Come to You
1-800-CALL-SAM
Our Family Help You
HISTORIC CORKTOWN
MOTEL
The Bible Says. WHAT MUST I DO TO BE SAVED ?
NEW LIFE RESCUE MISSION
The Bible Says BELIEVE ON THE LORD JESU CHRIST, AND THO SHALT BE SAVED
NEW LIFE RESCUE MISSION

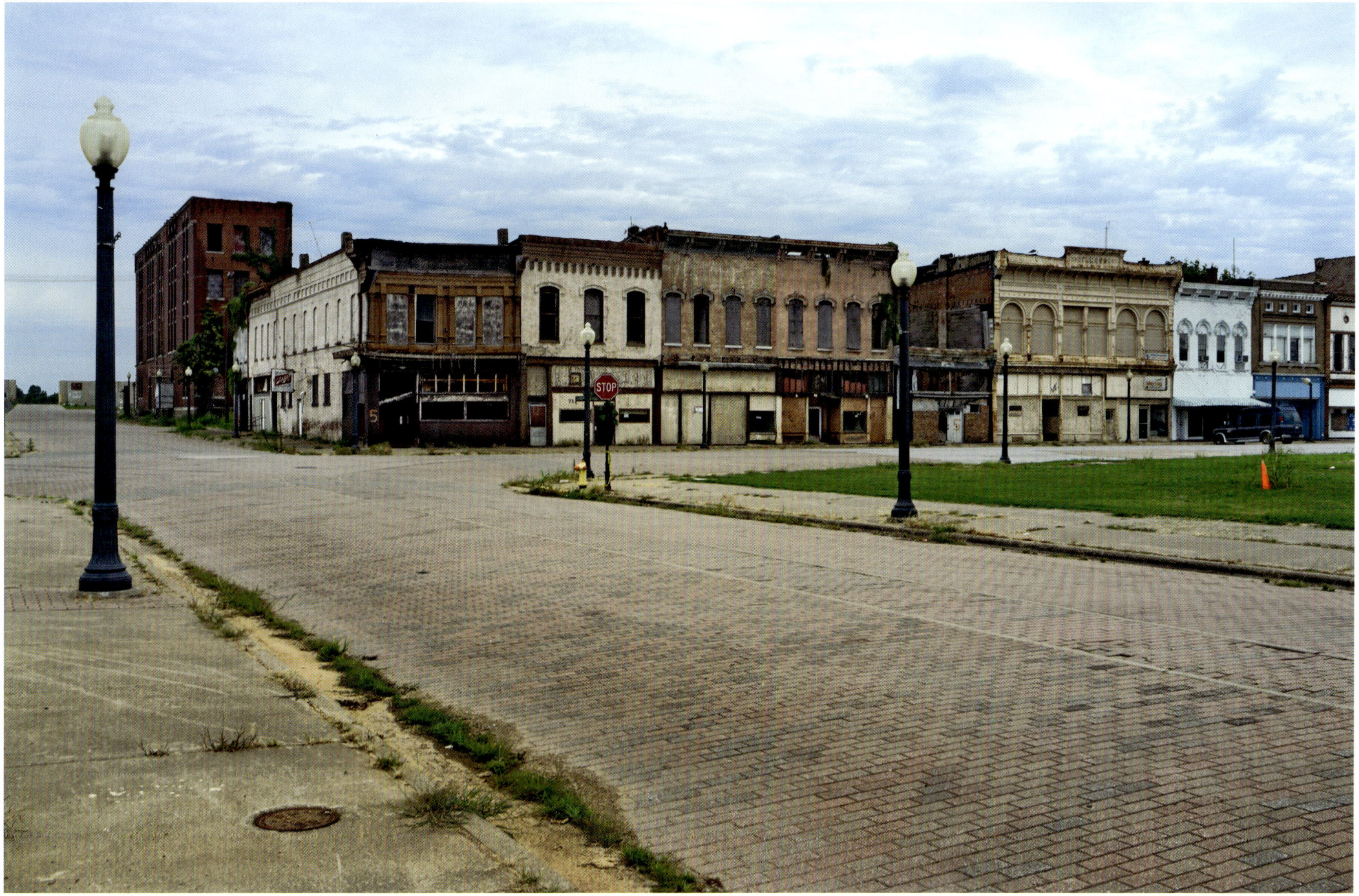

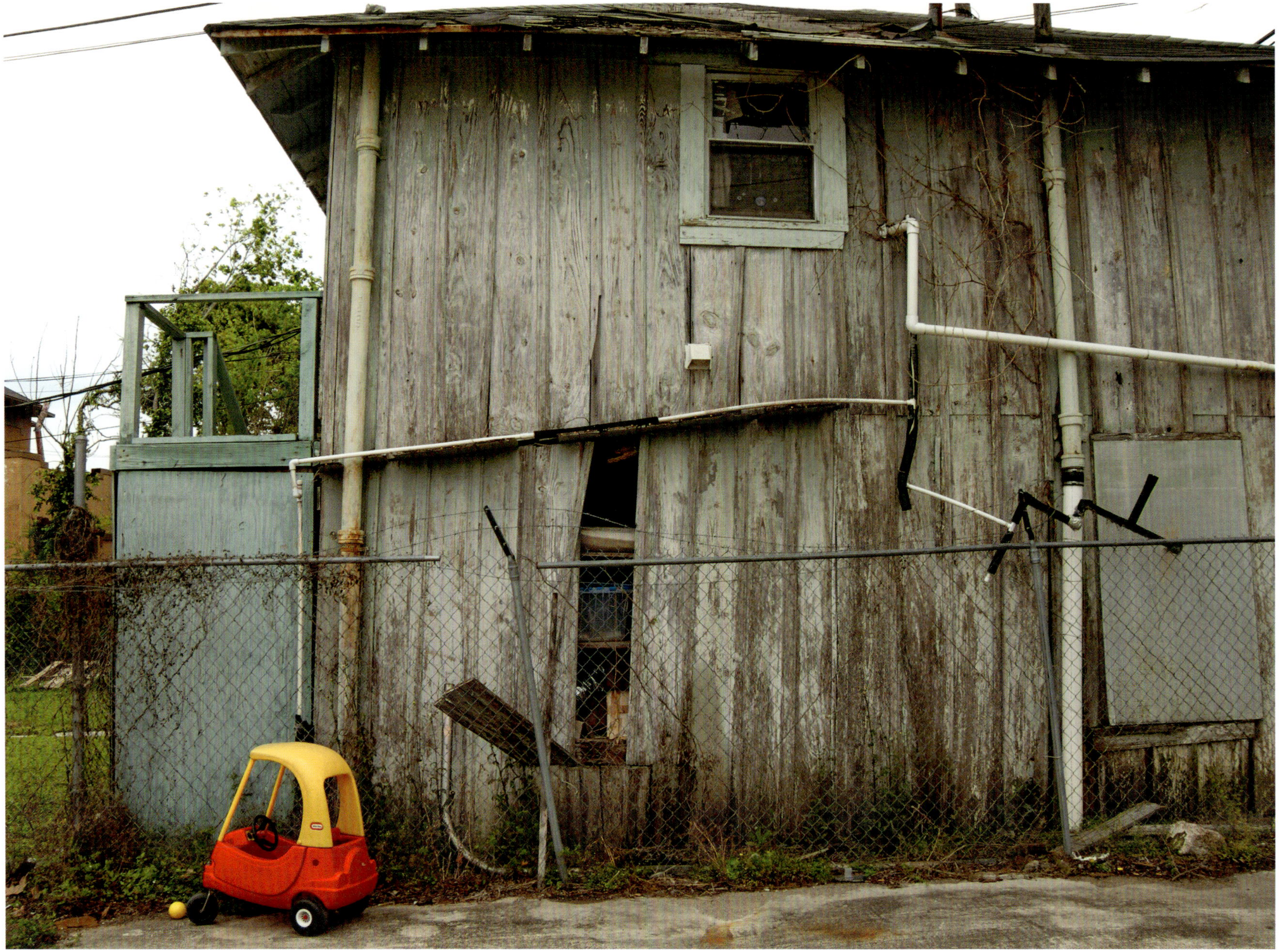

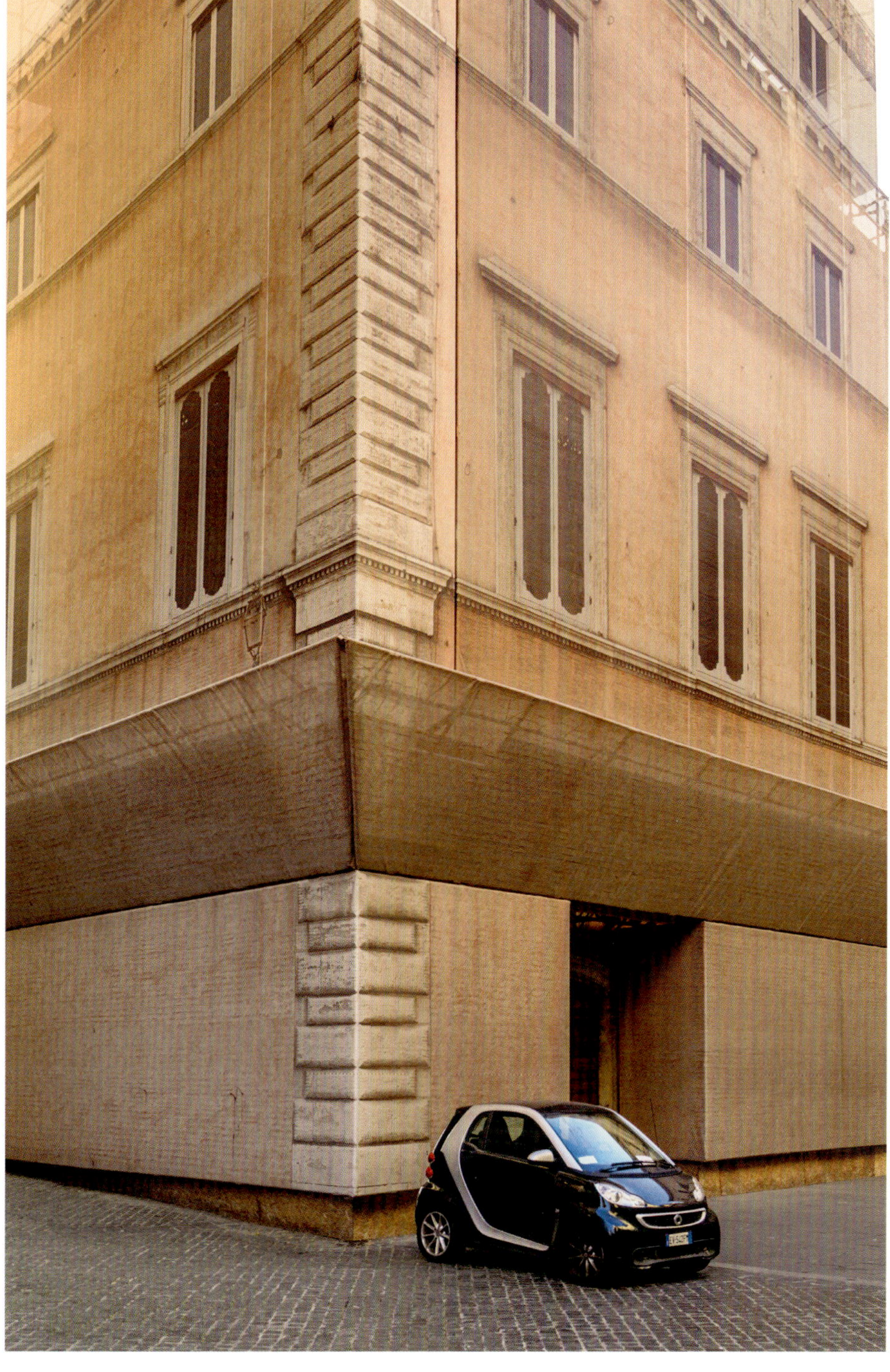

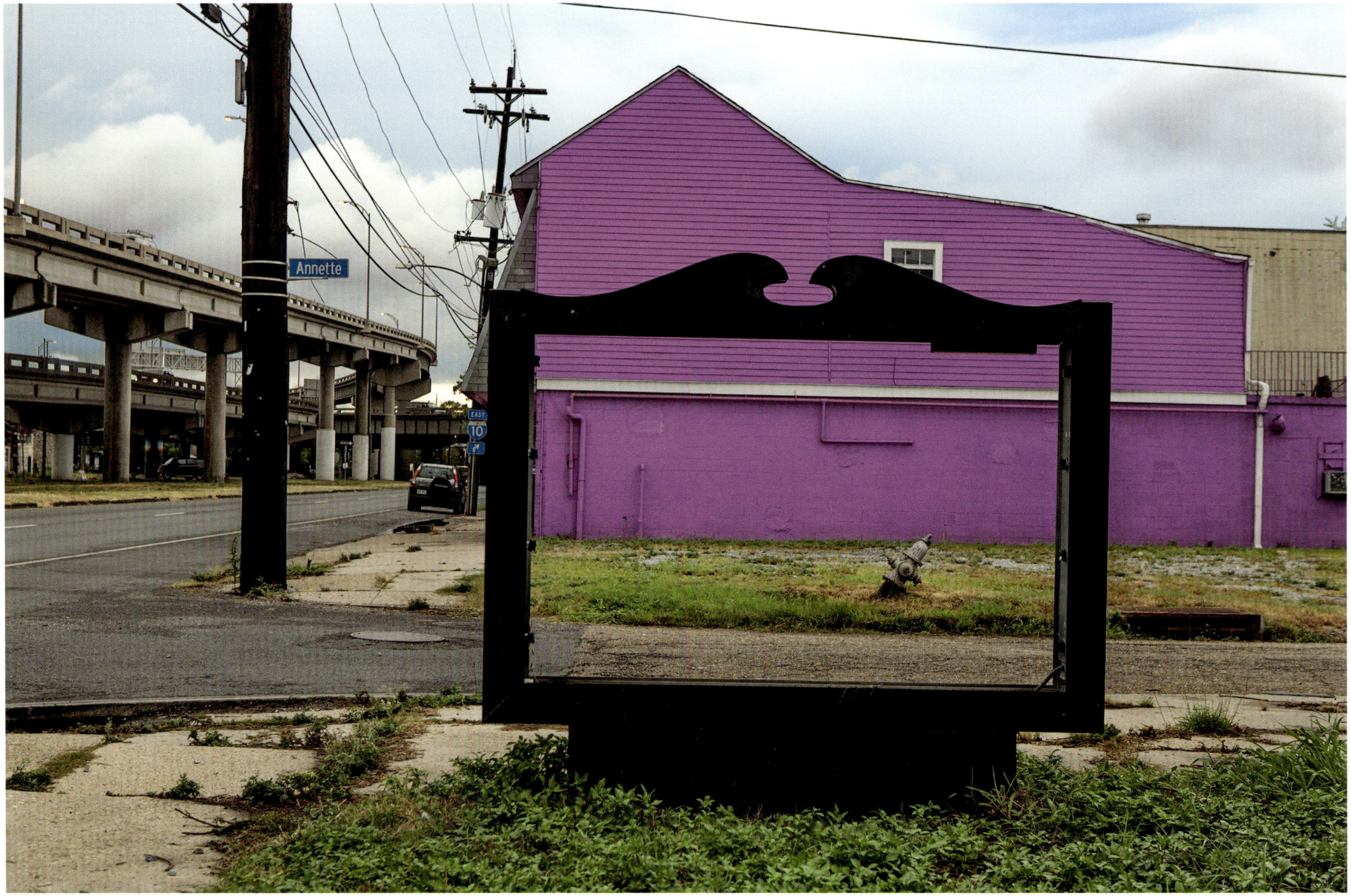

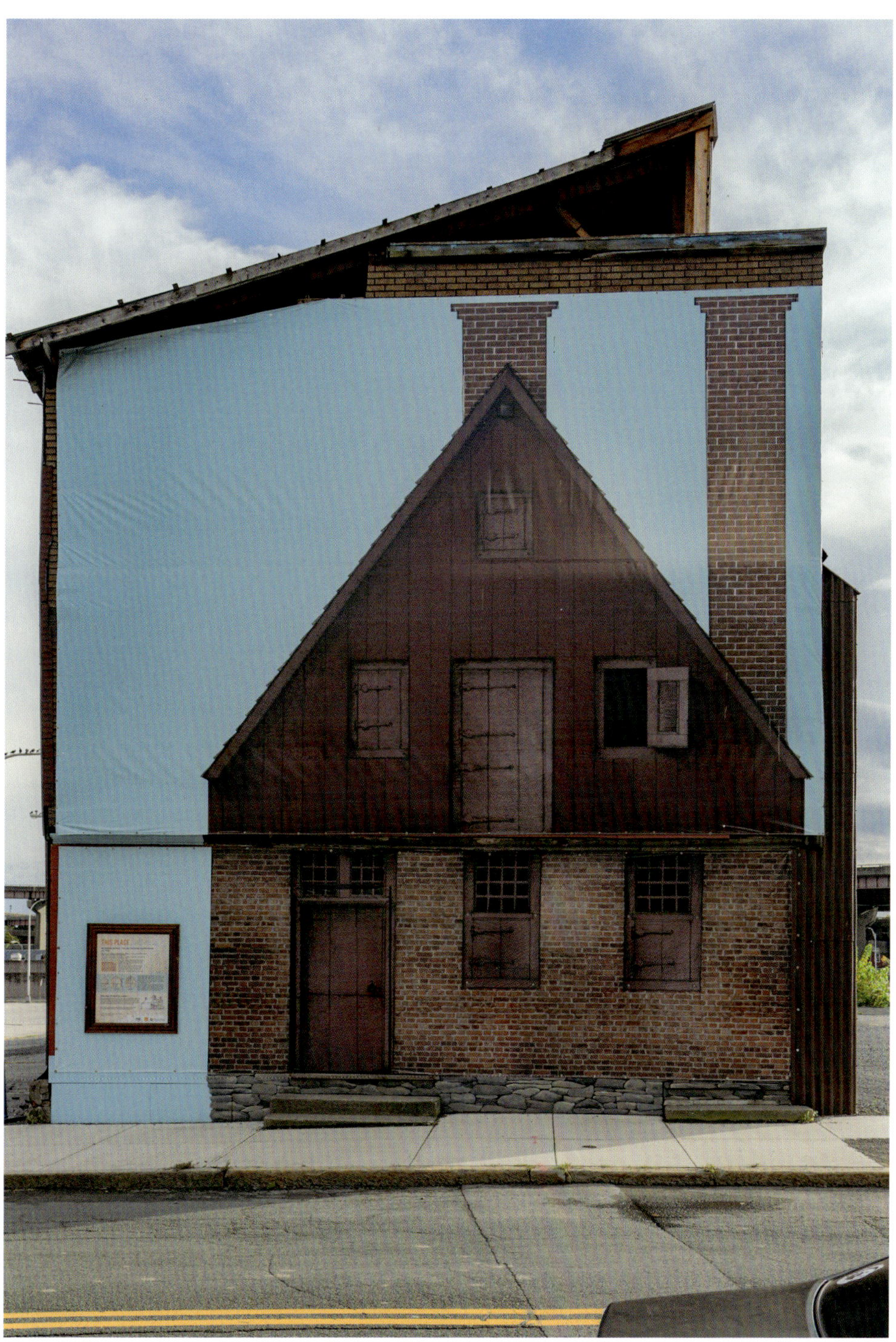

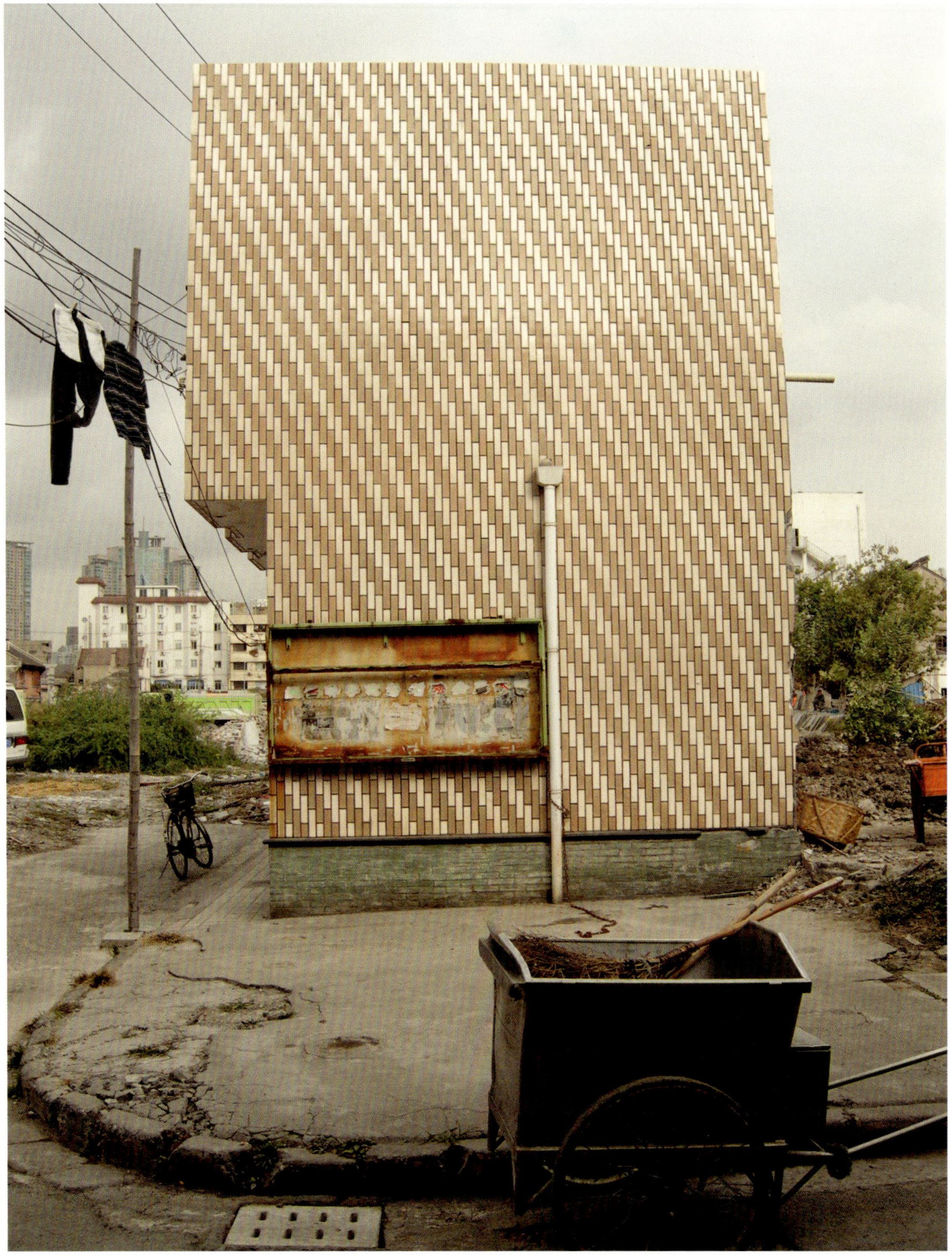

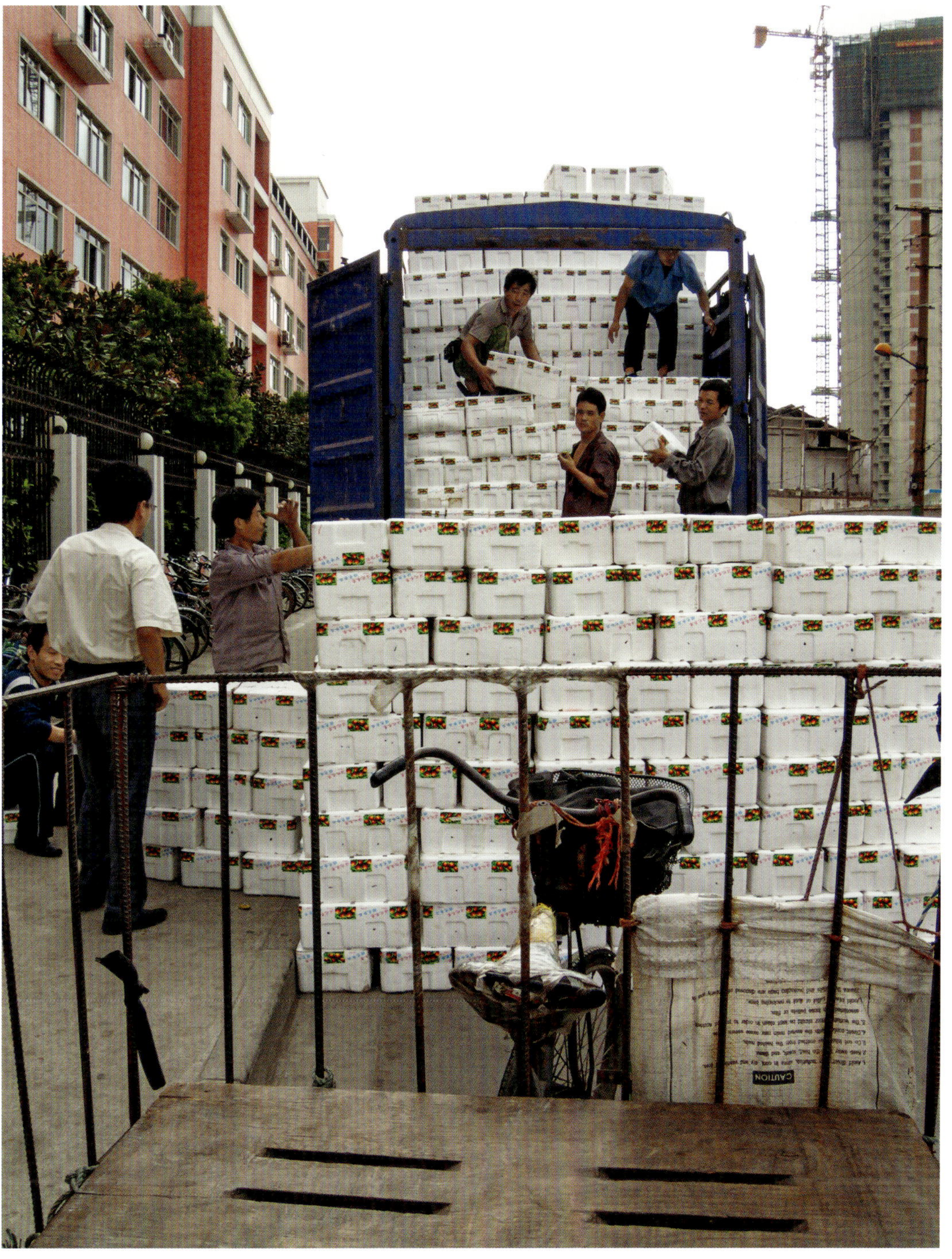

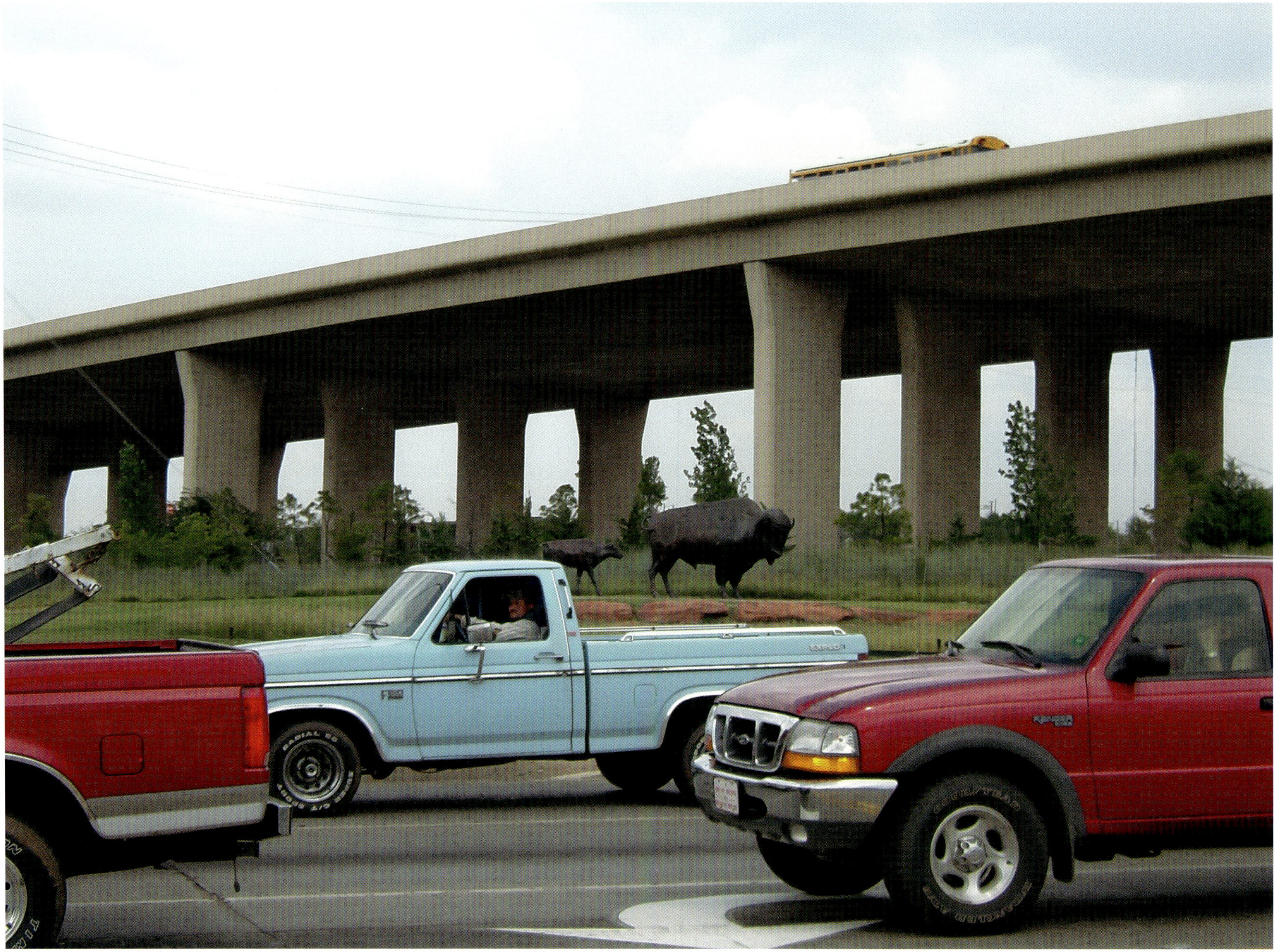

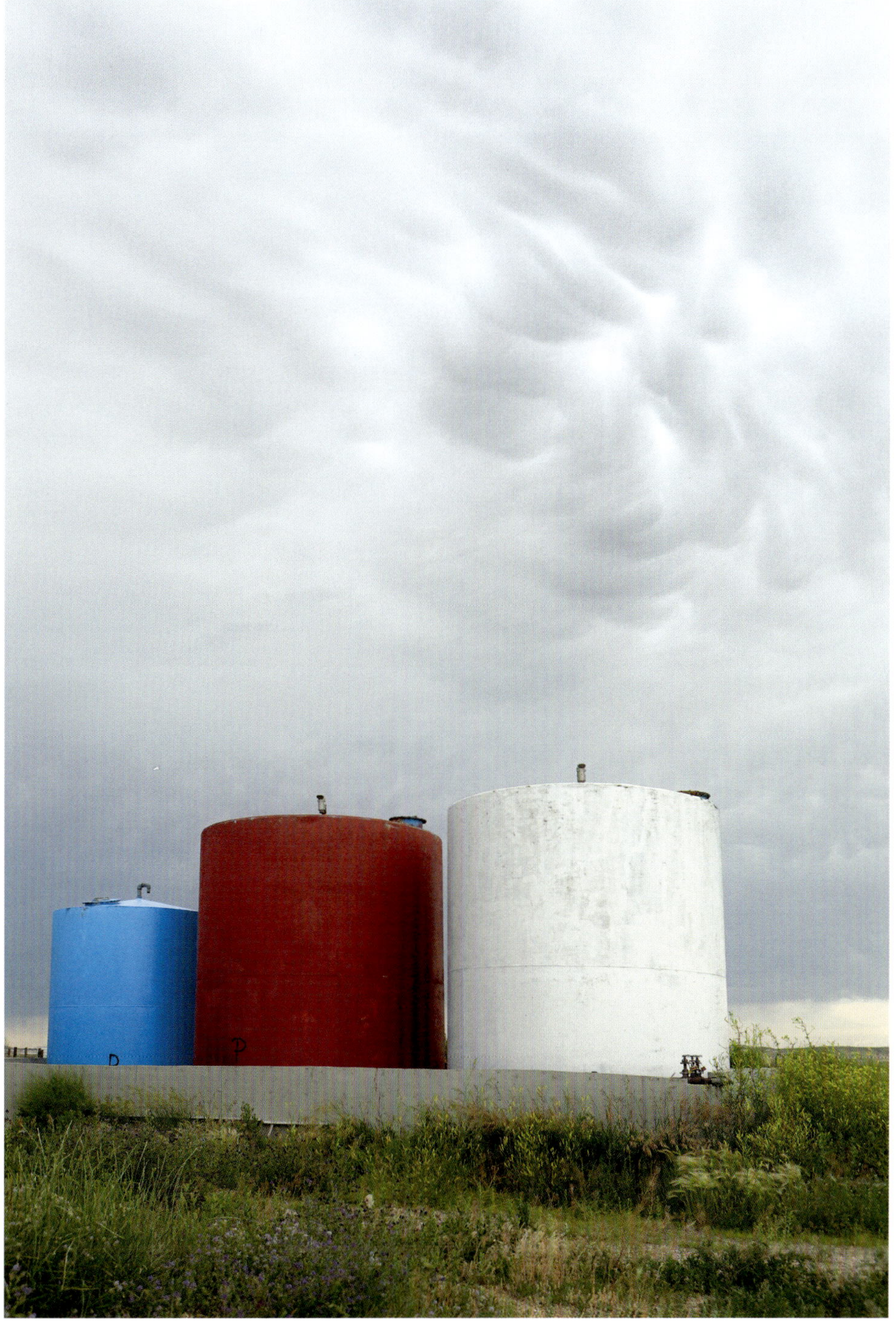

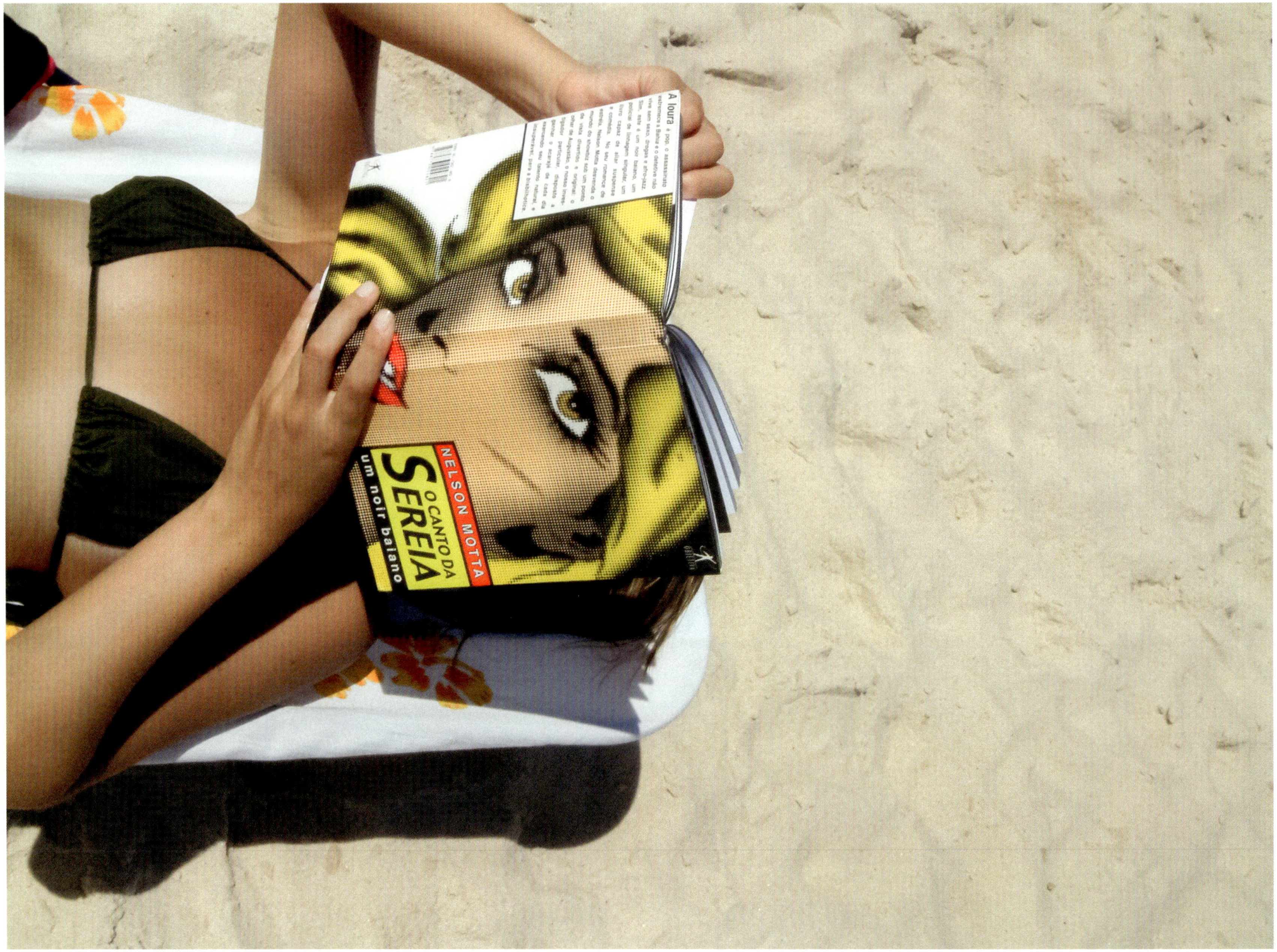

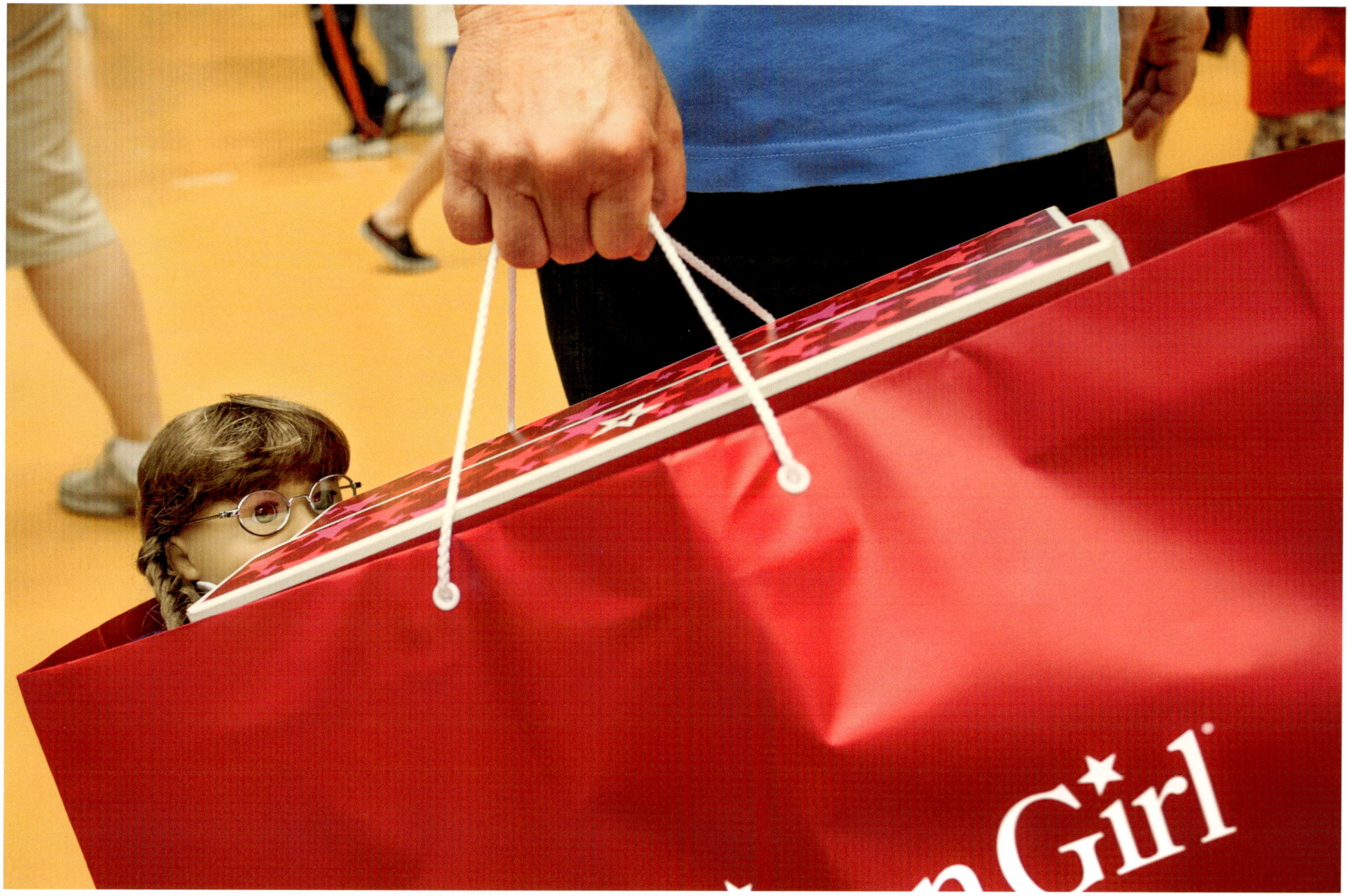

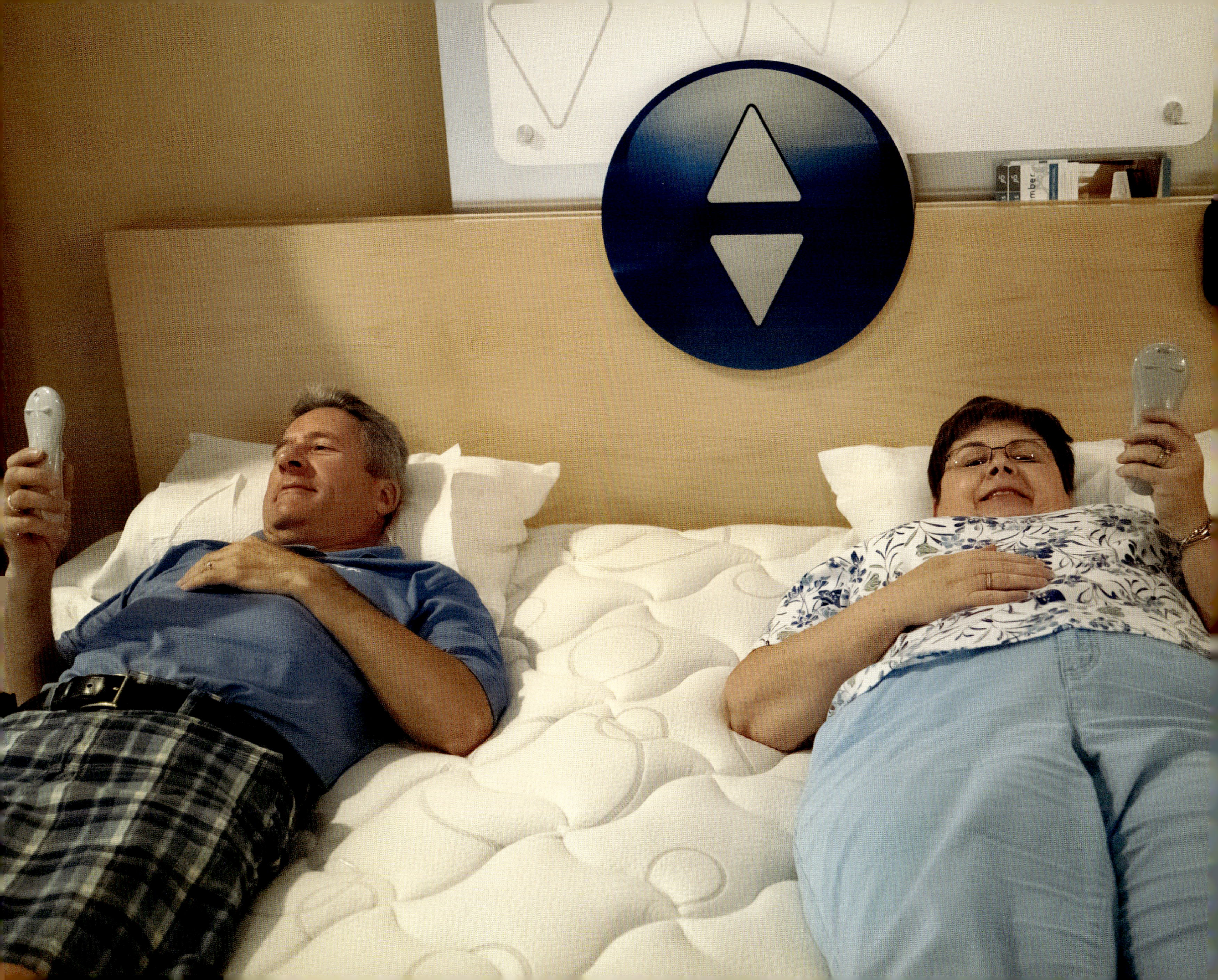

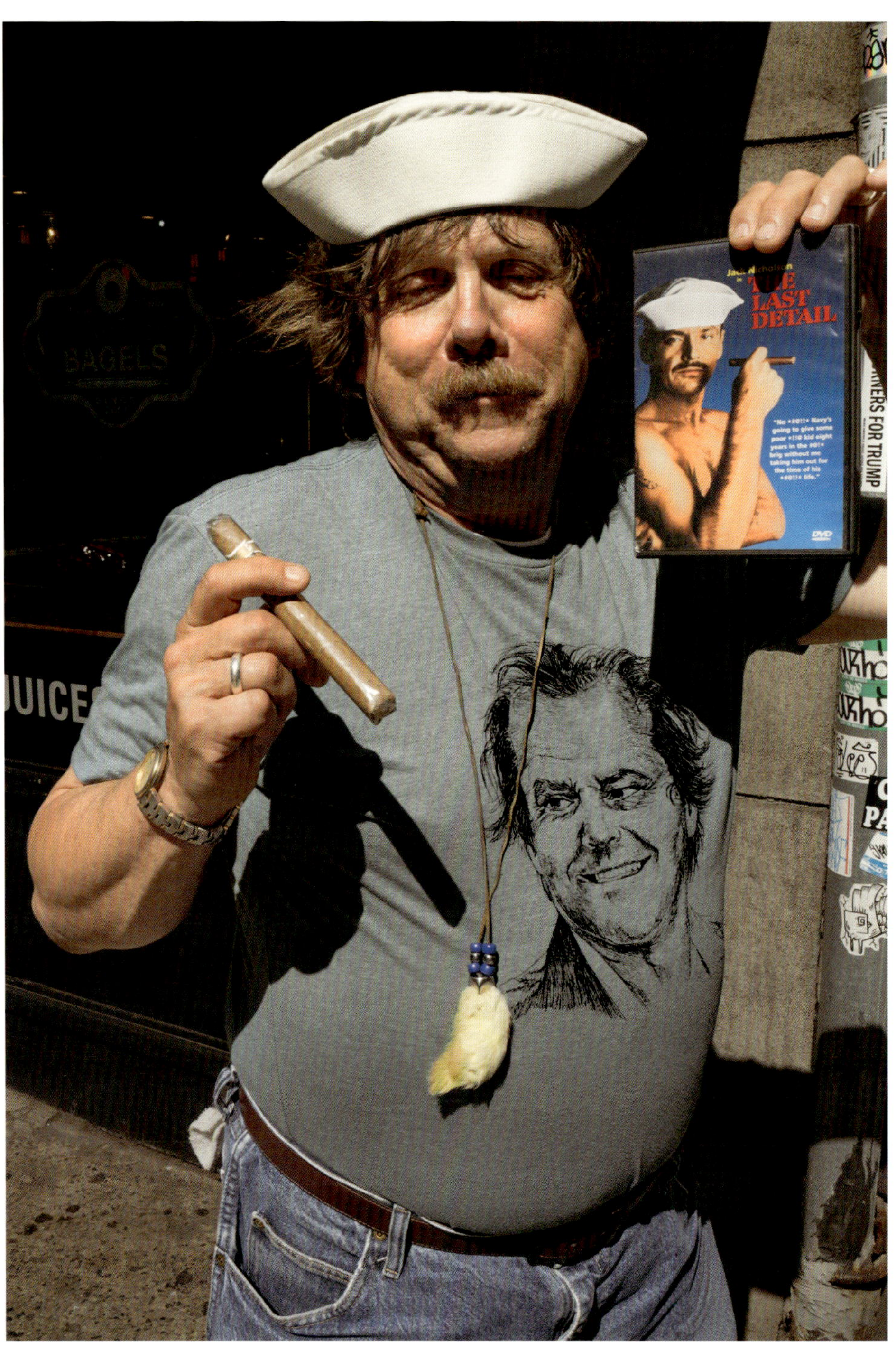
BAGELS
LAST DETAIL
DVD

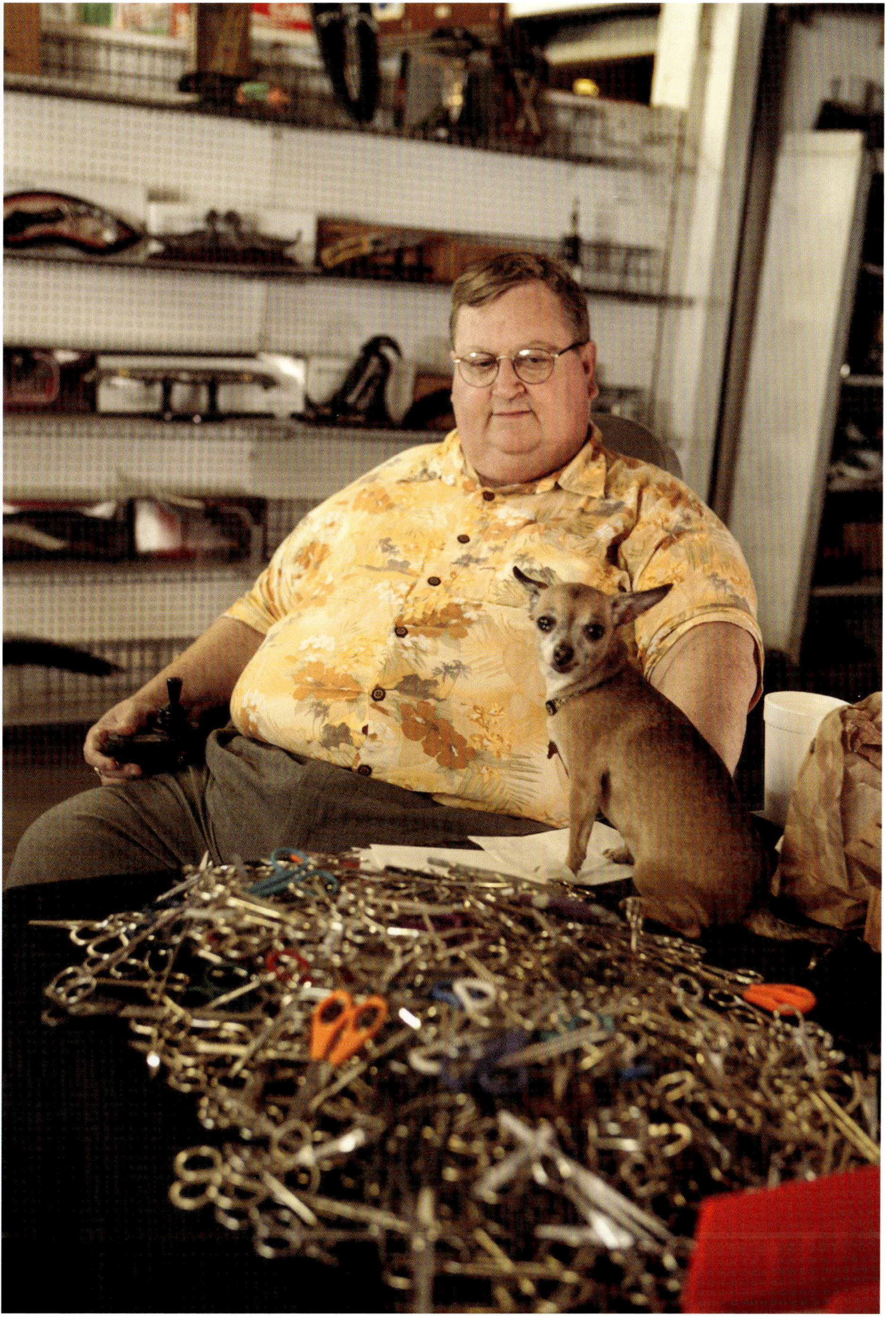

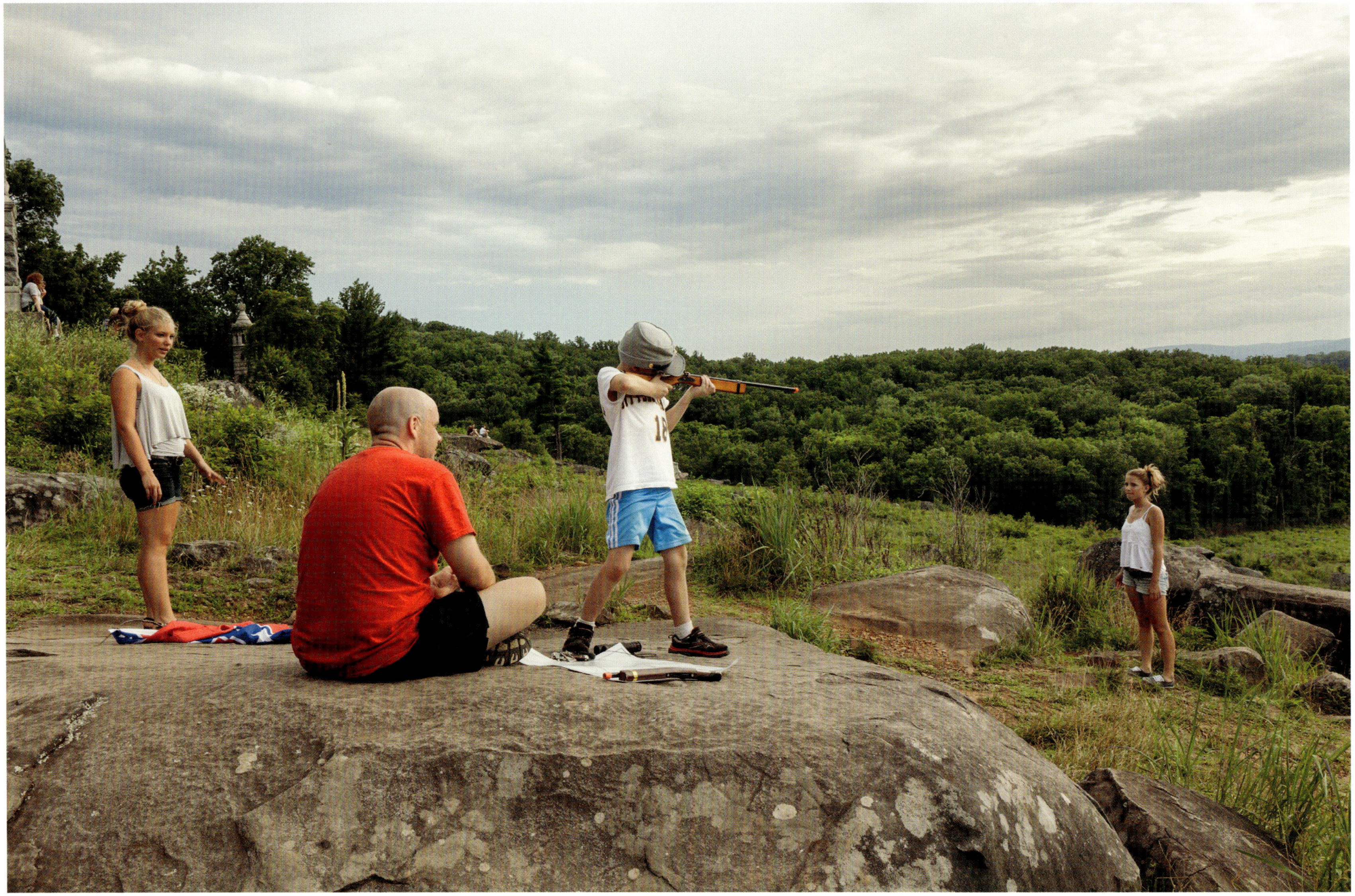

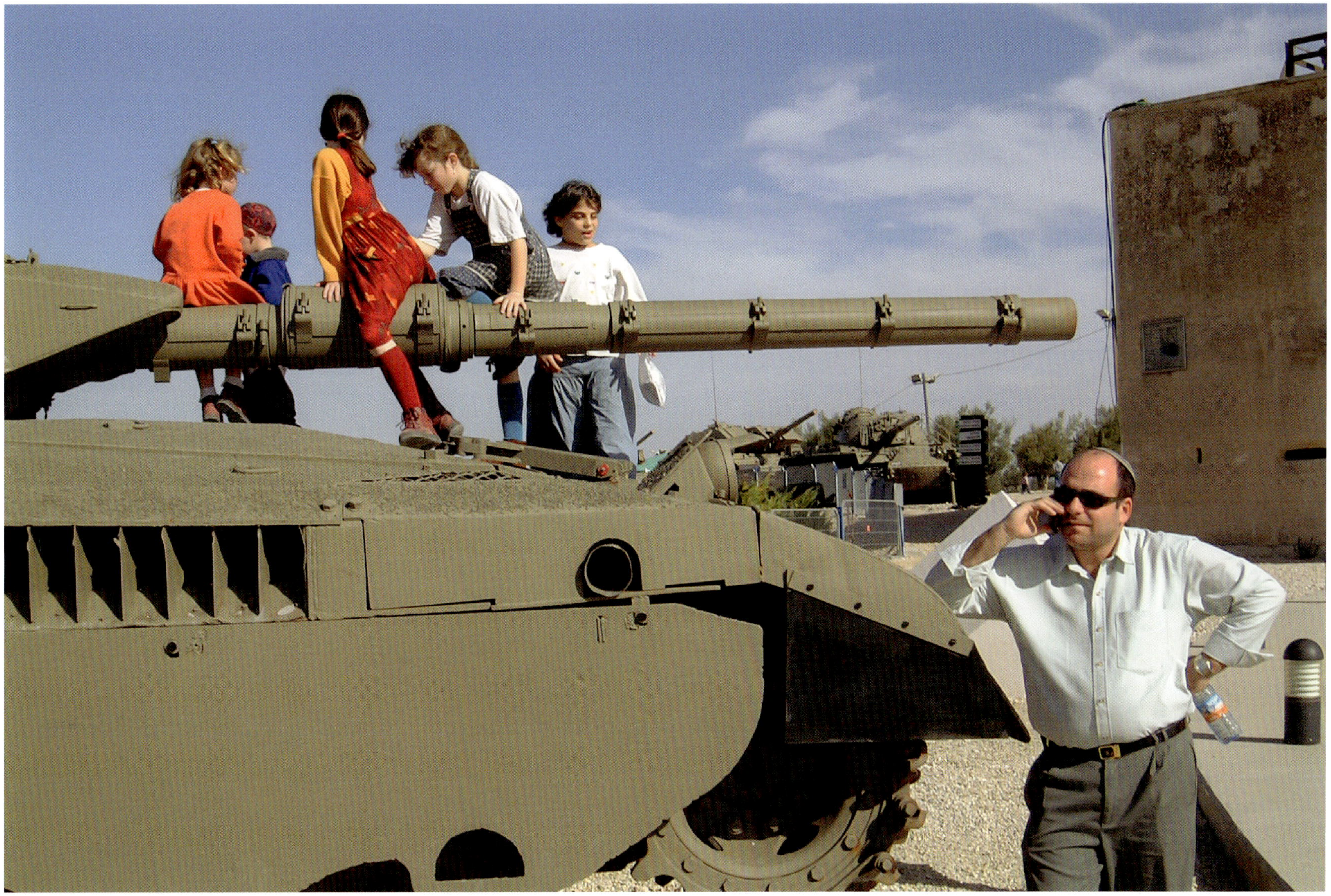

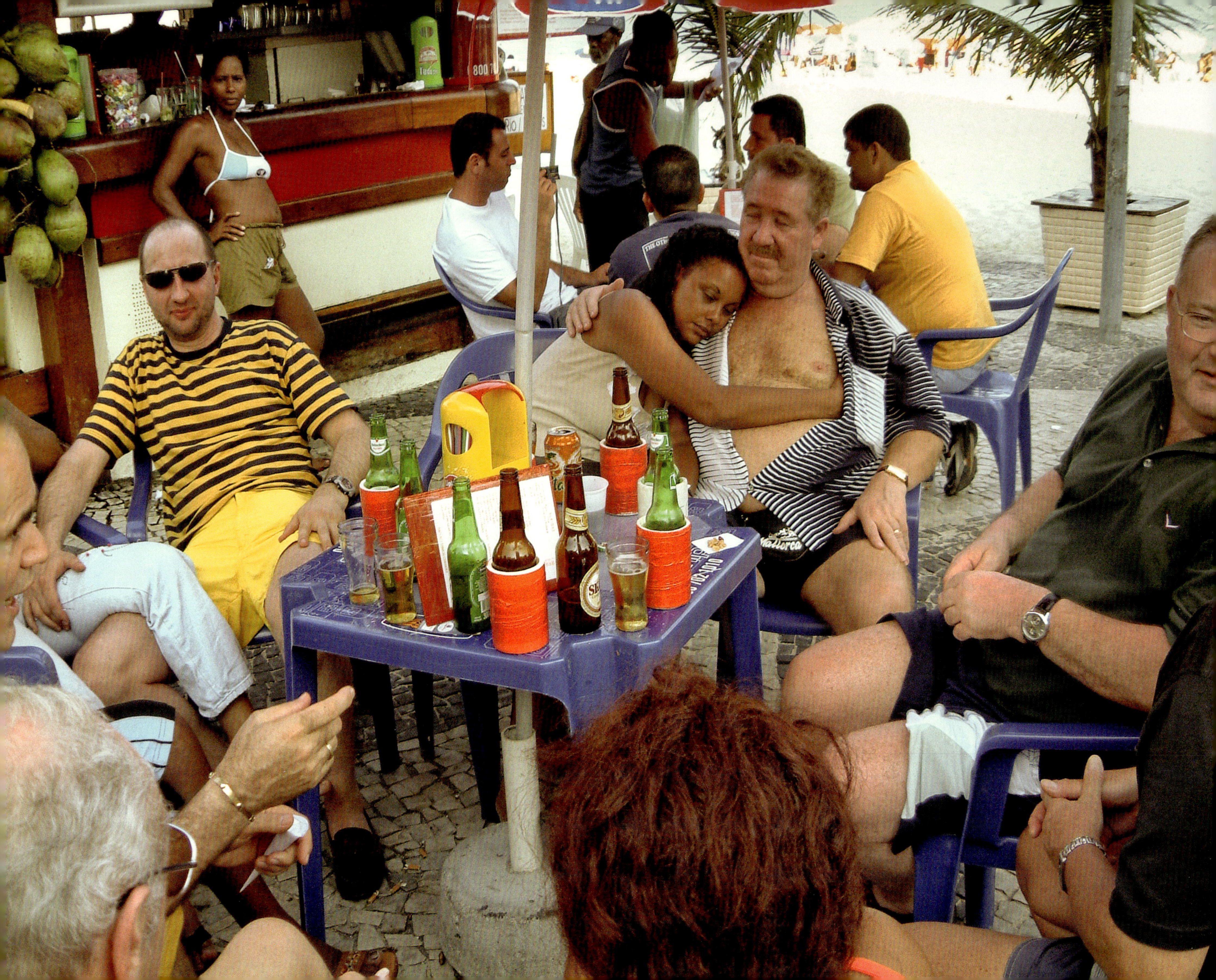

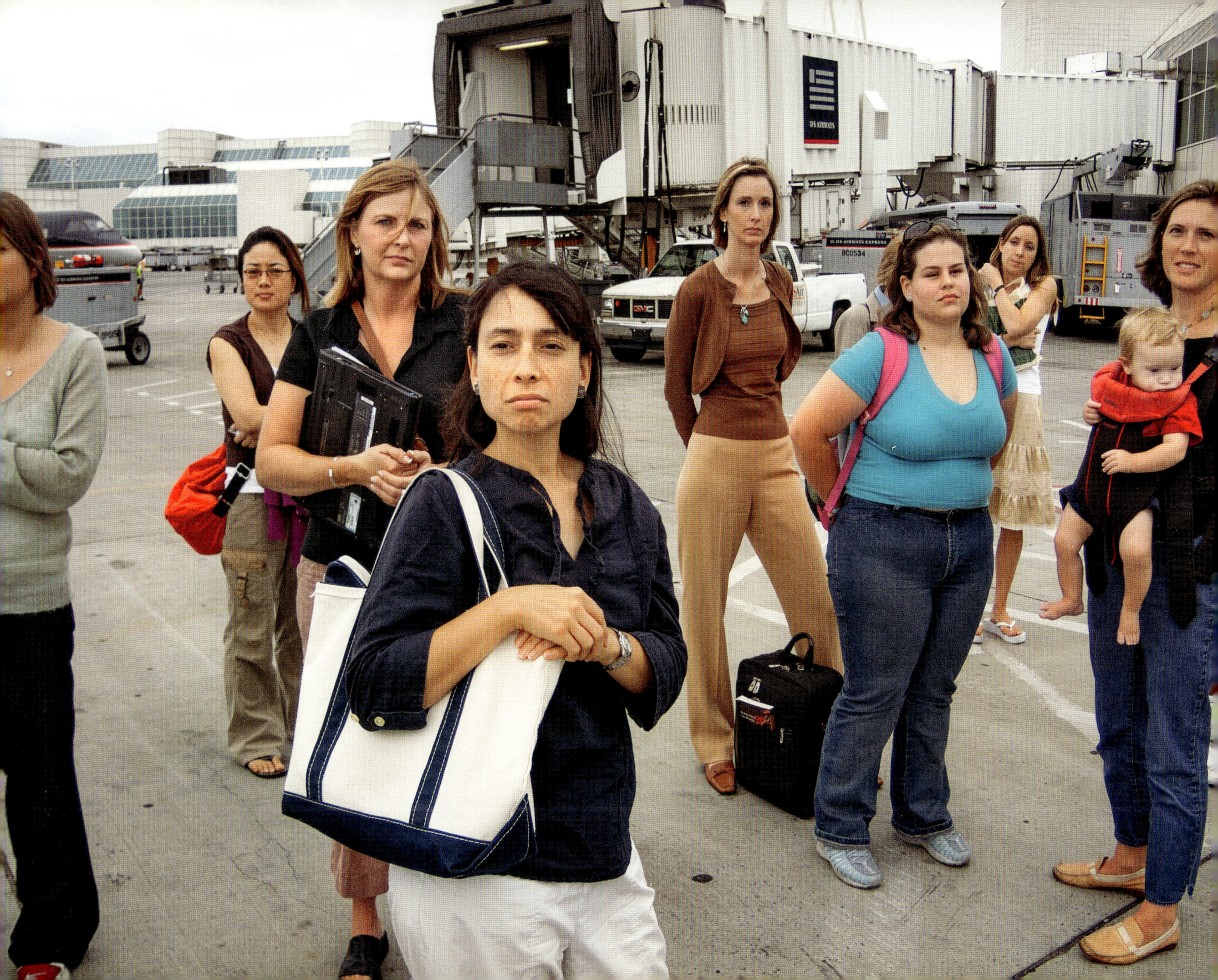
US AIRWAYS
US AIRWAYS EXPRESS
8C0534
GMC

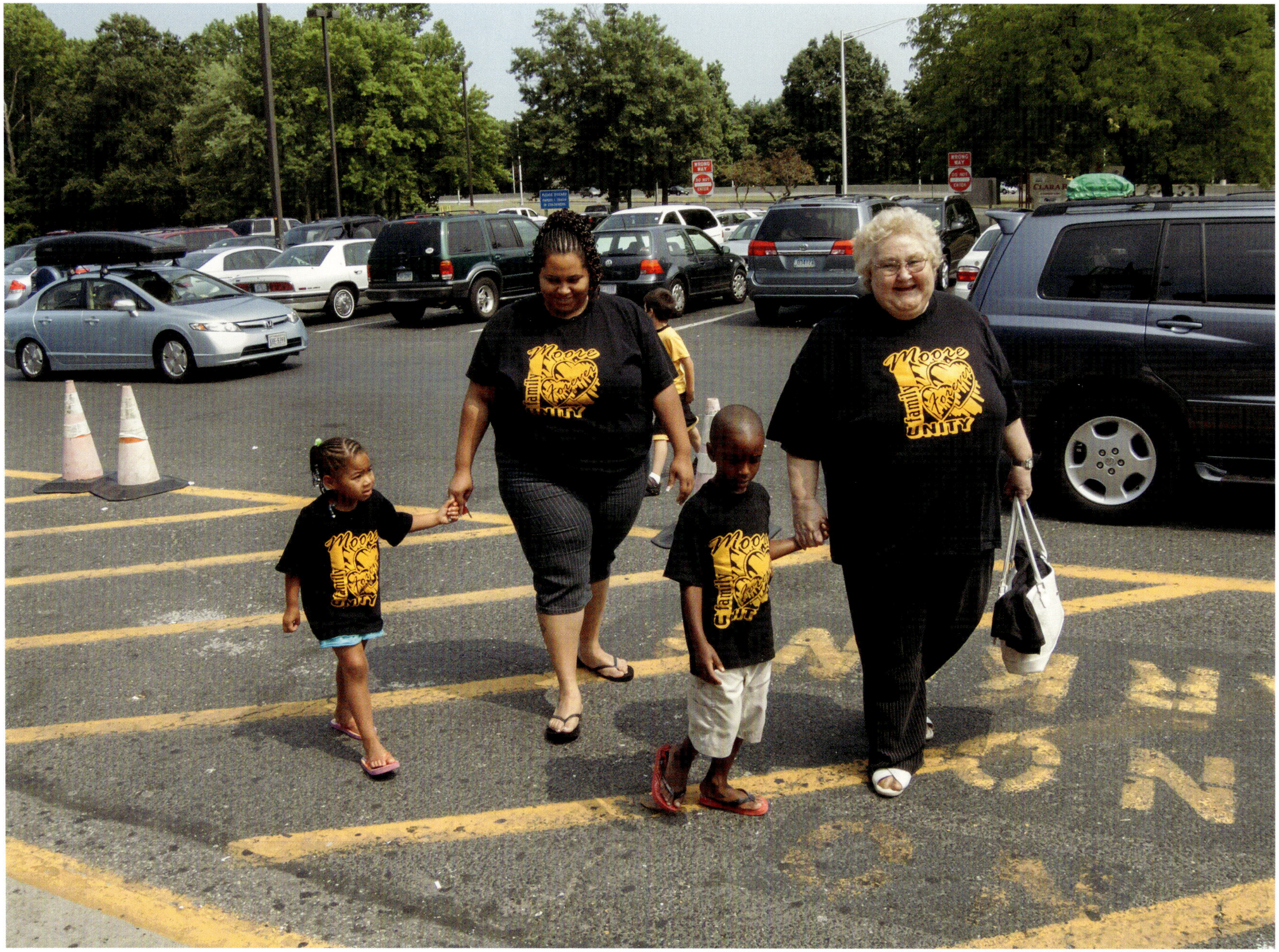

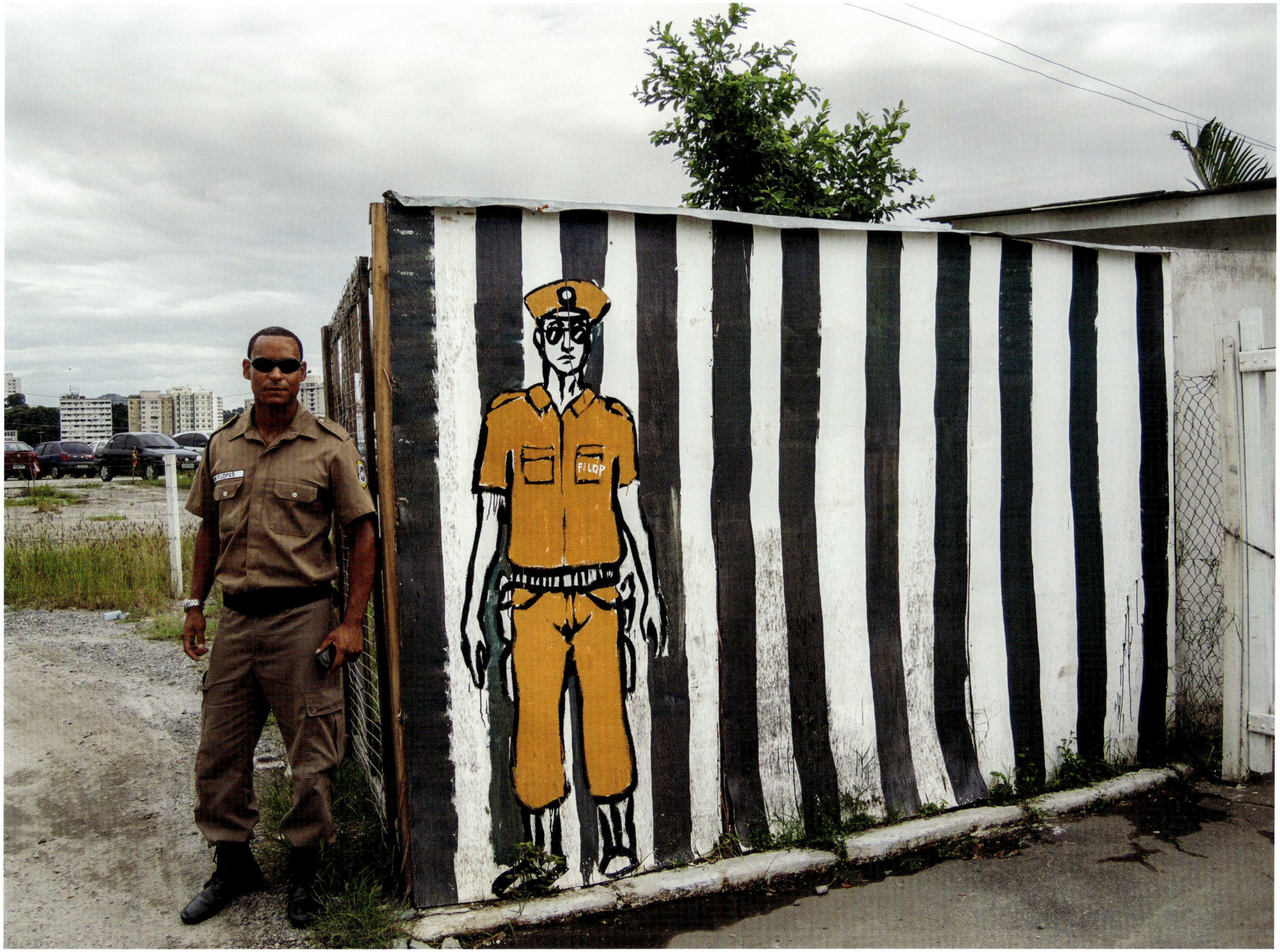

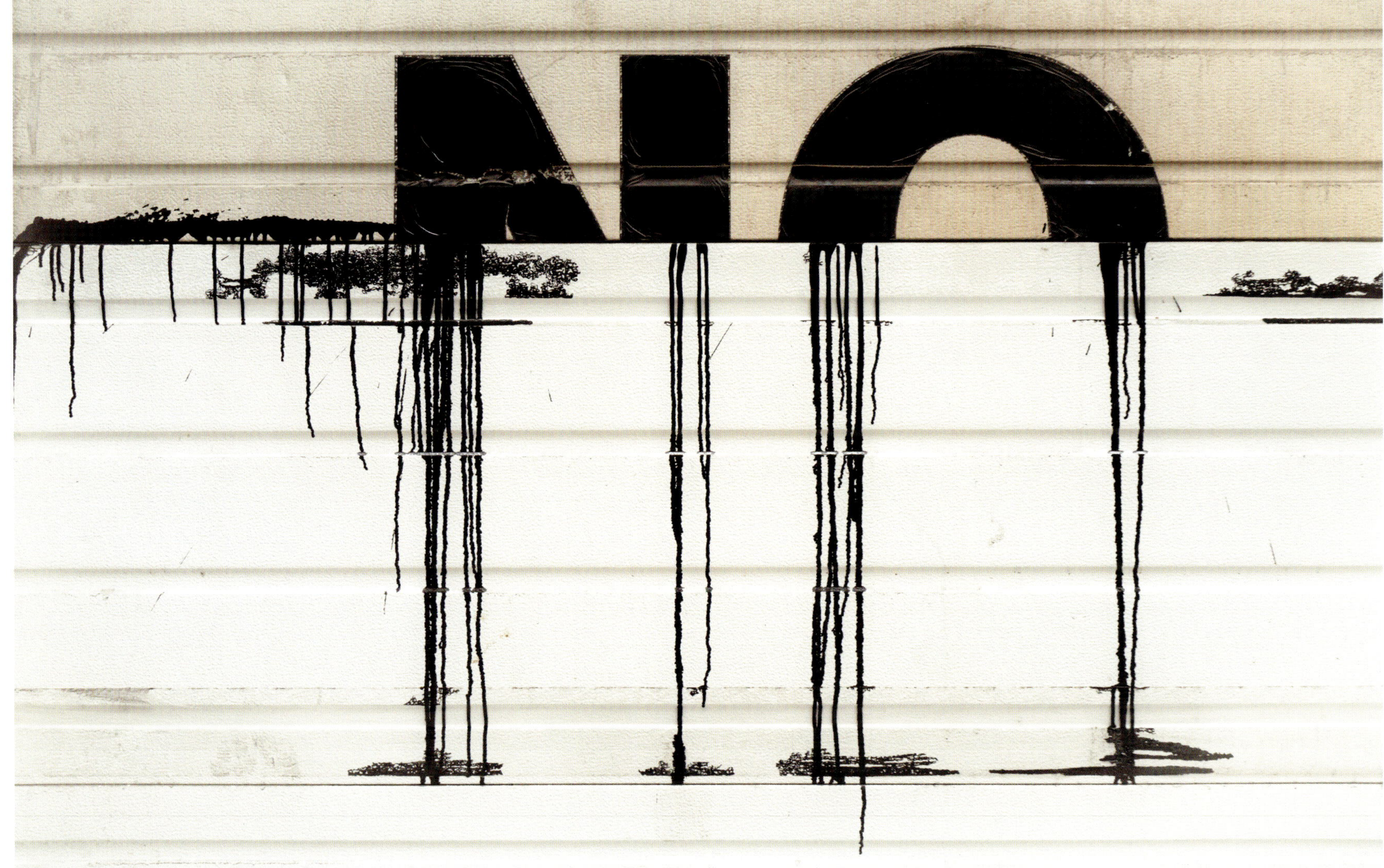

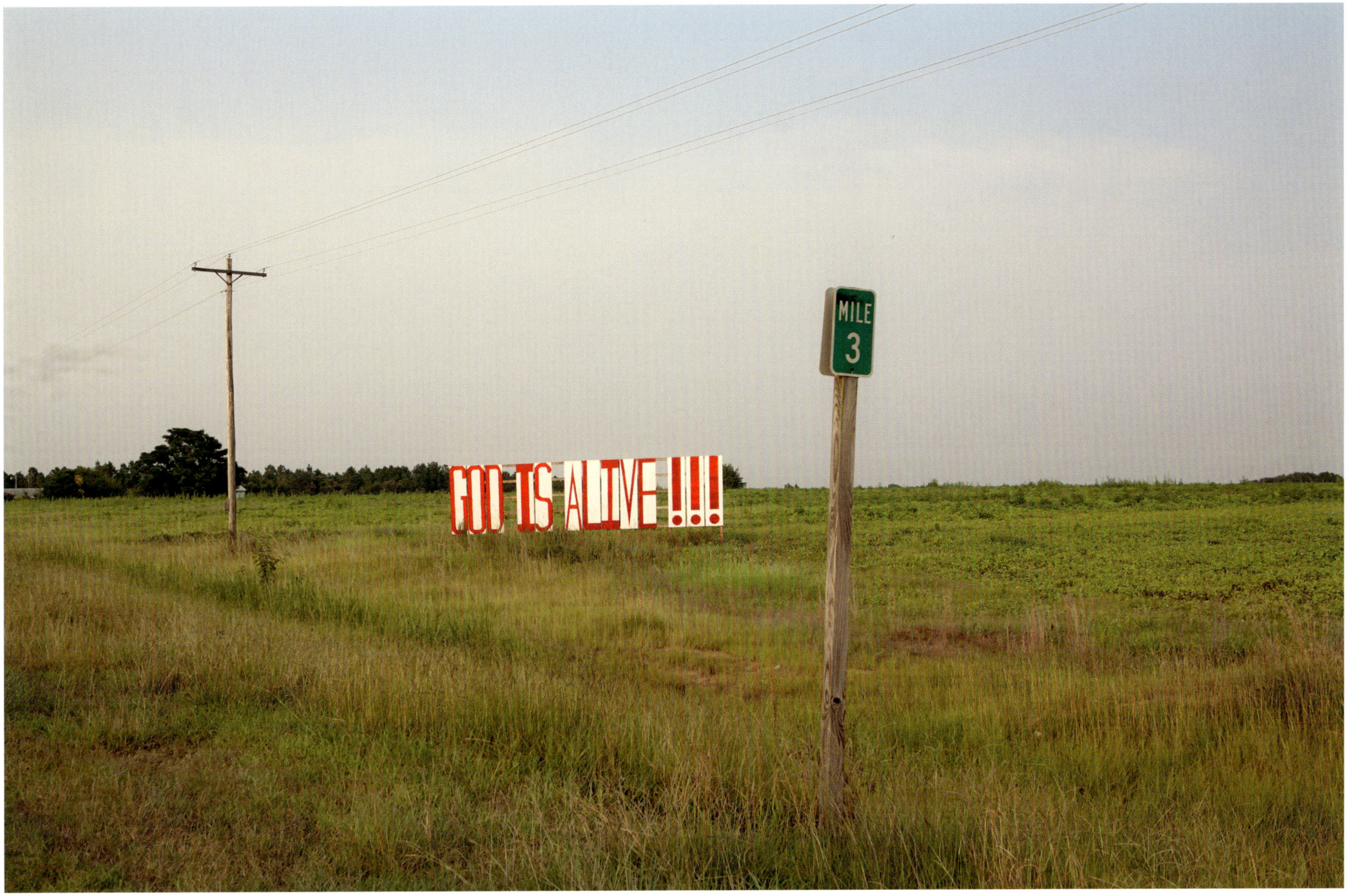

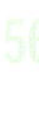

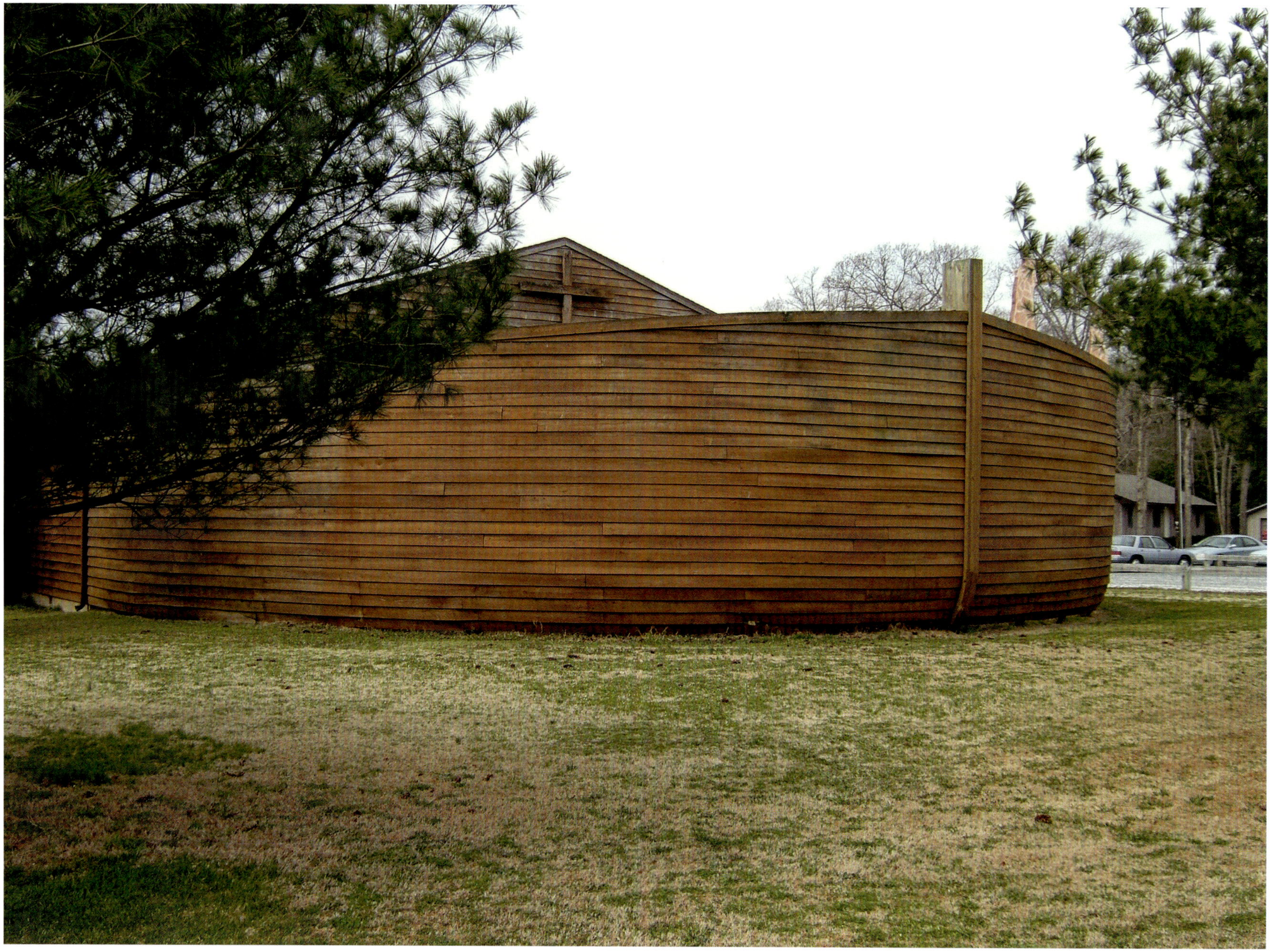

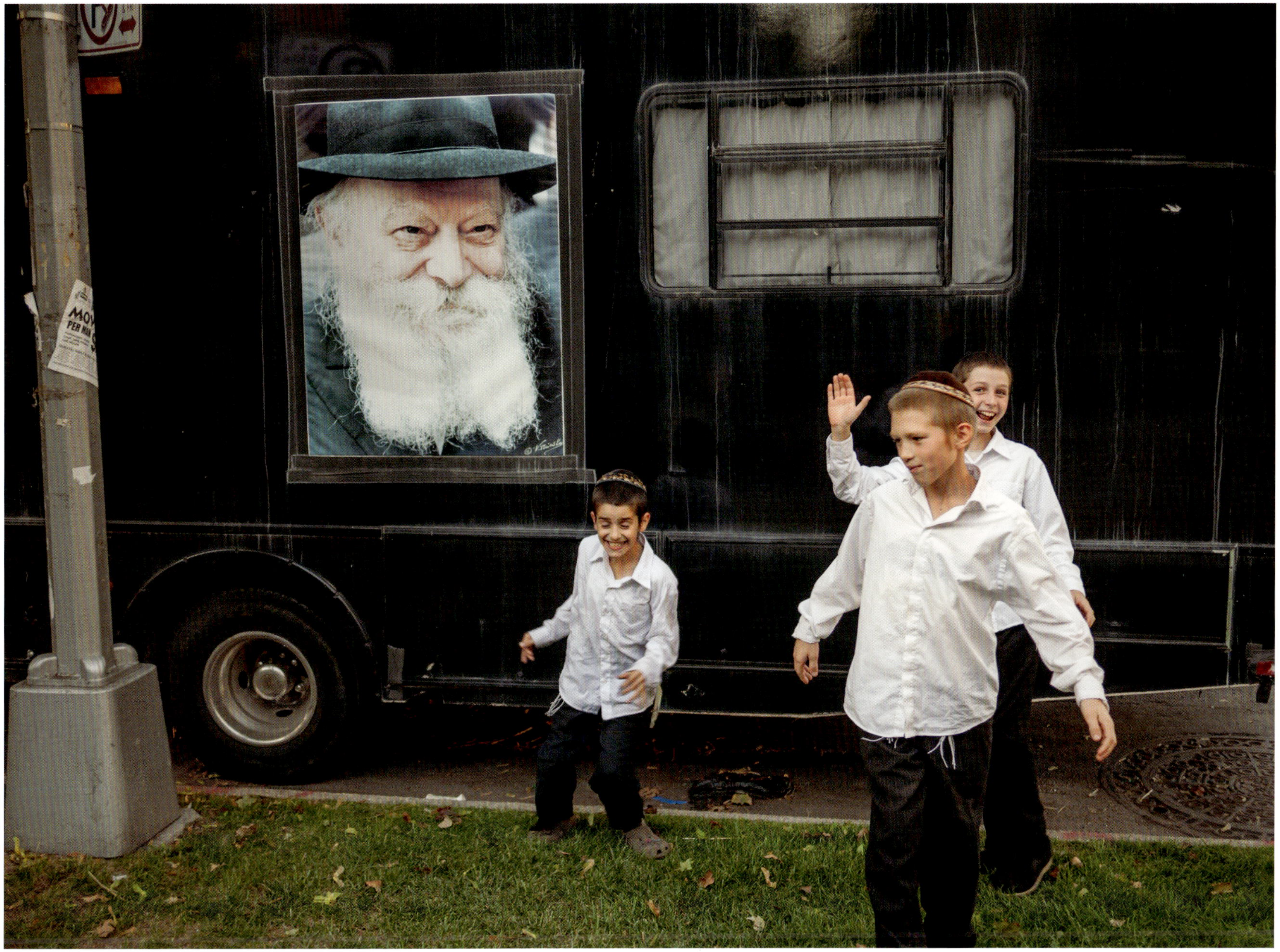

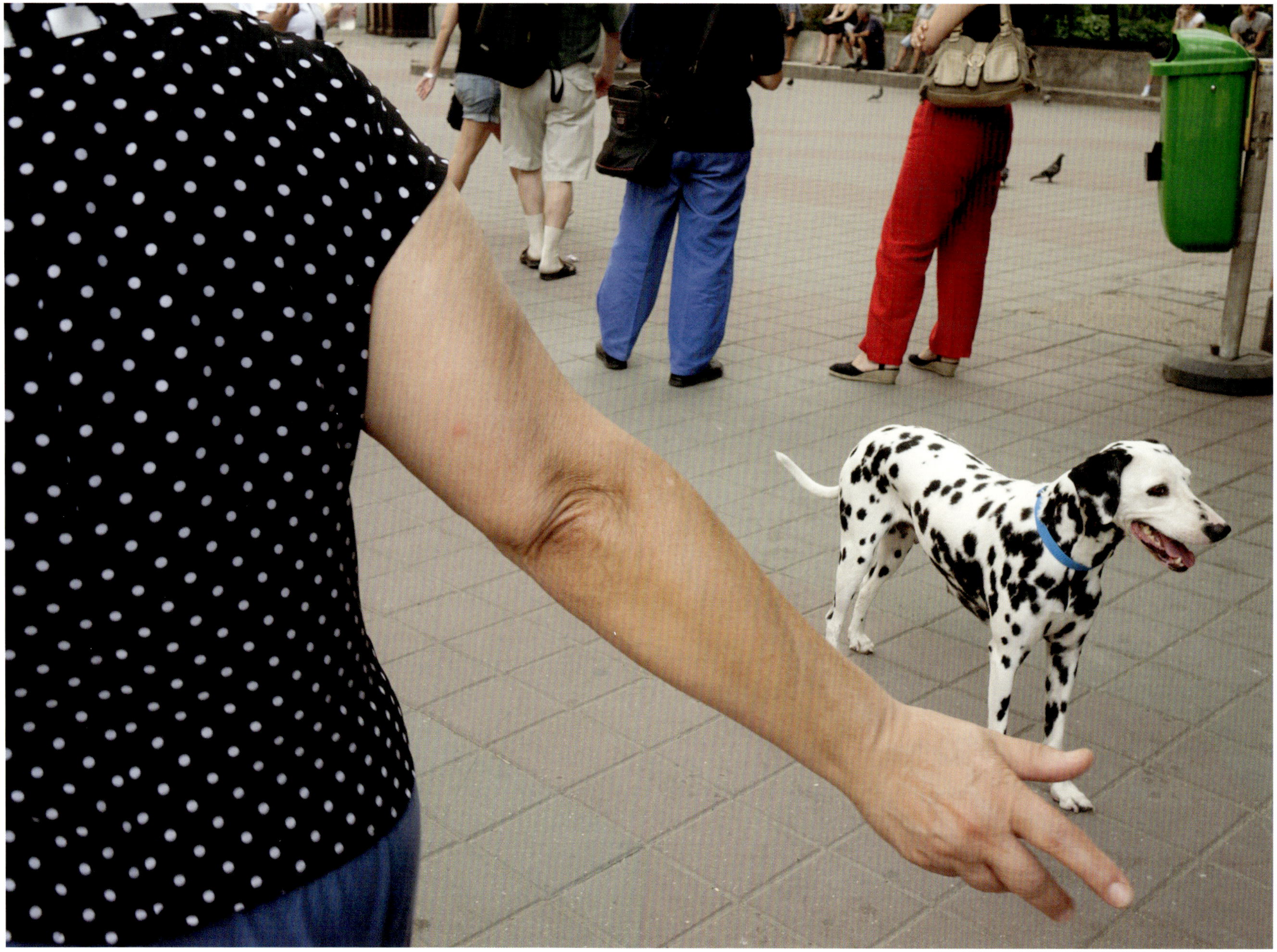

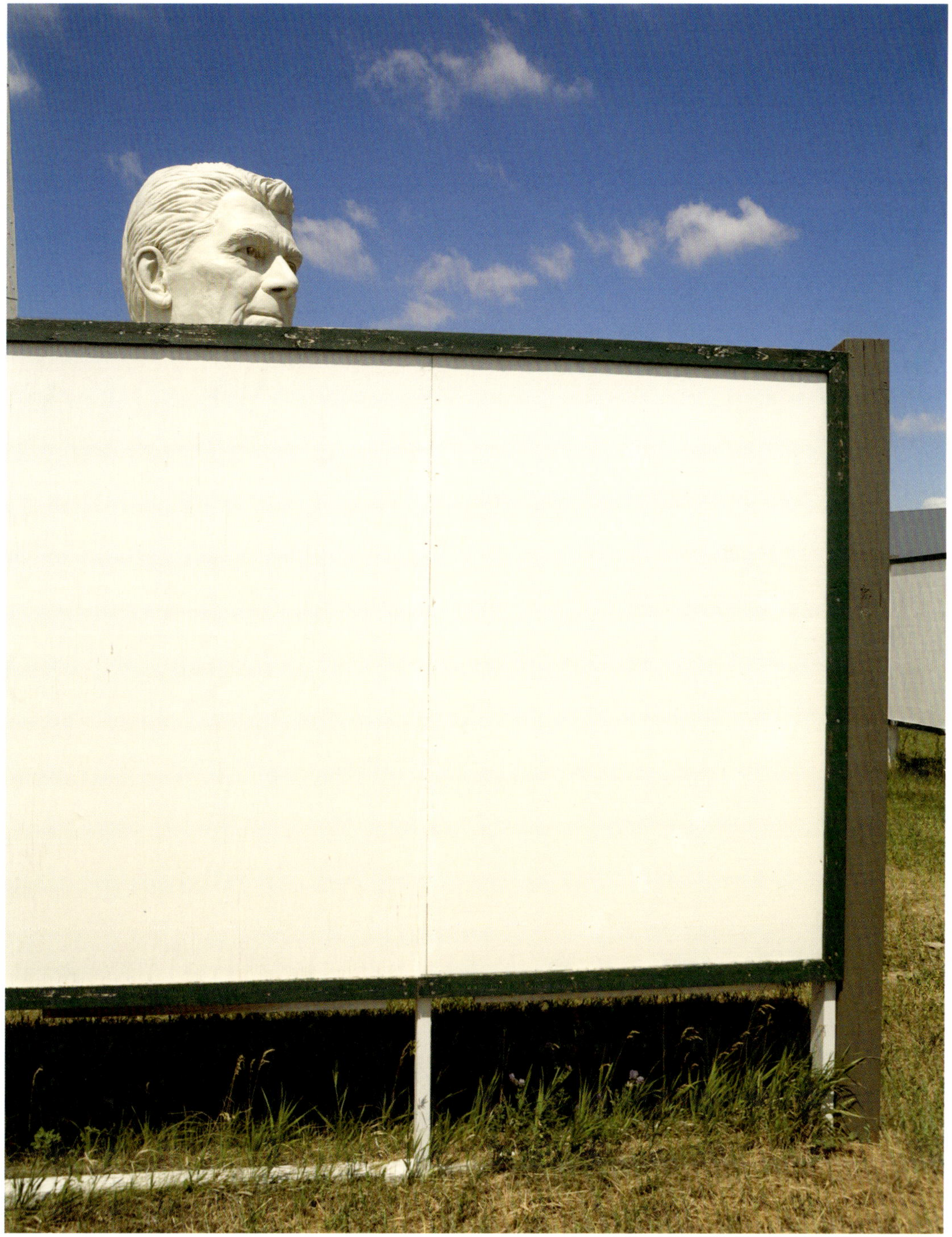

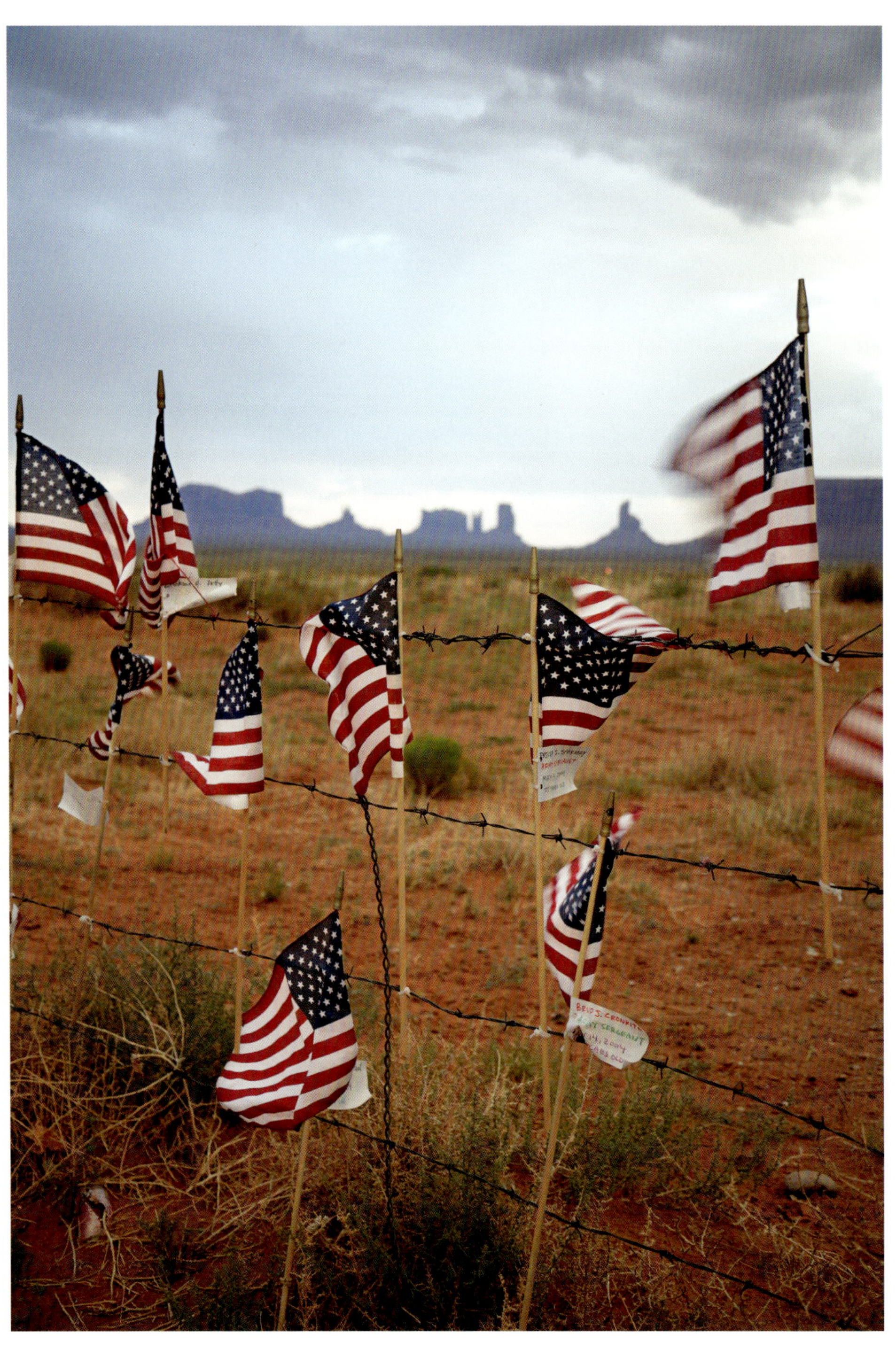

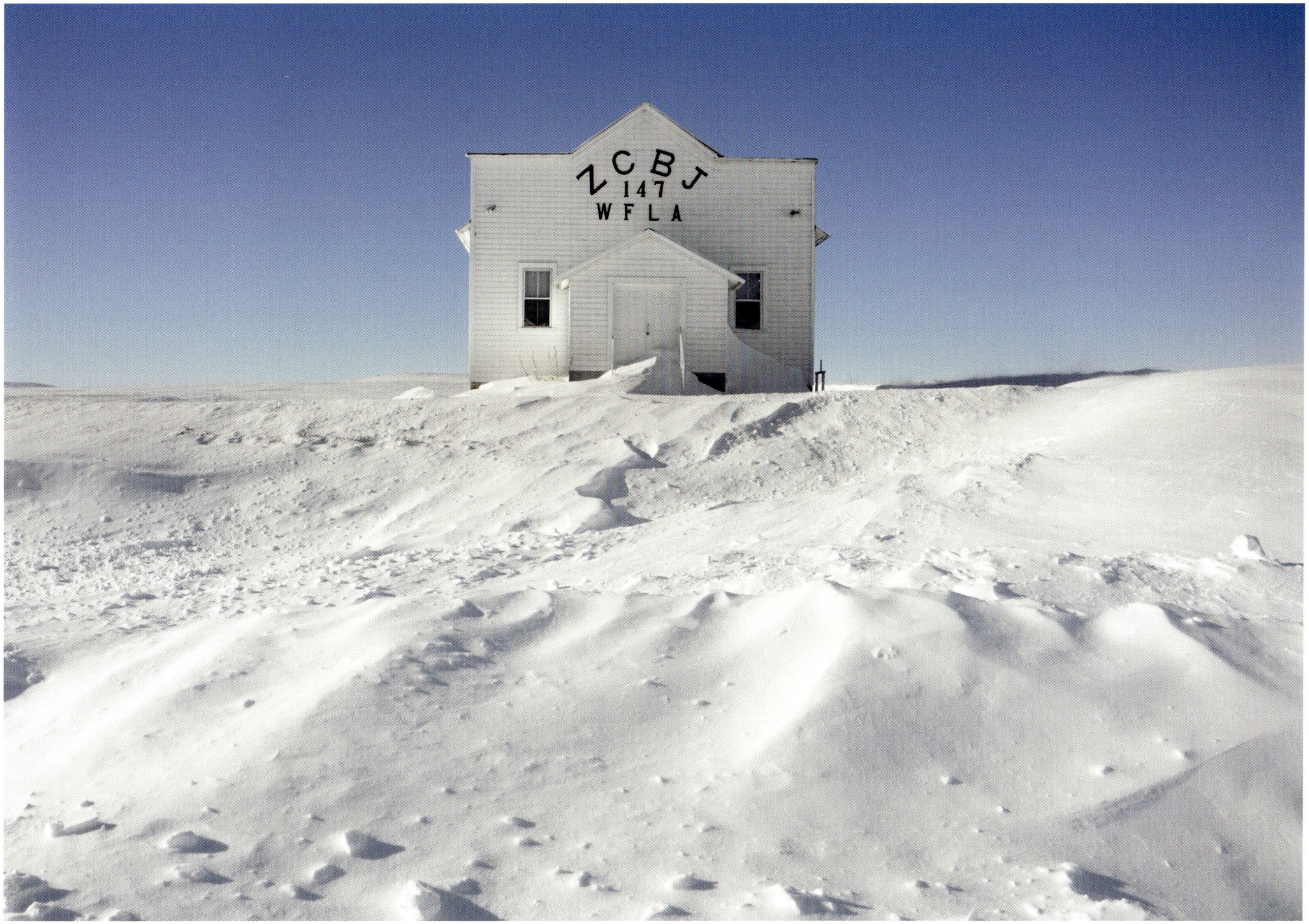

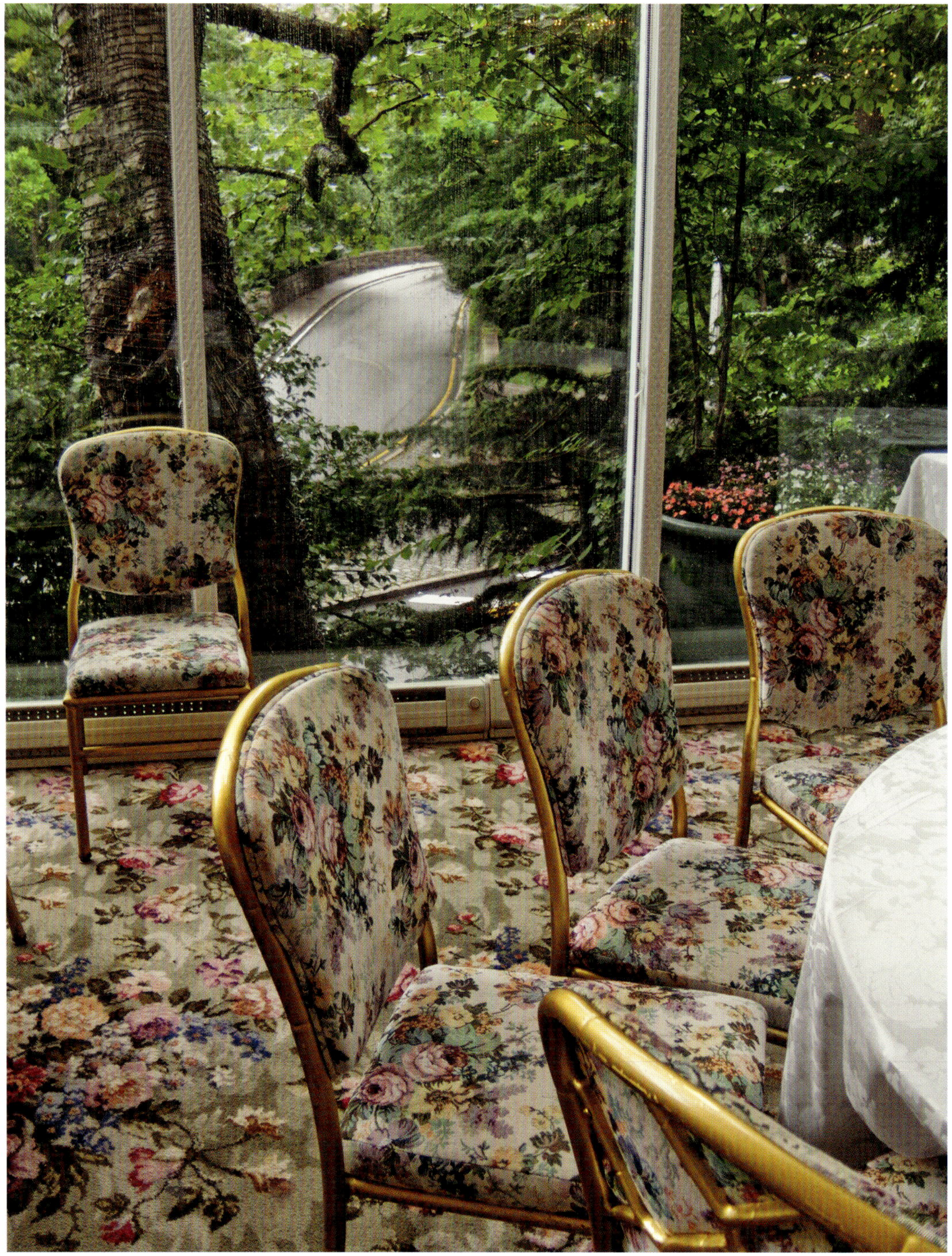

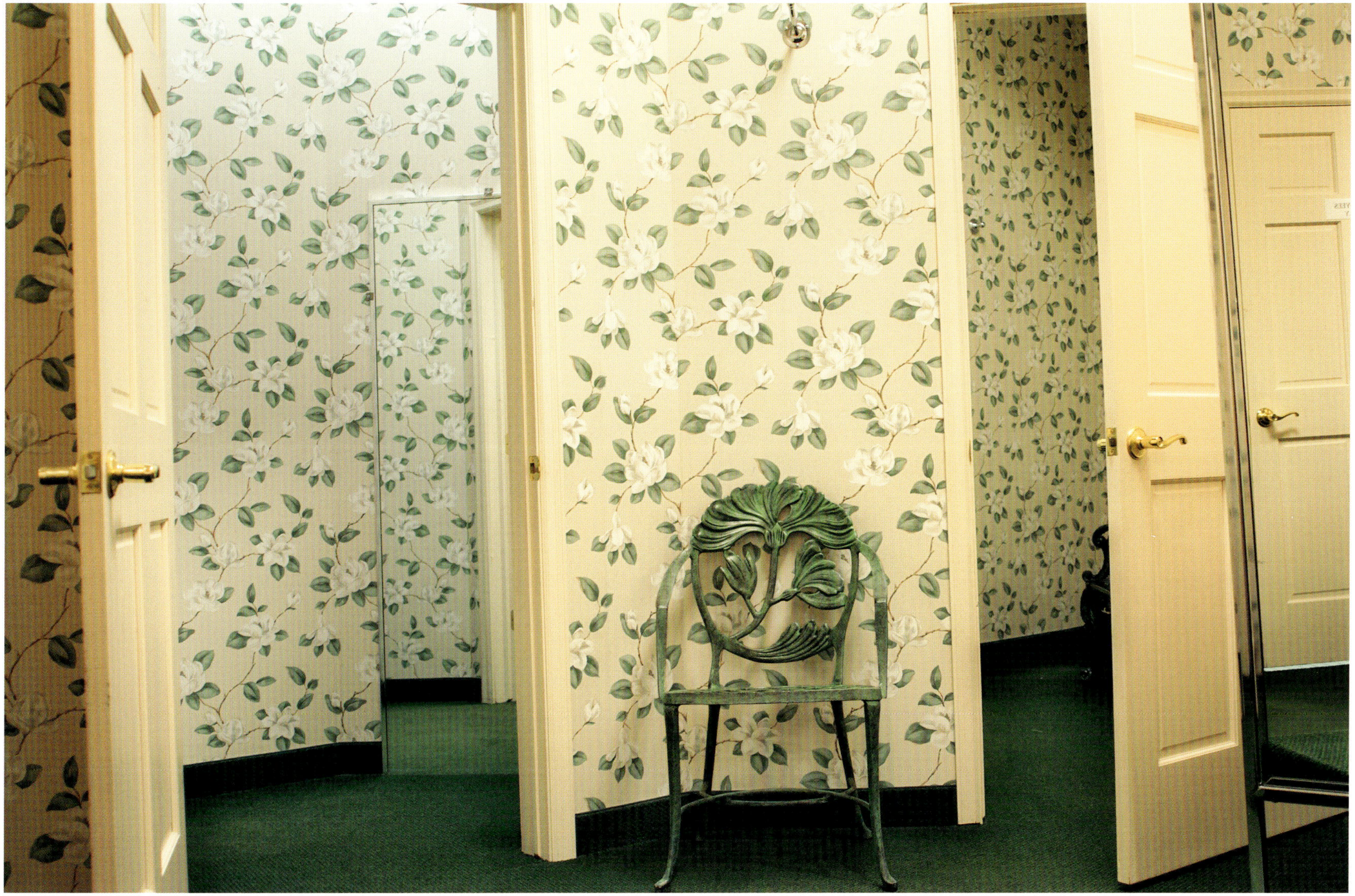

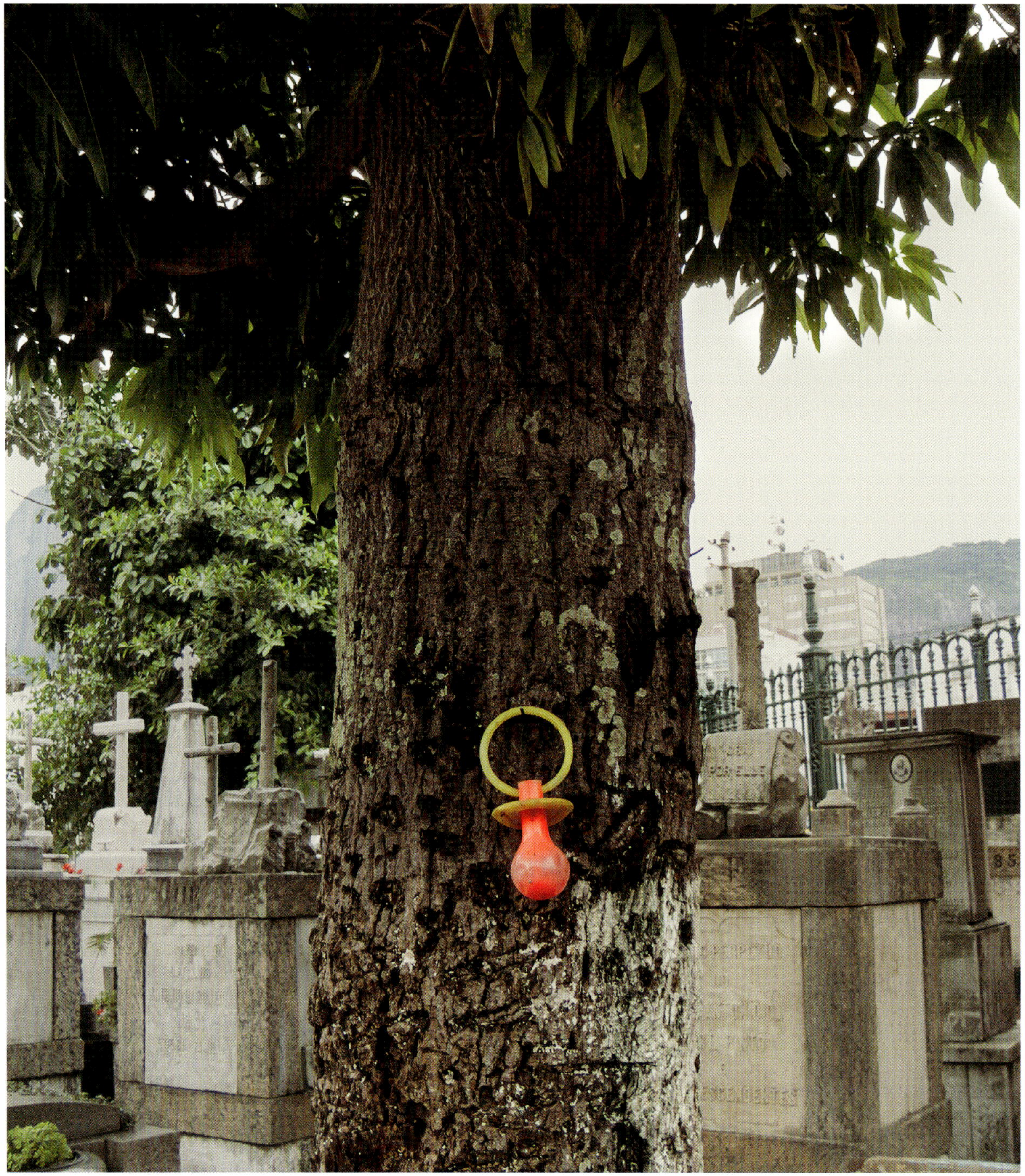

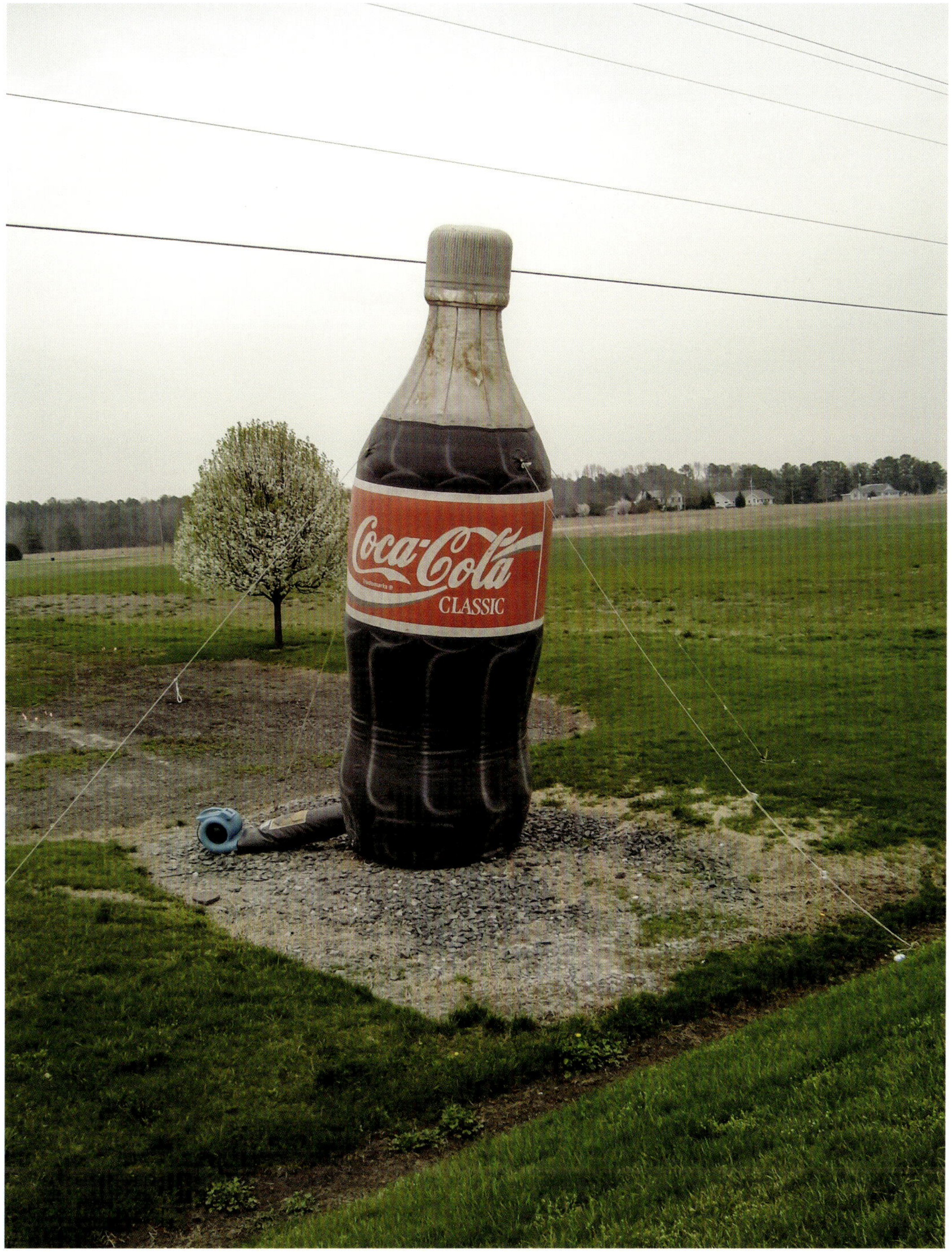

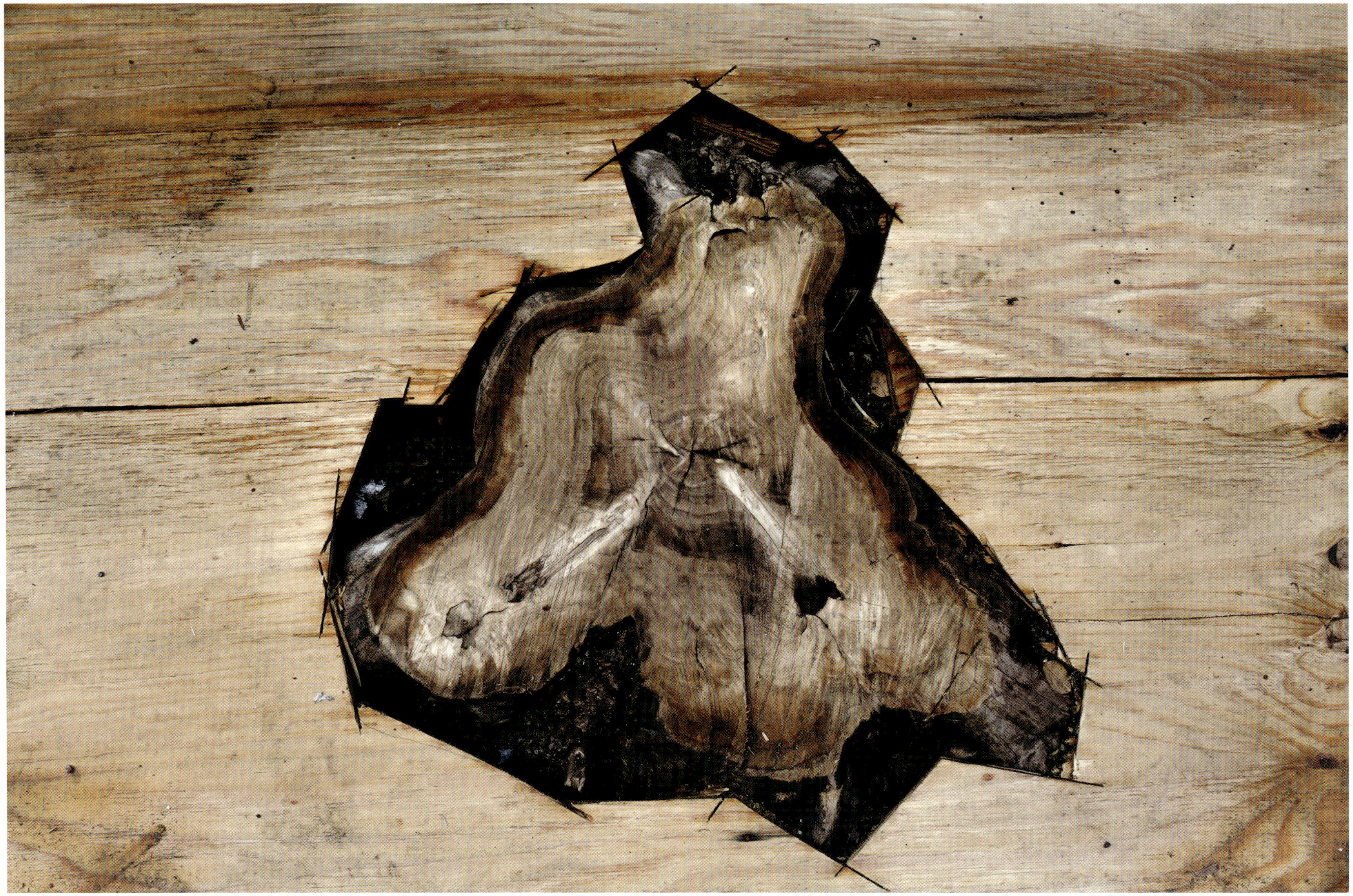

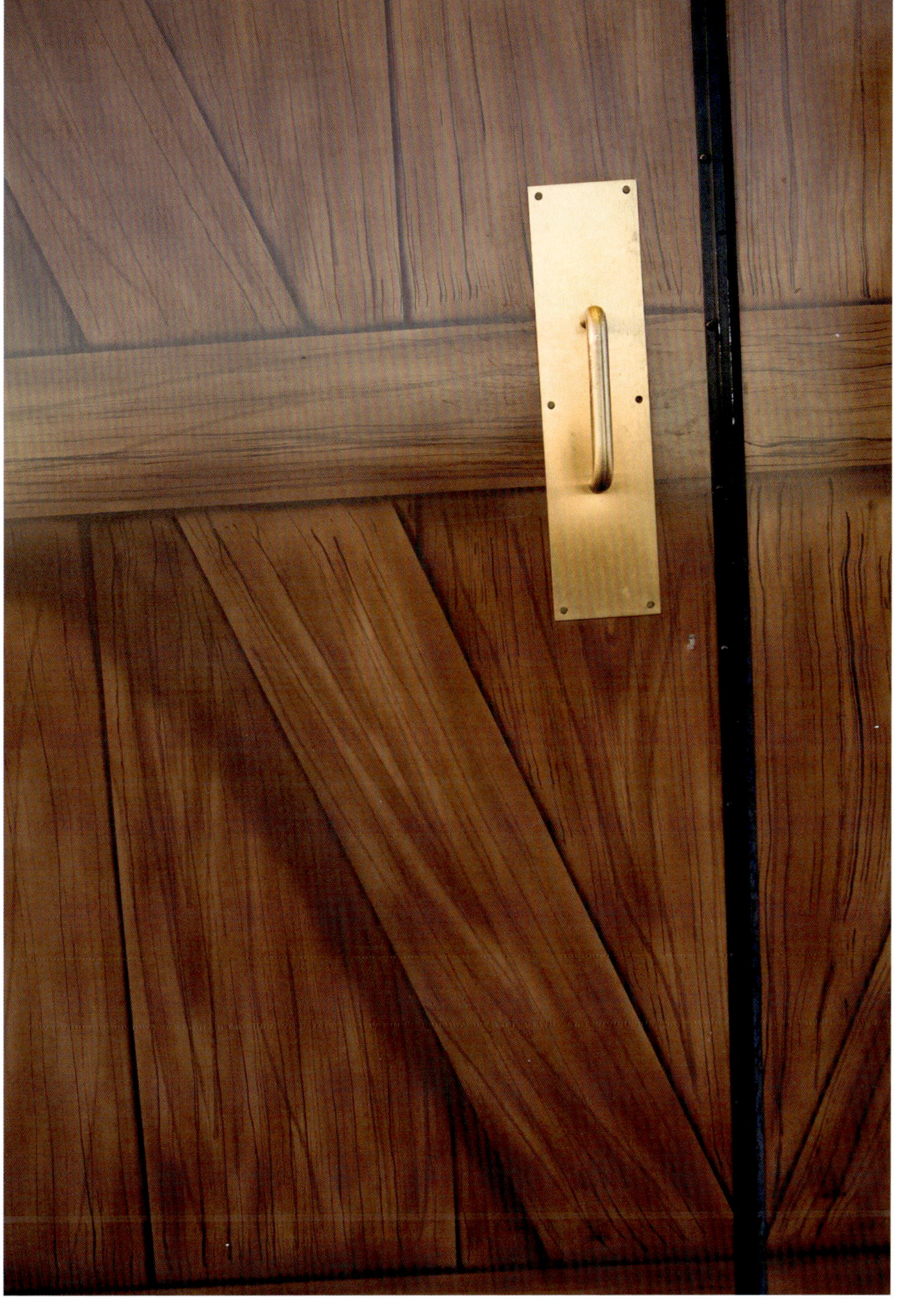

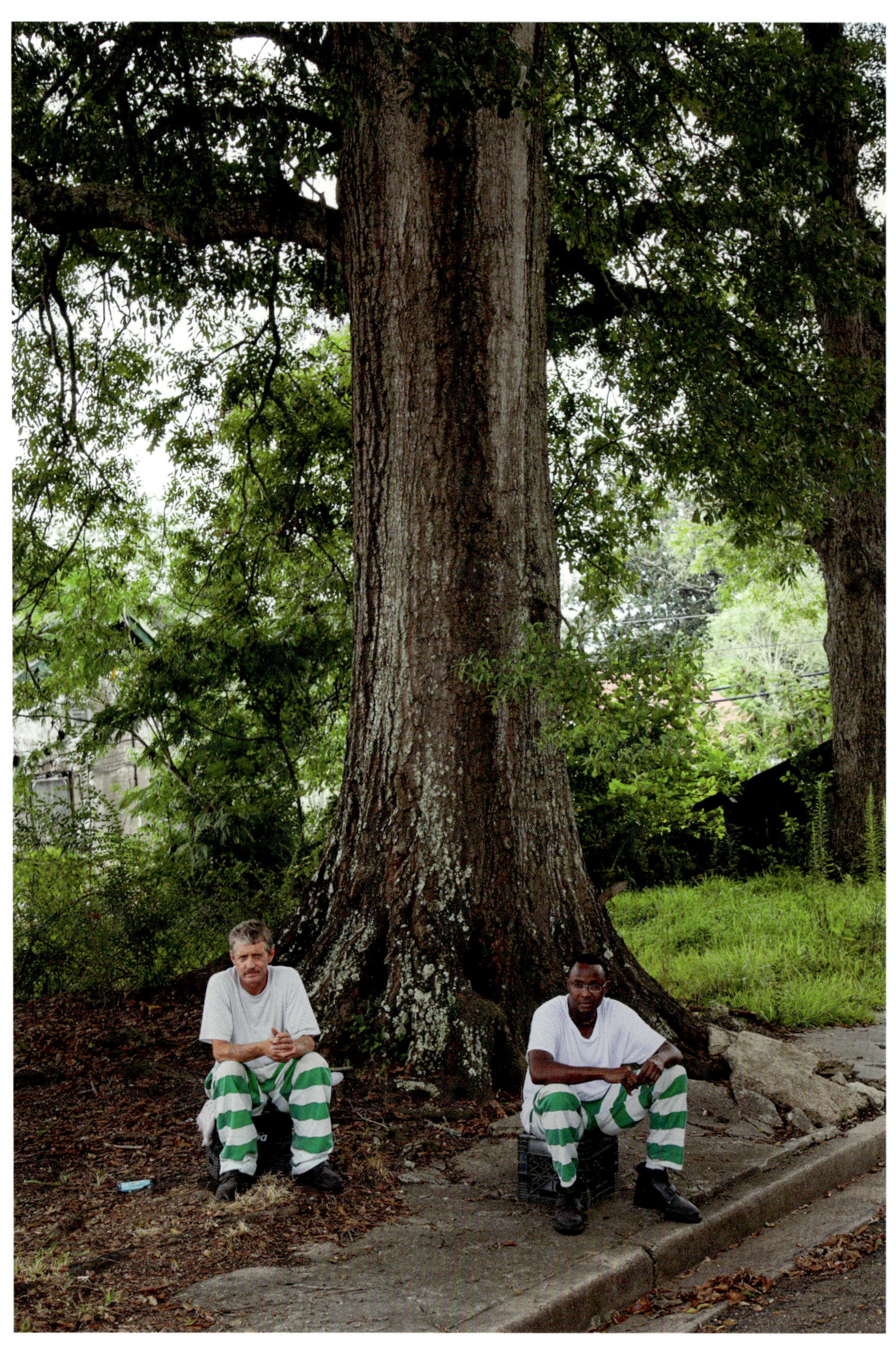

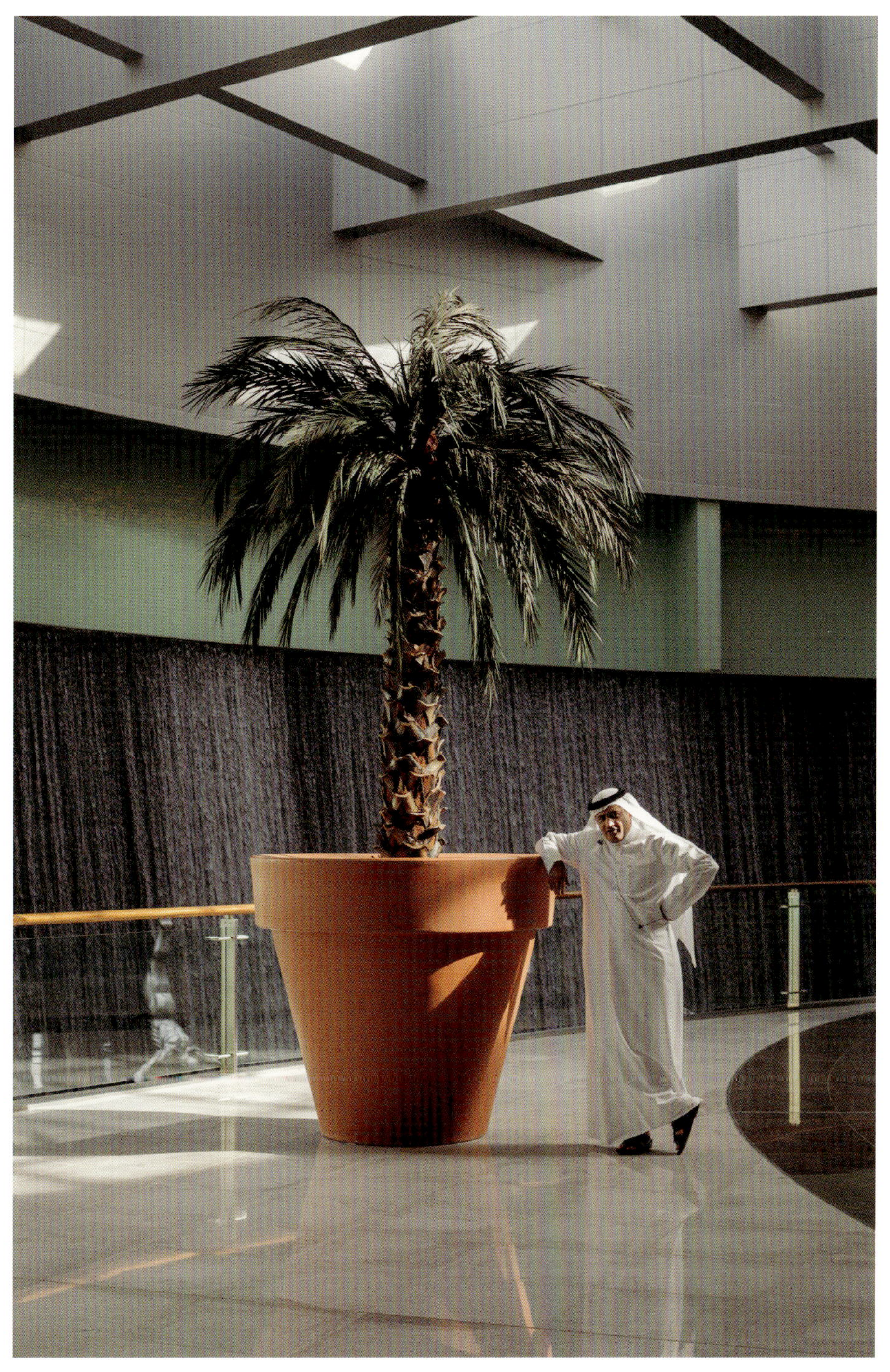

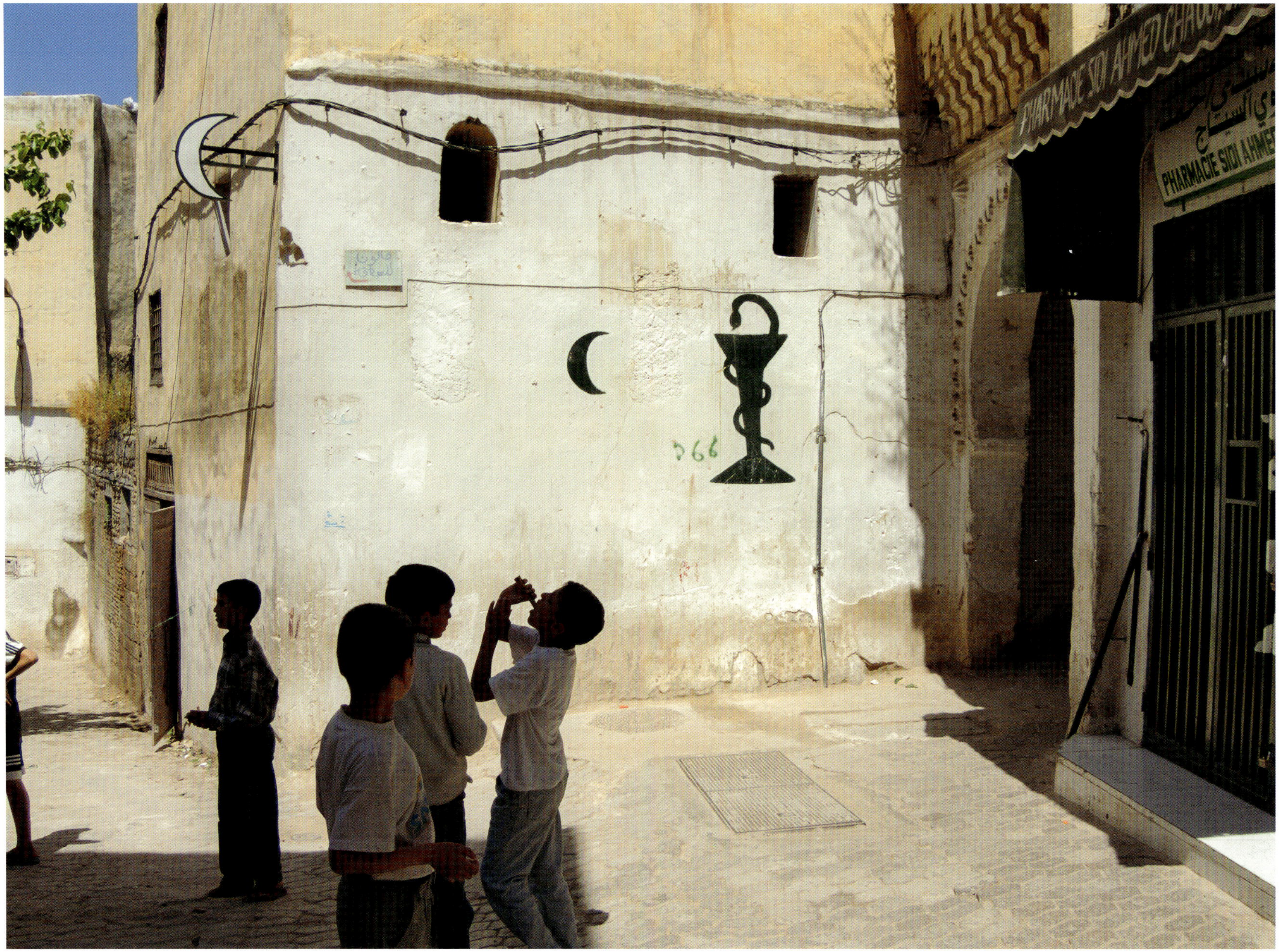

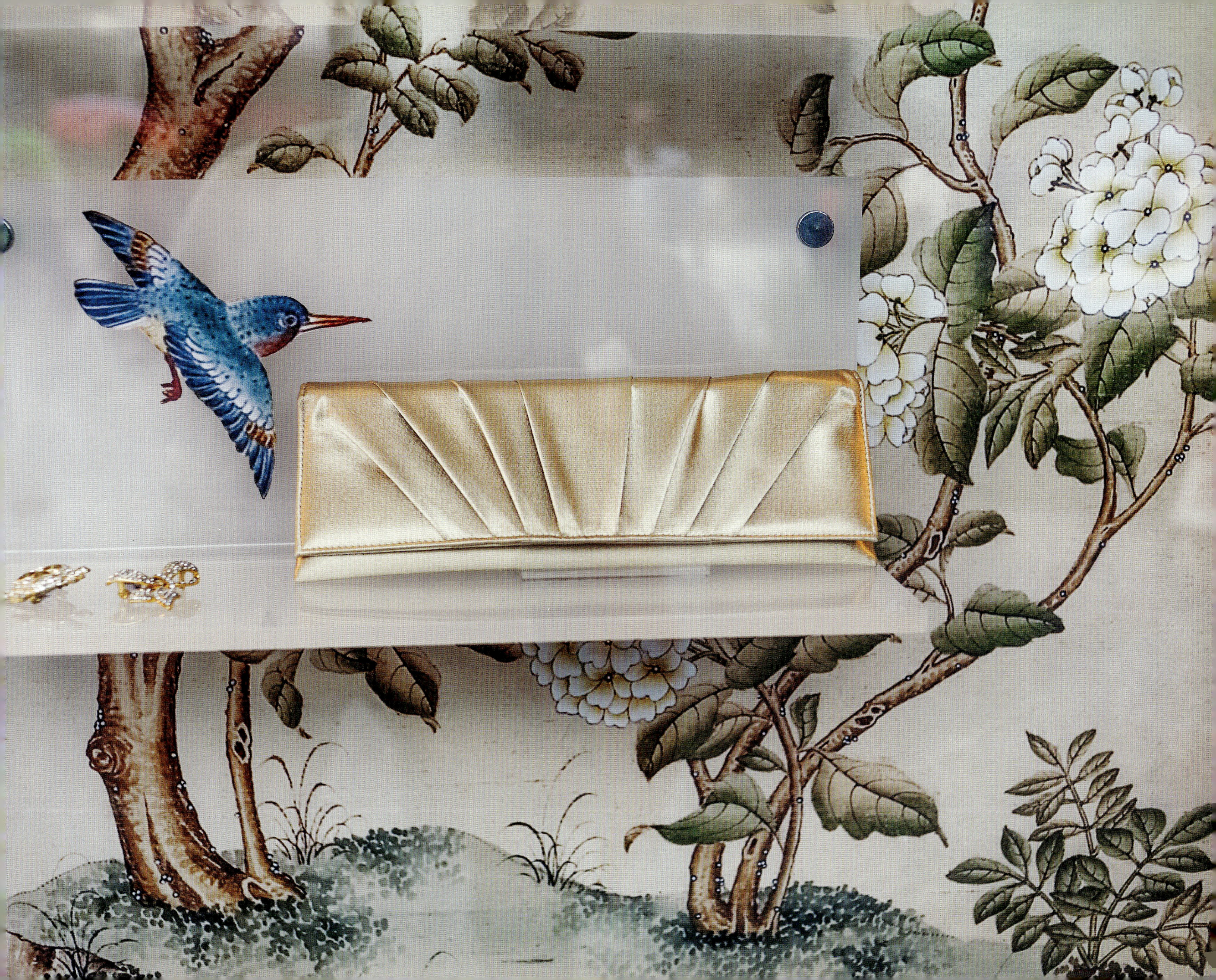

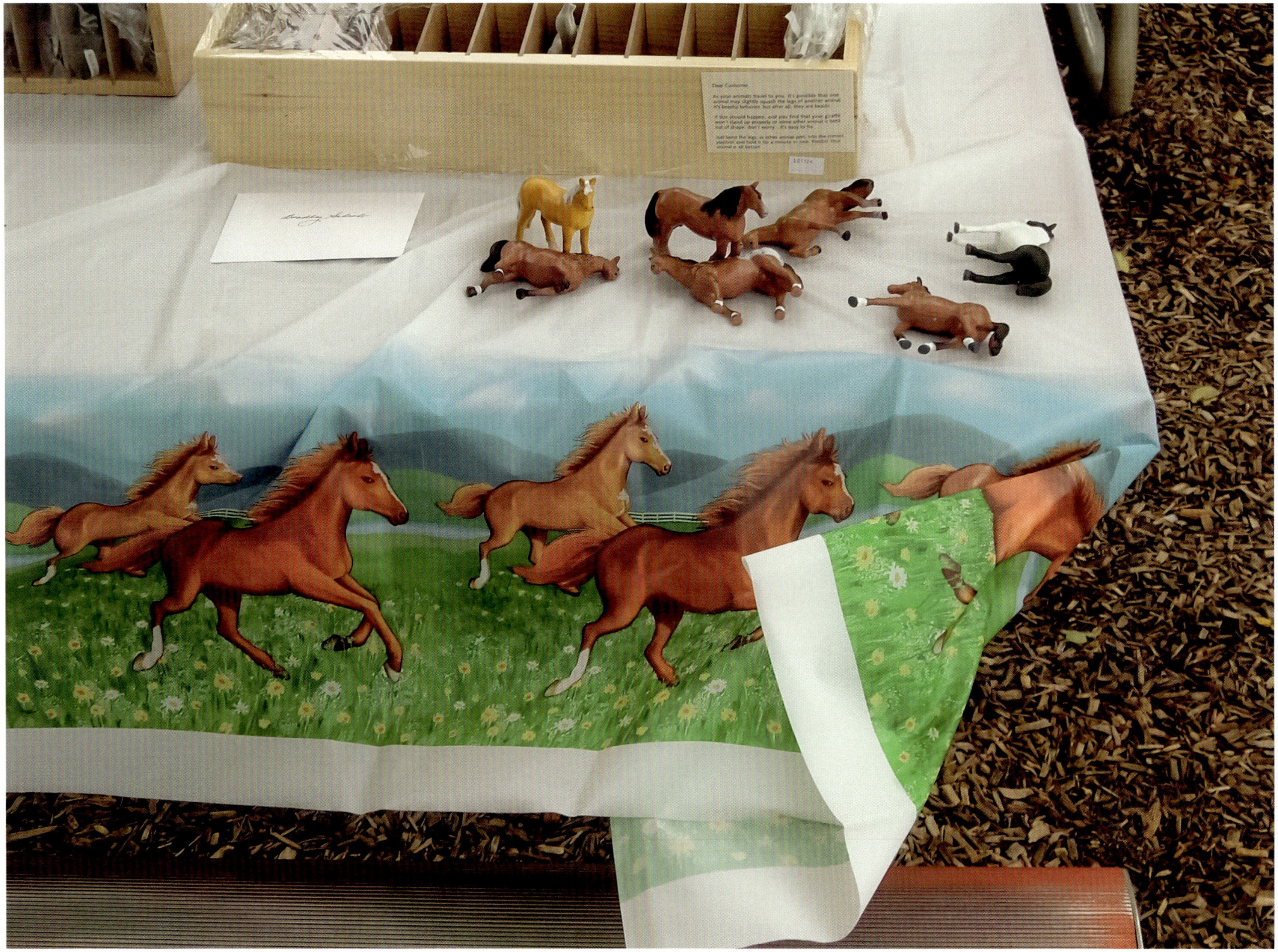

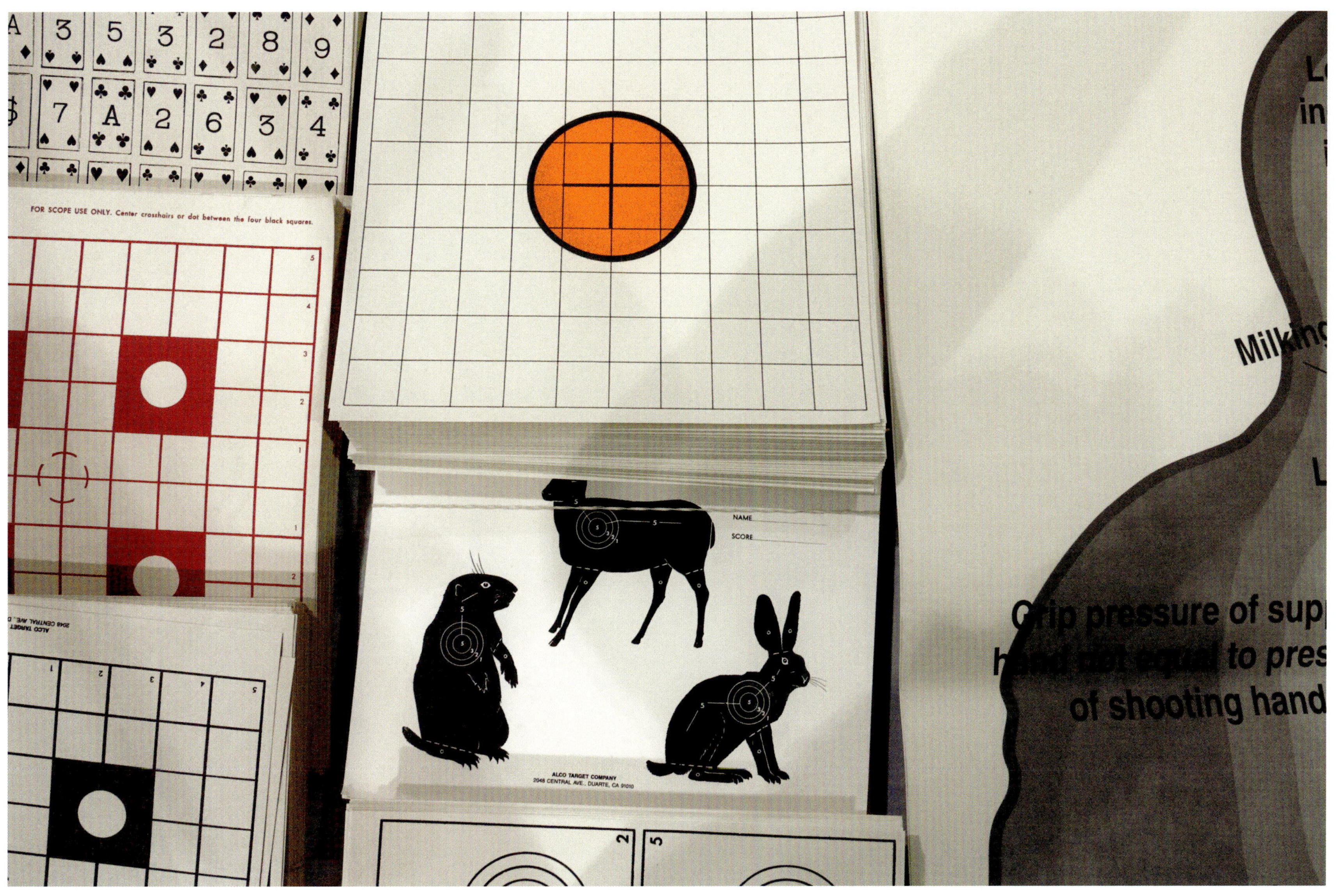
FOR SCOPE USE ONLY. Center crosshairs or dot between the four black squares.
NAME
SCORE
ALCO TARGET COMPANY
2048 CENTRAL AVE., DUARTE, CA 91010
of shooting hand

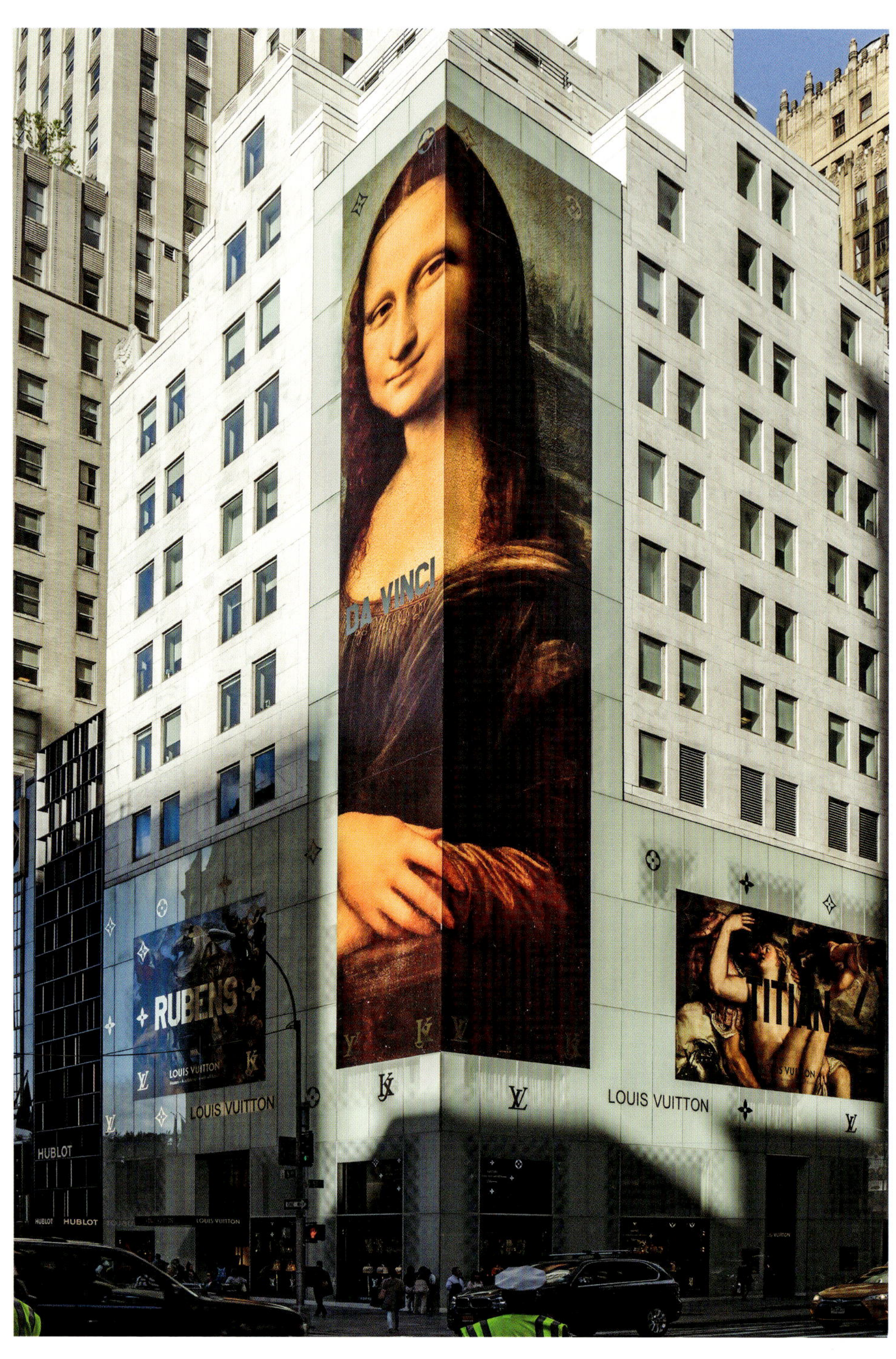
DA VINCI
RUBENS
LOUIS VUITTON
TITIAN
LOUIS VUITTON
LOUIS VUITTON
HUBLOT

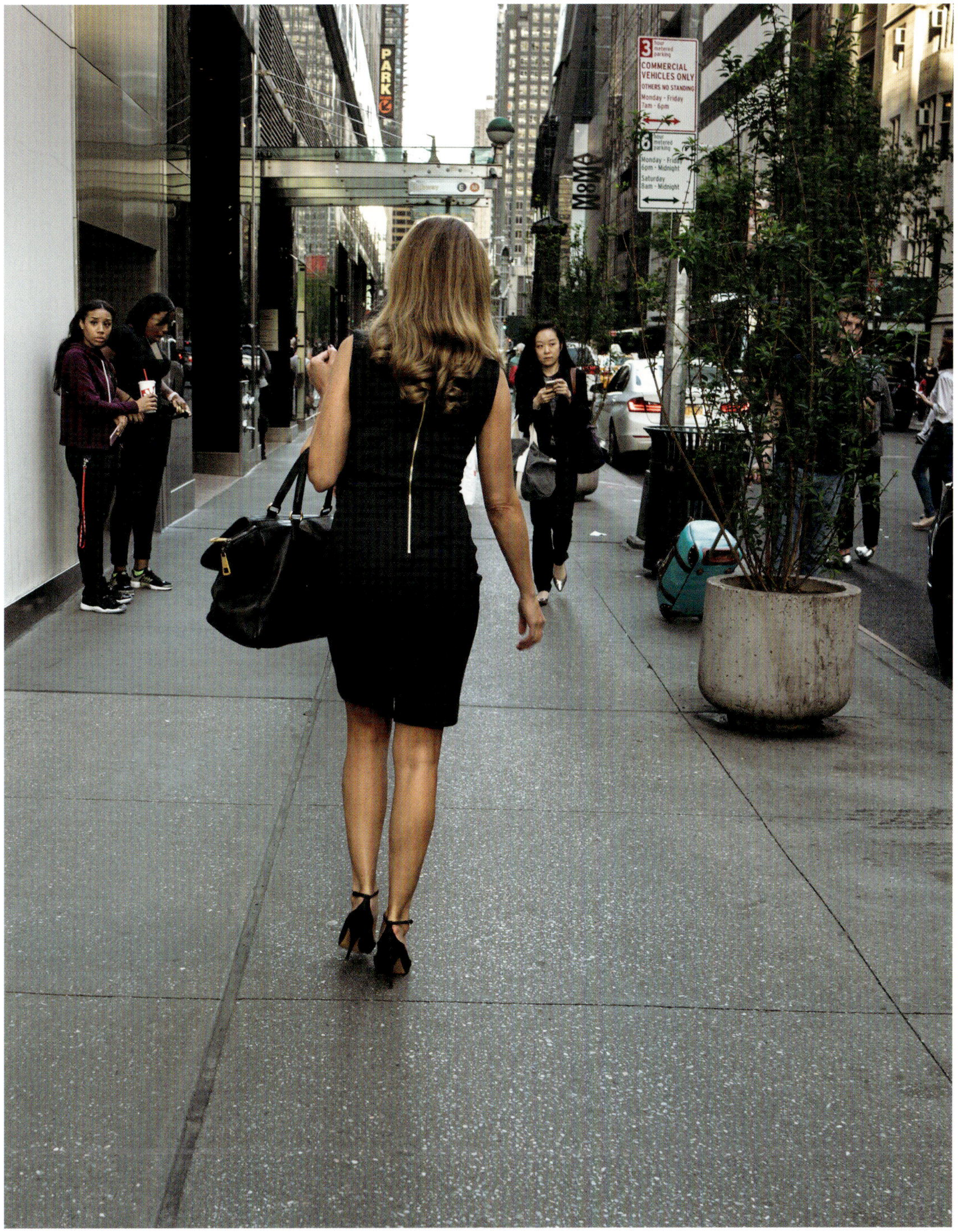

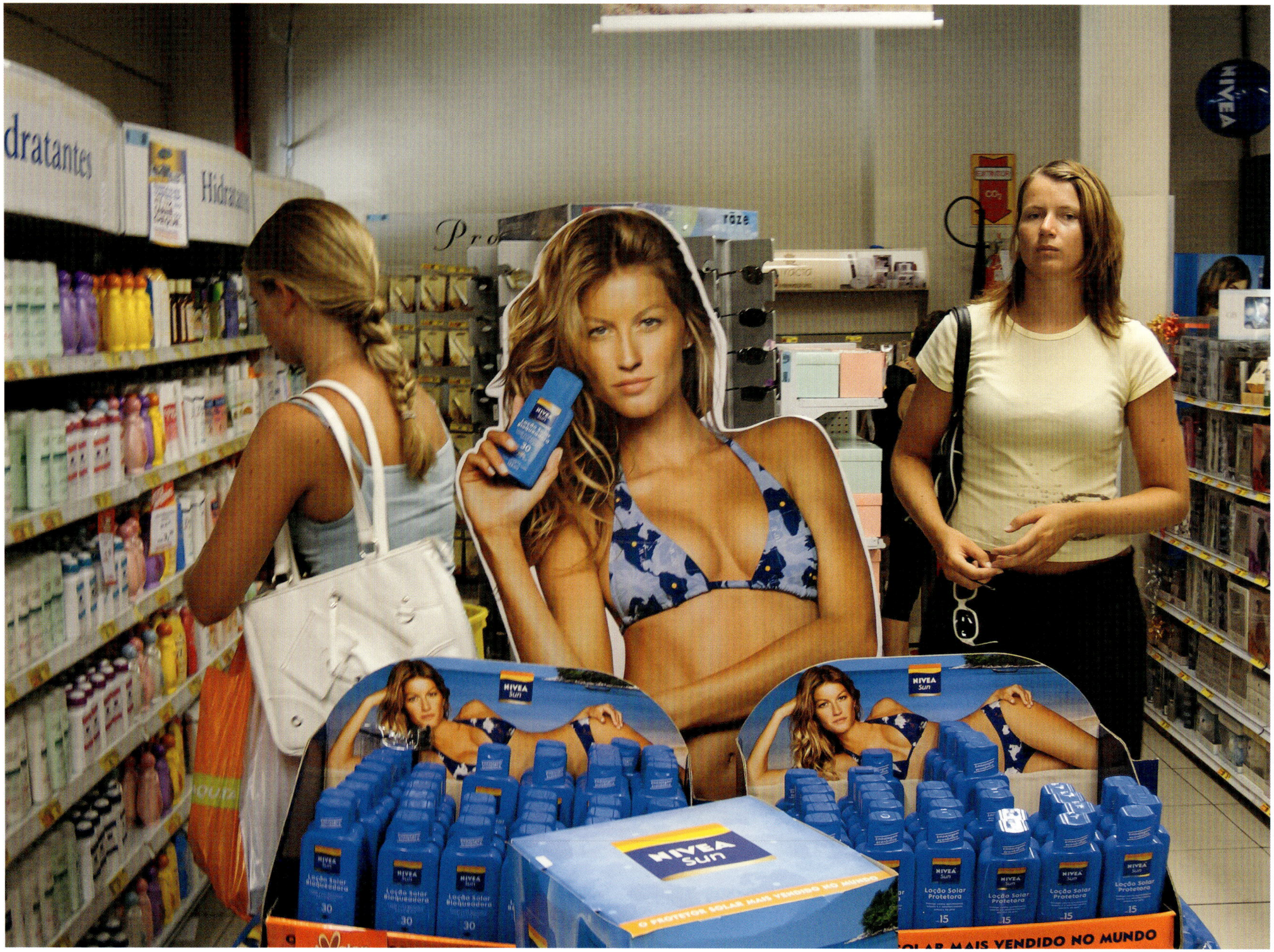

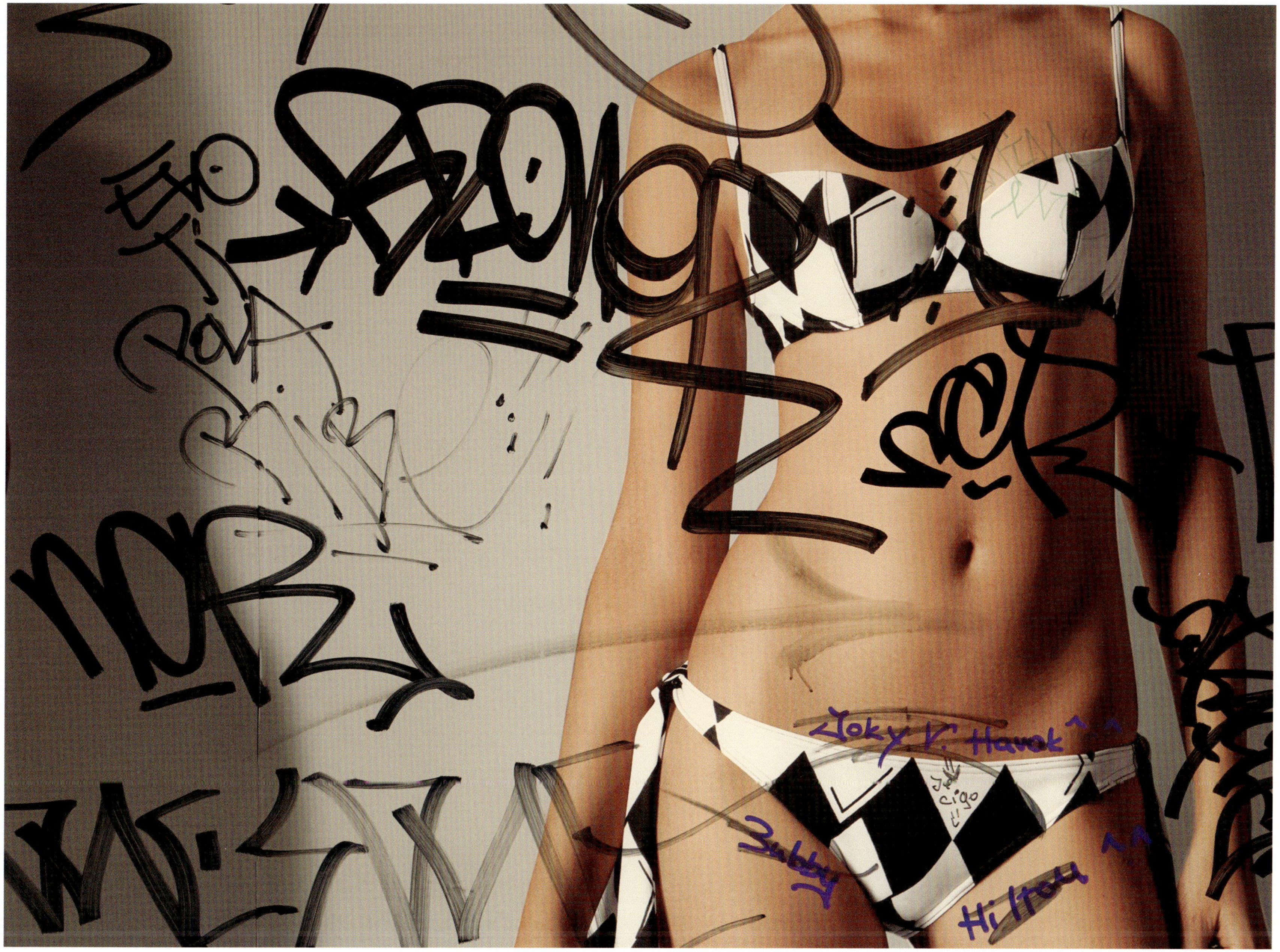

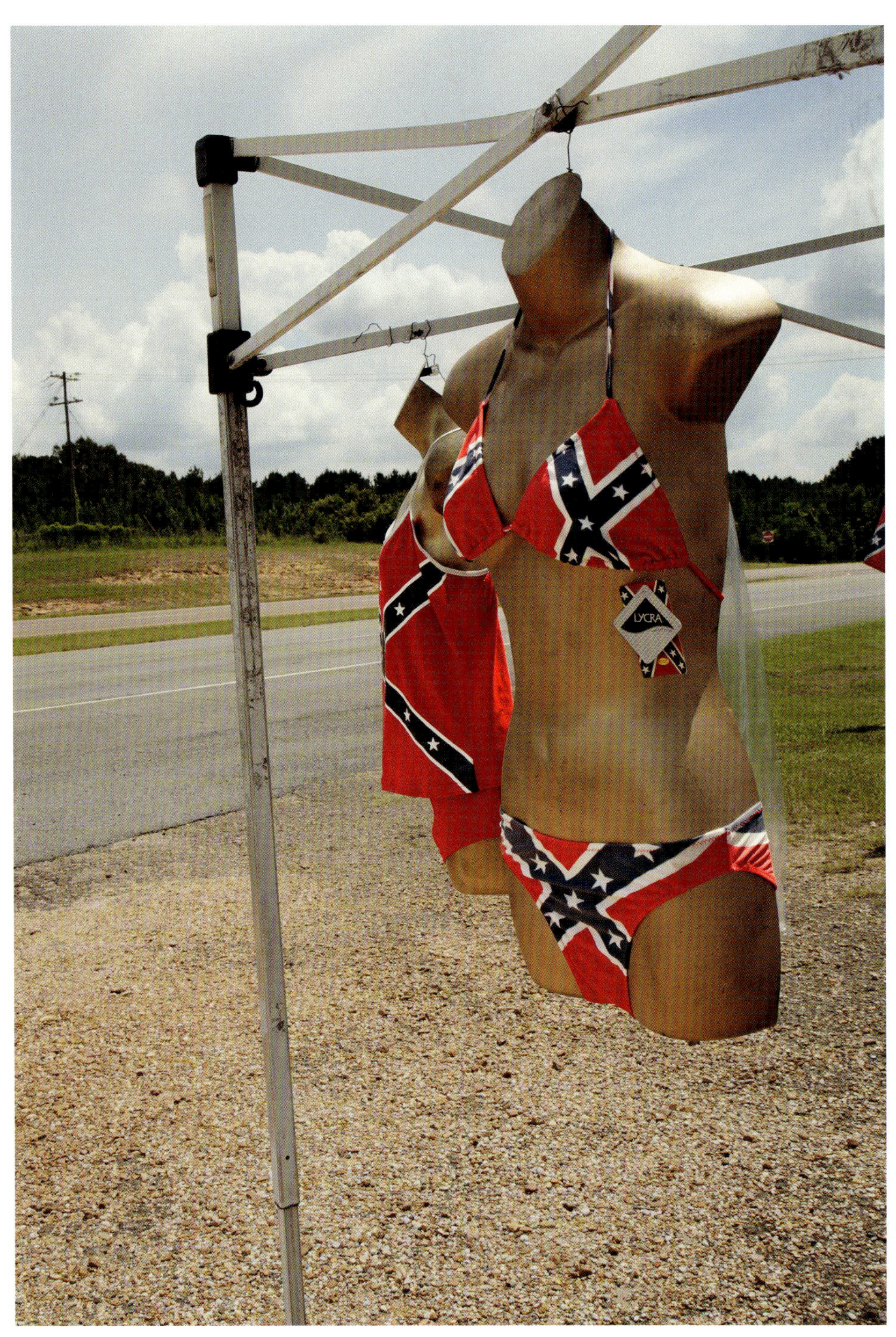
LYCRA

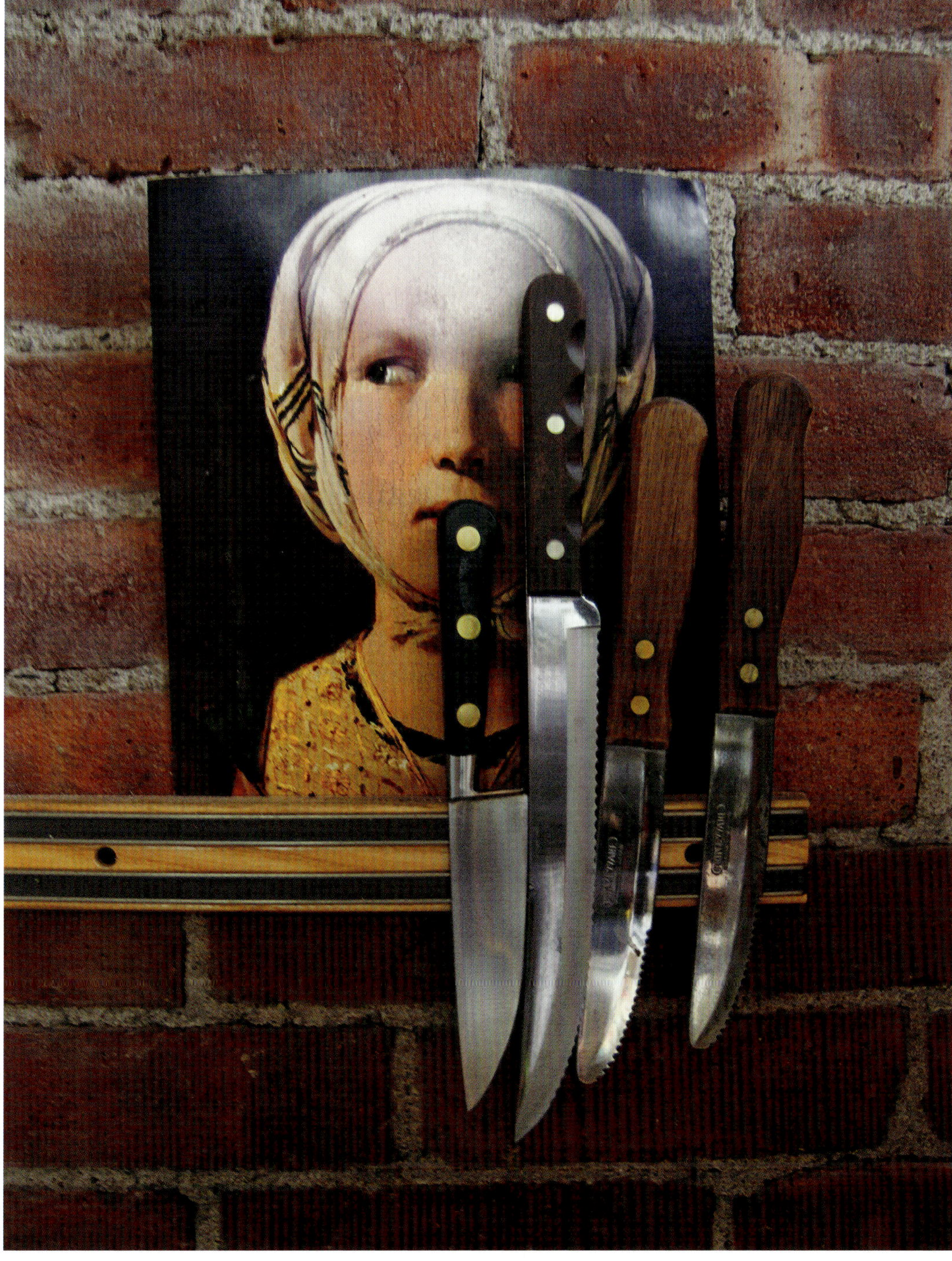

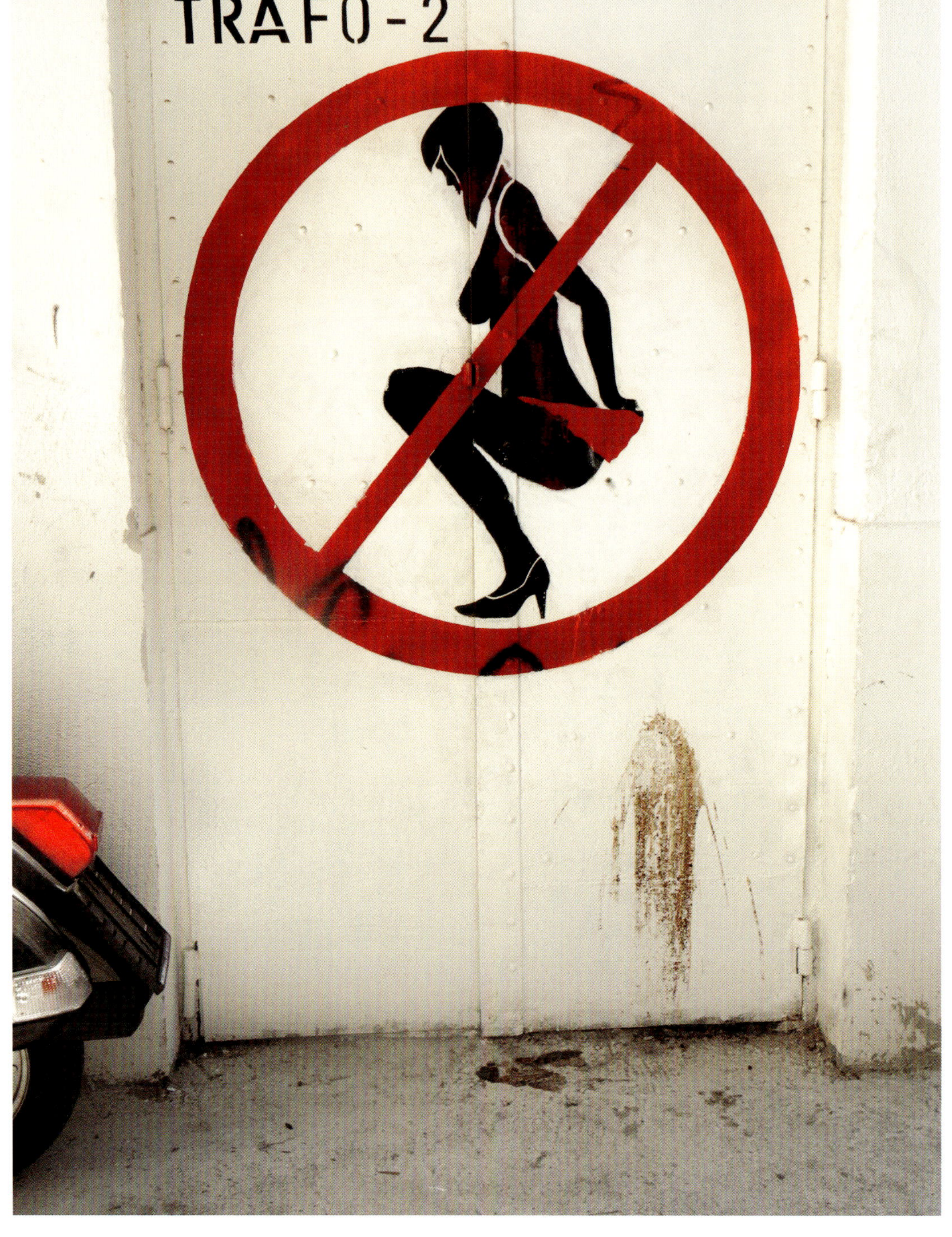
TRAFO-2

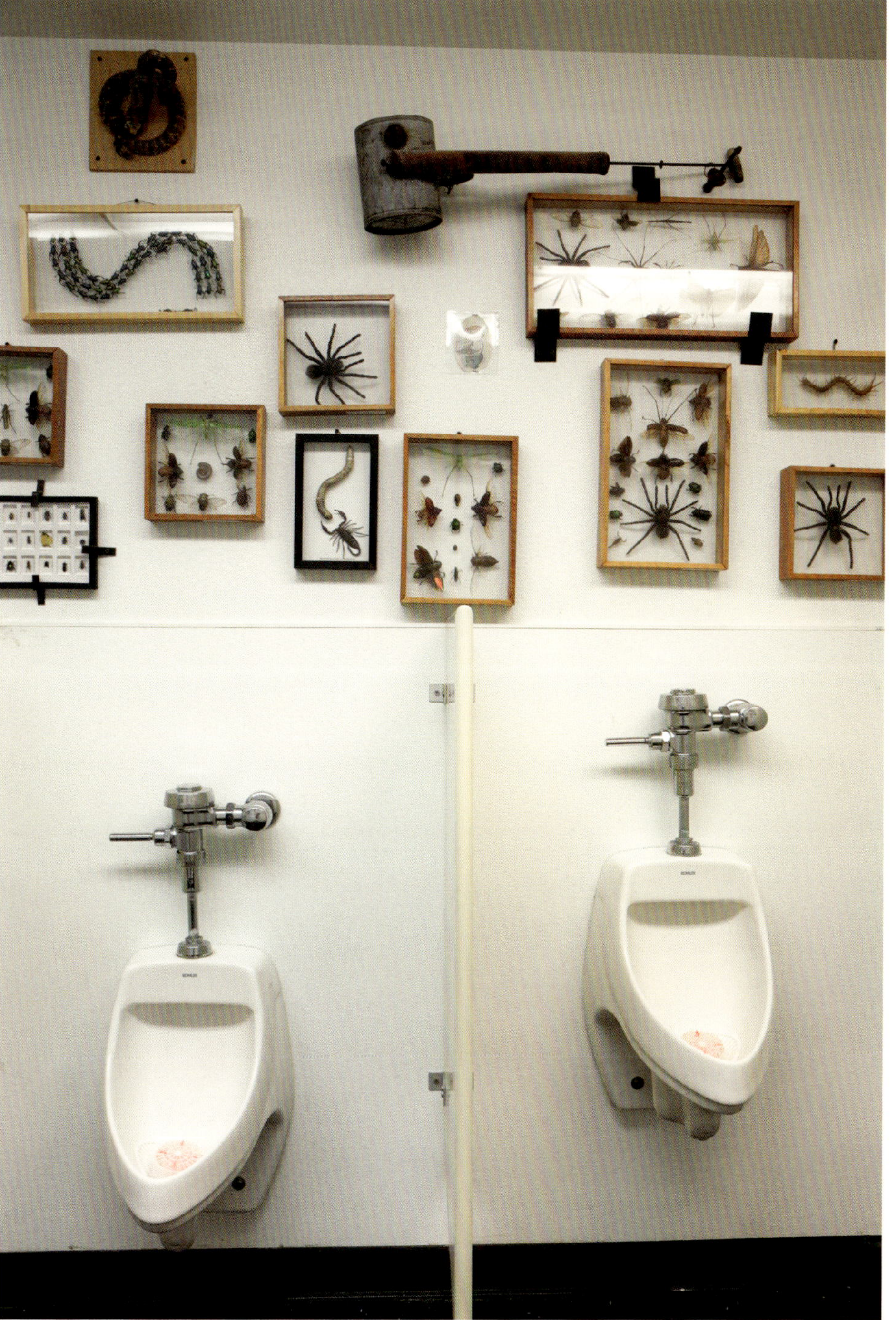

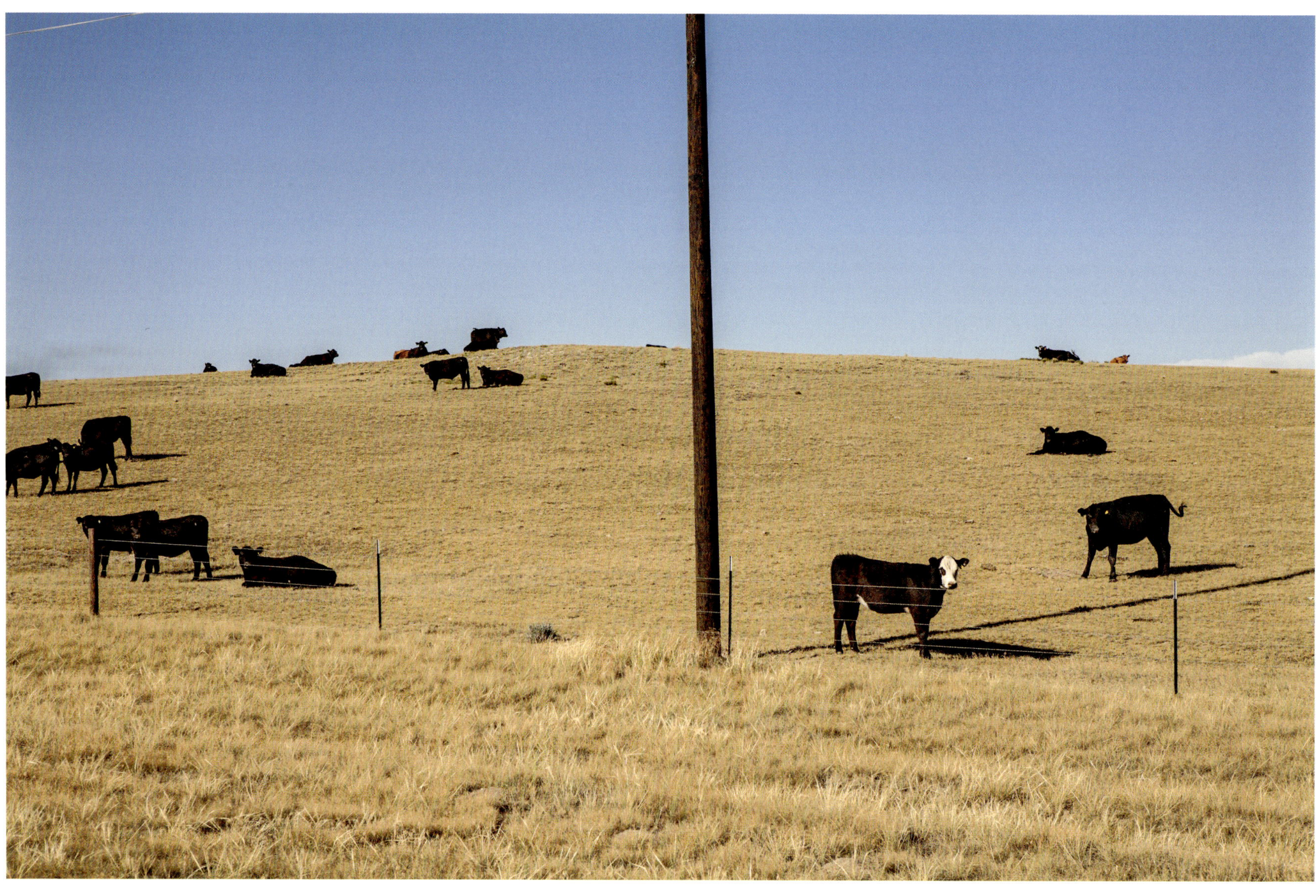

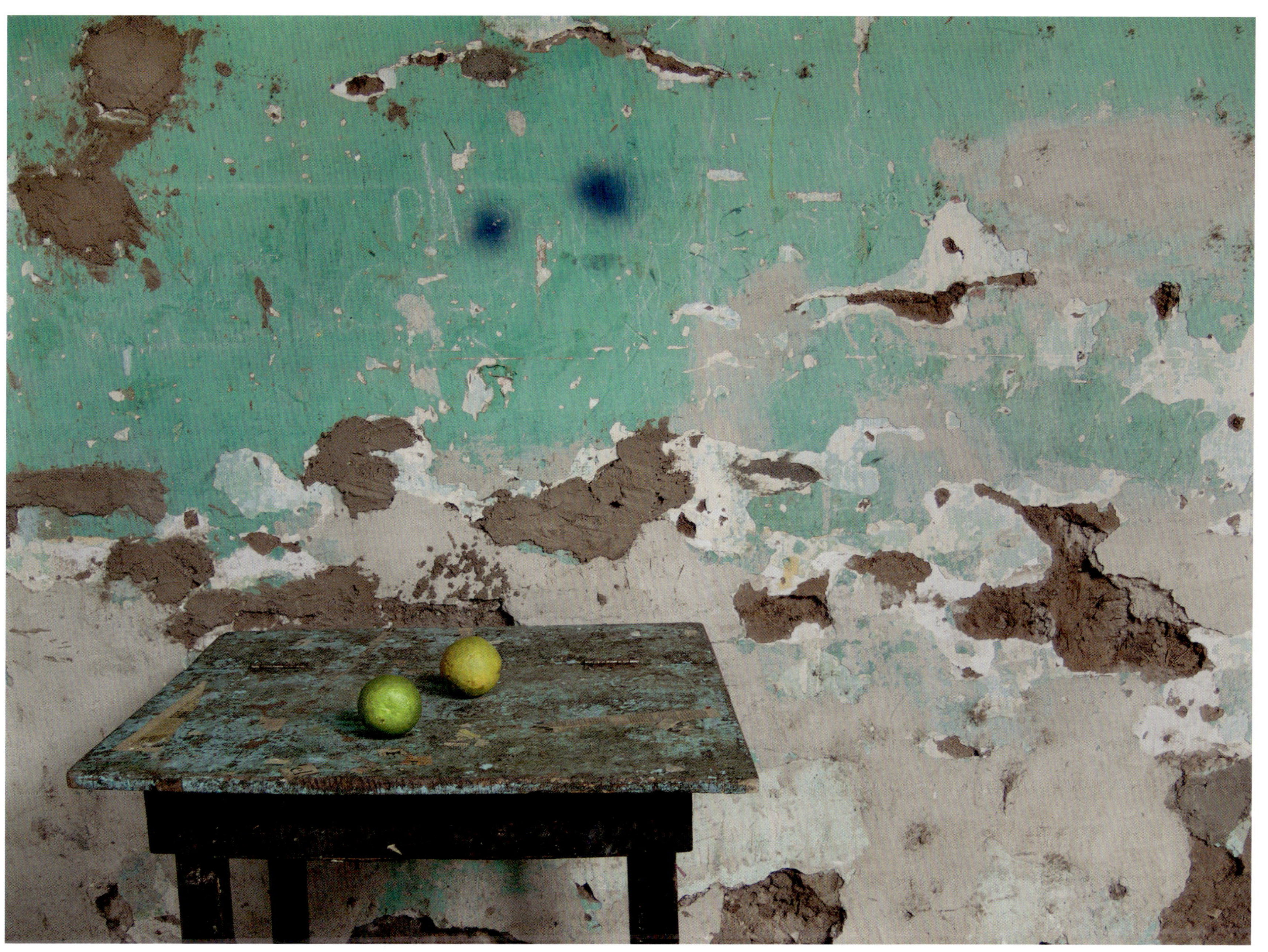

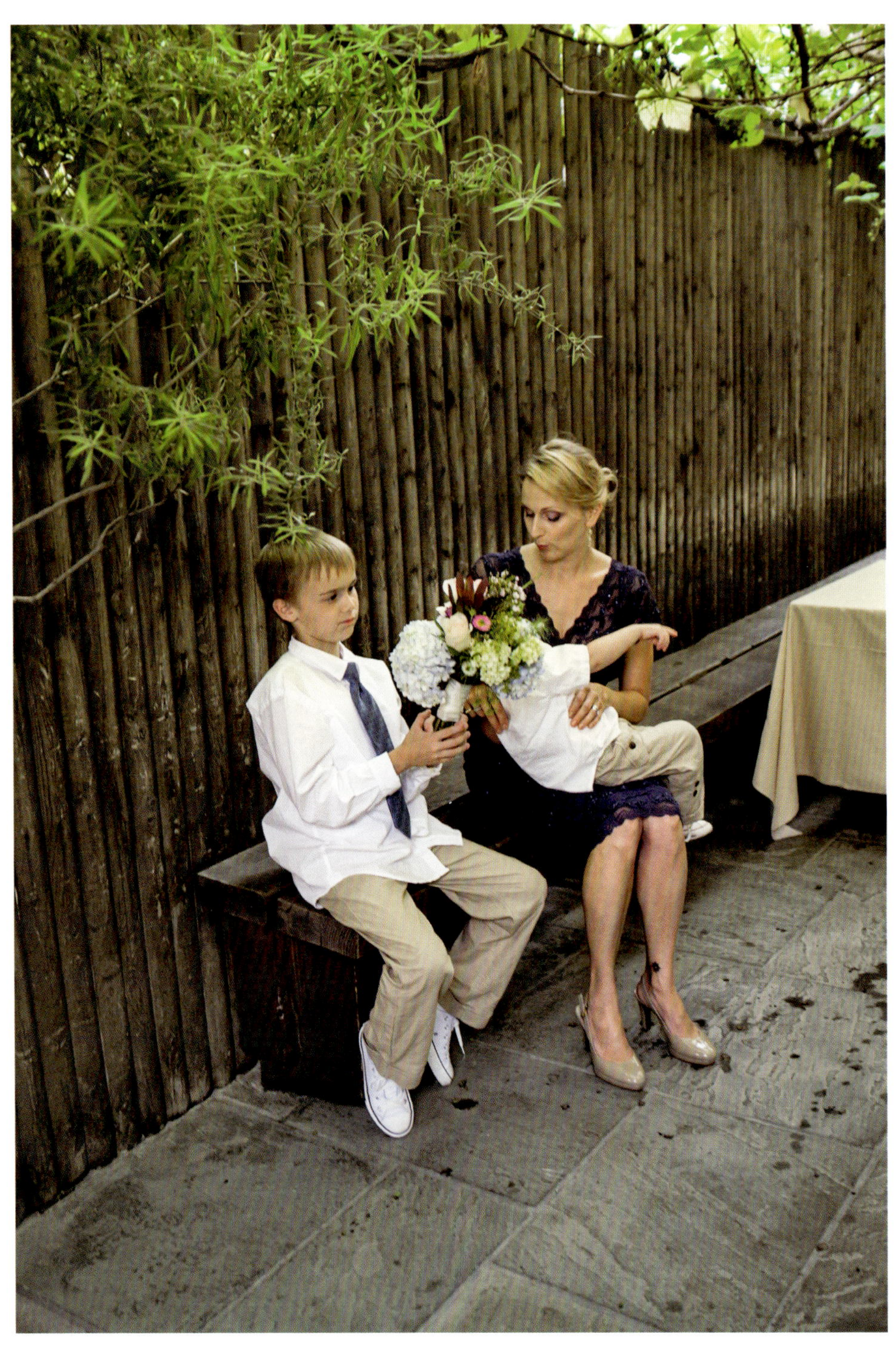

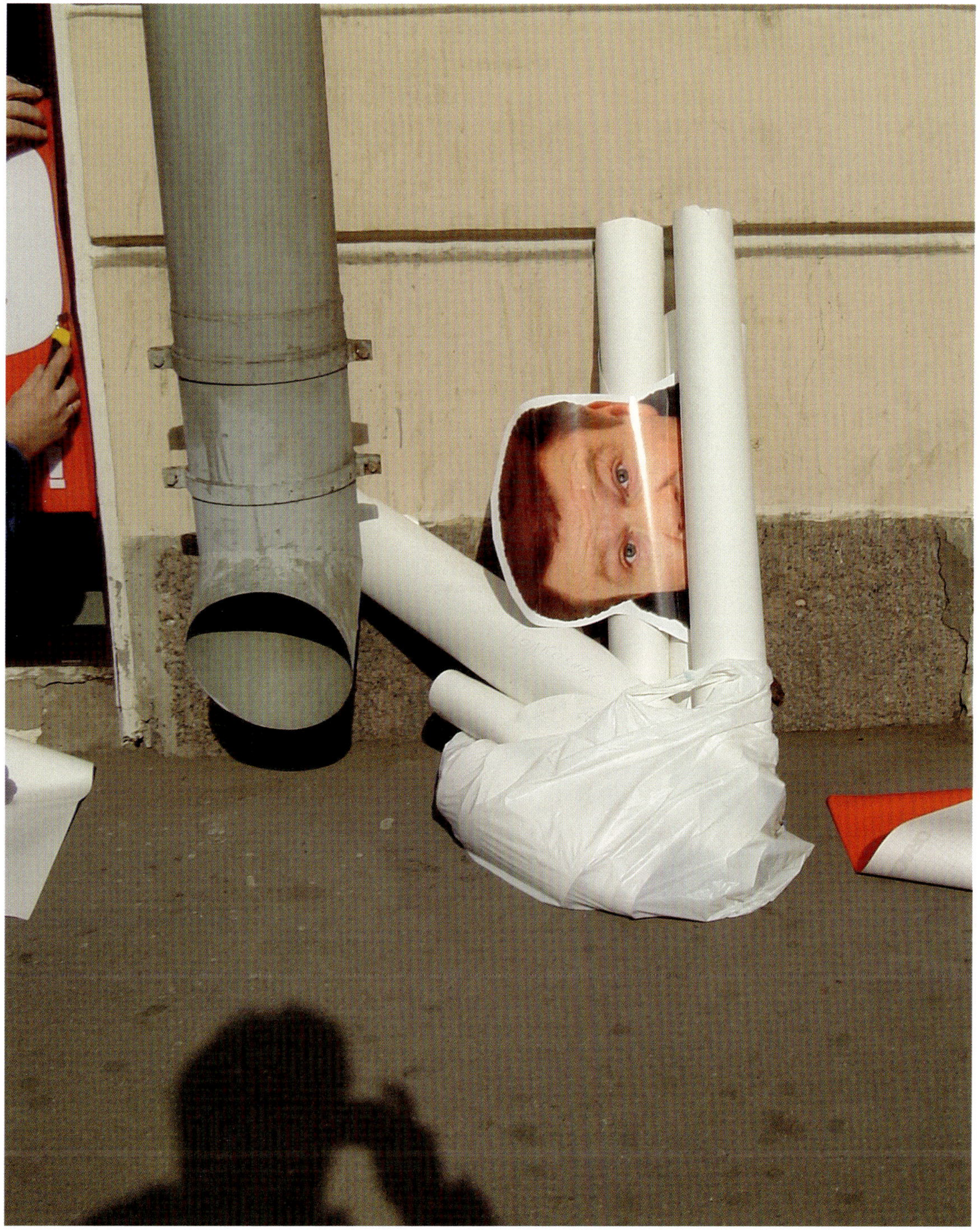

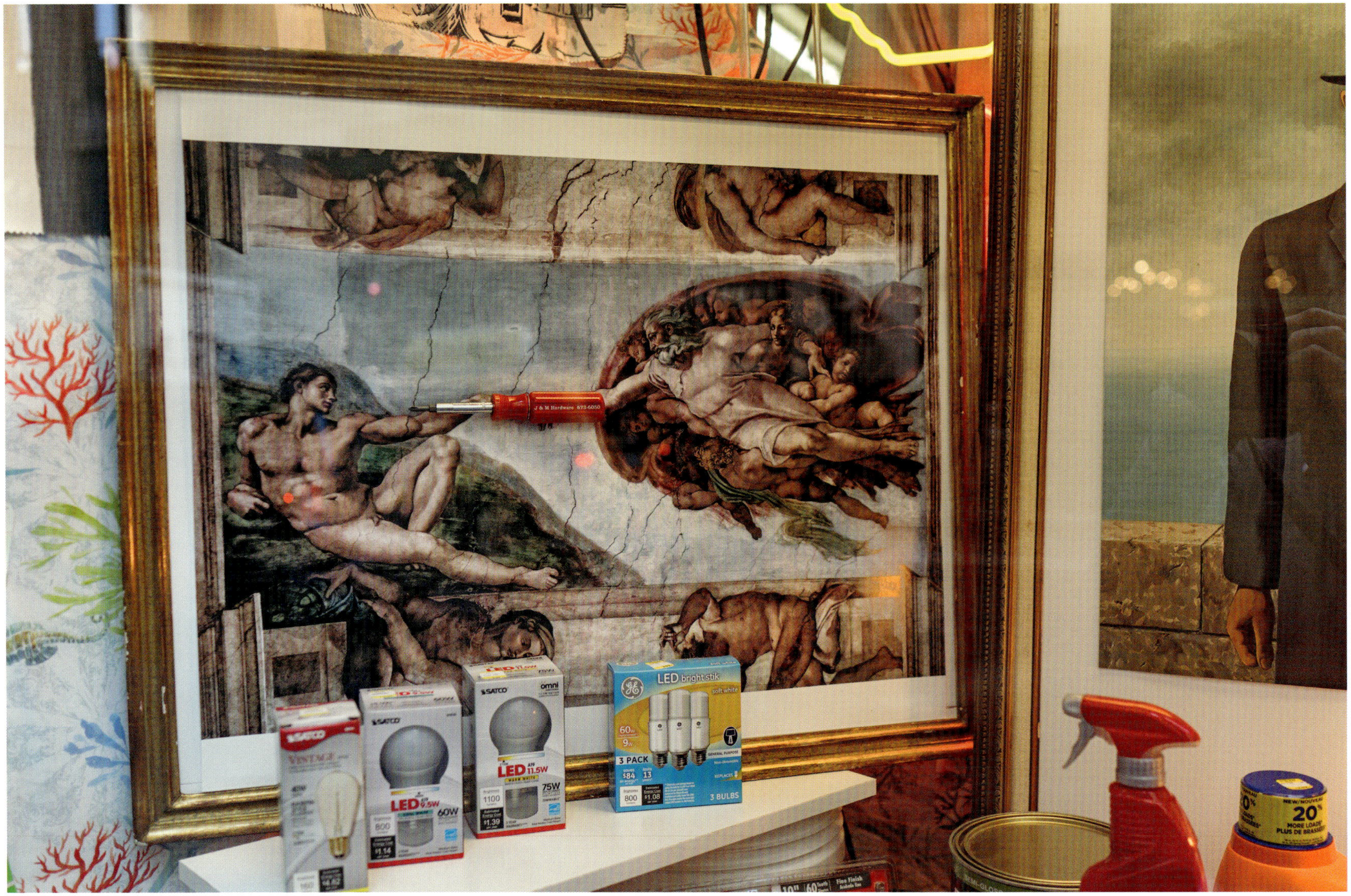

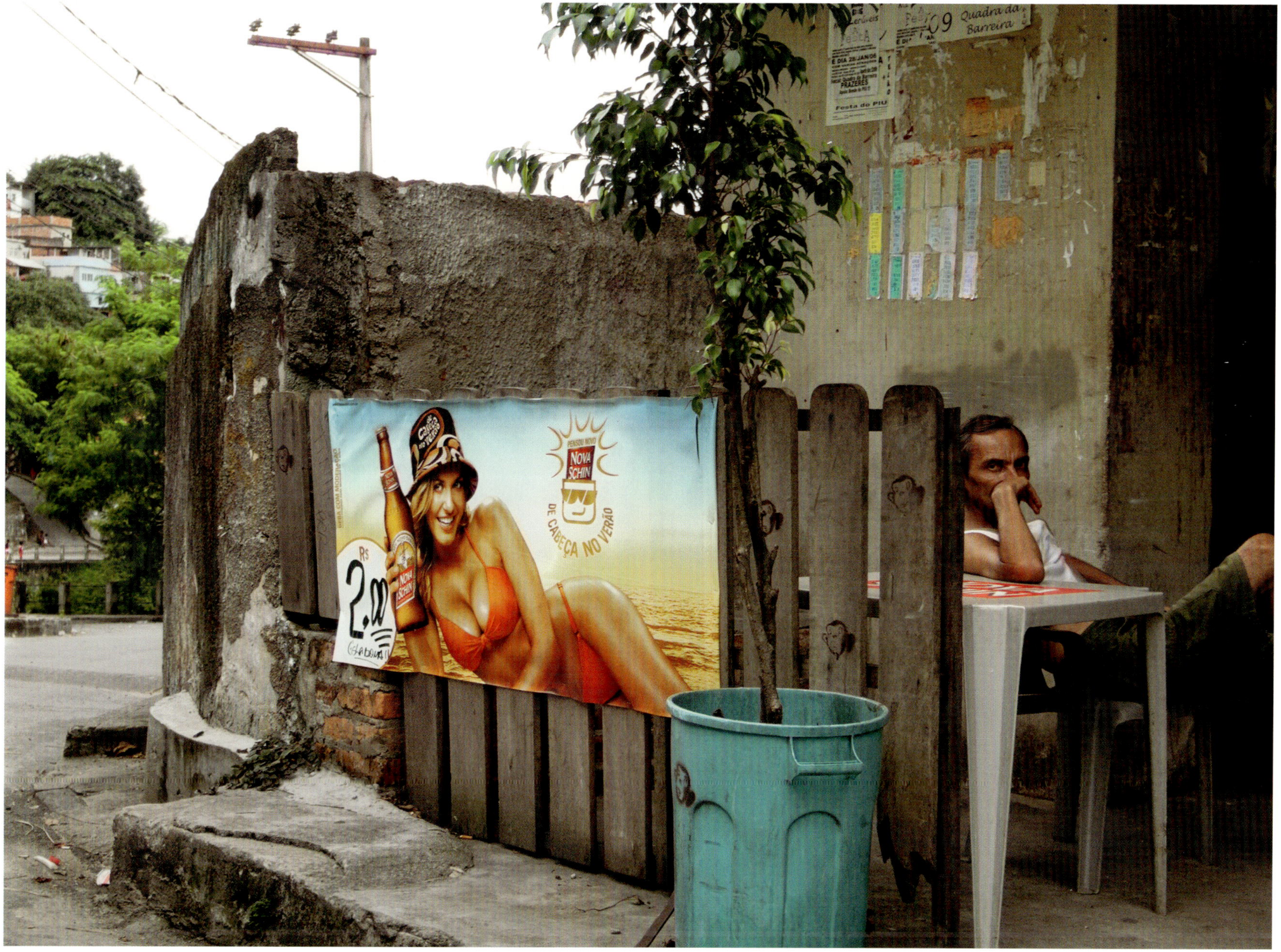

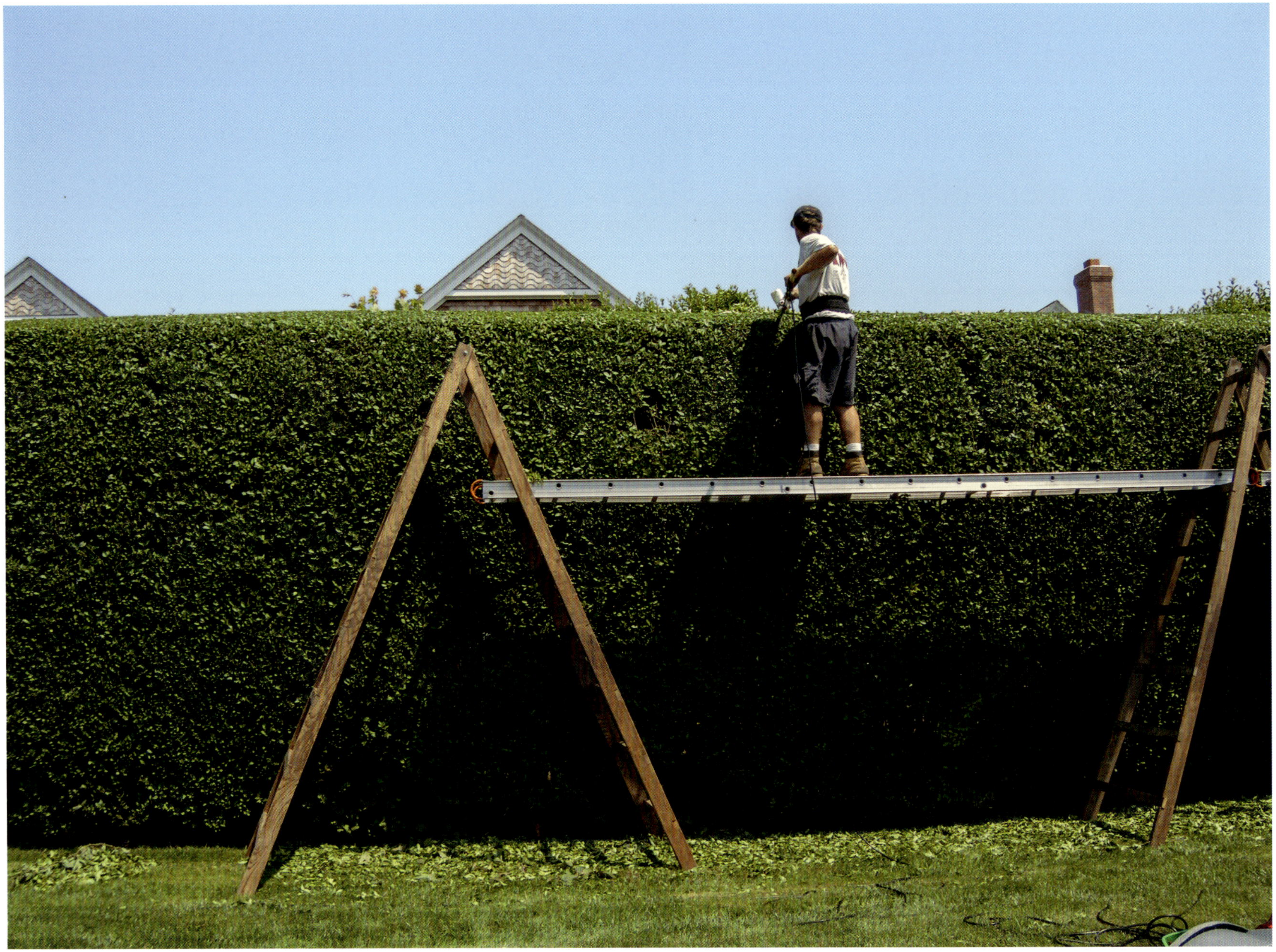

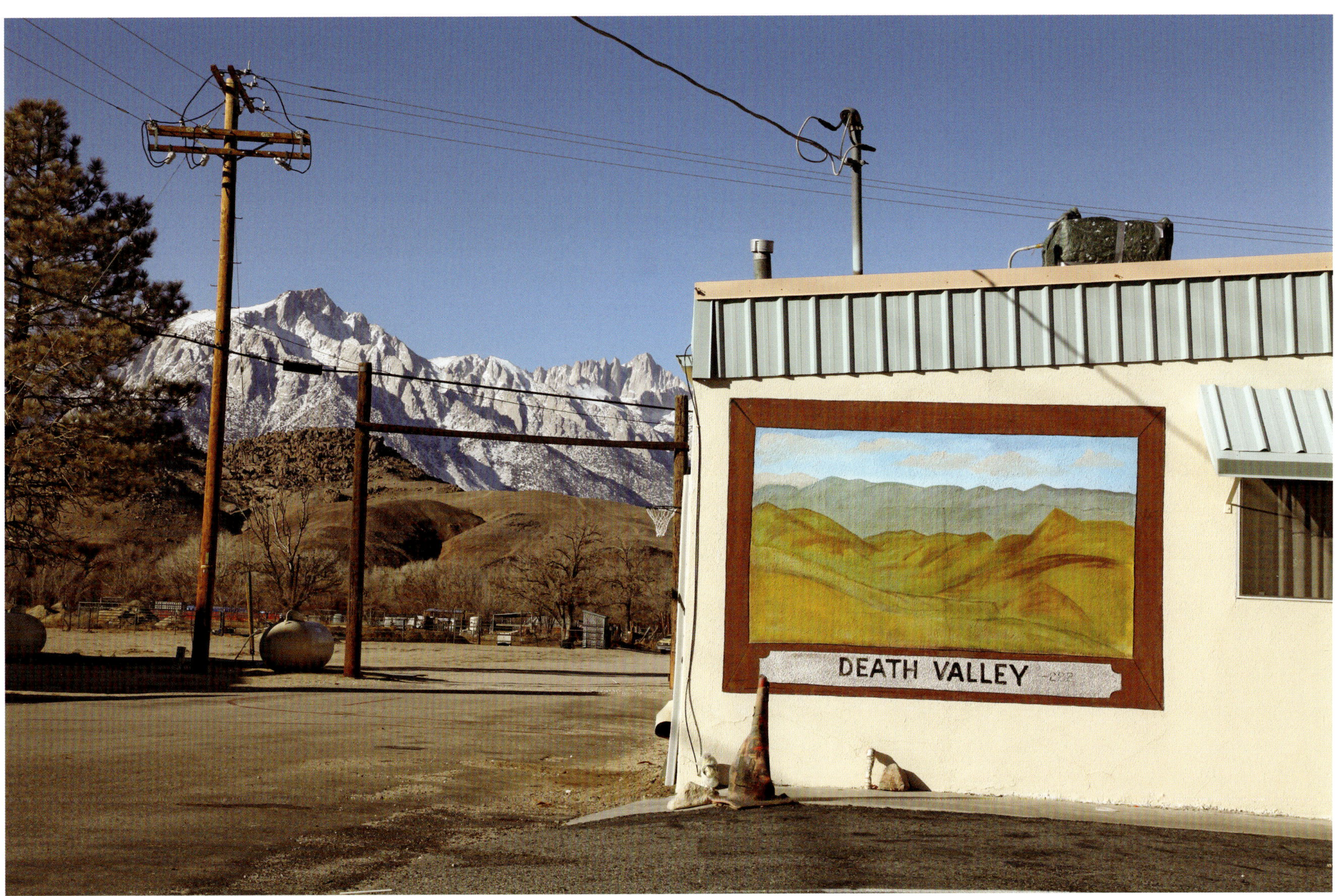
DEATH VALLEY

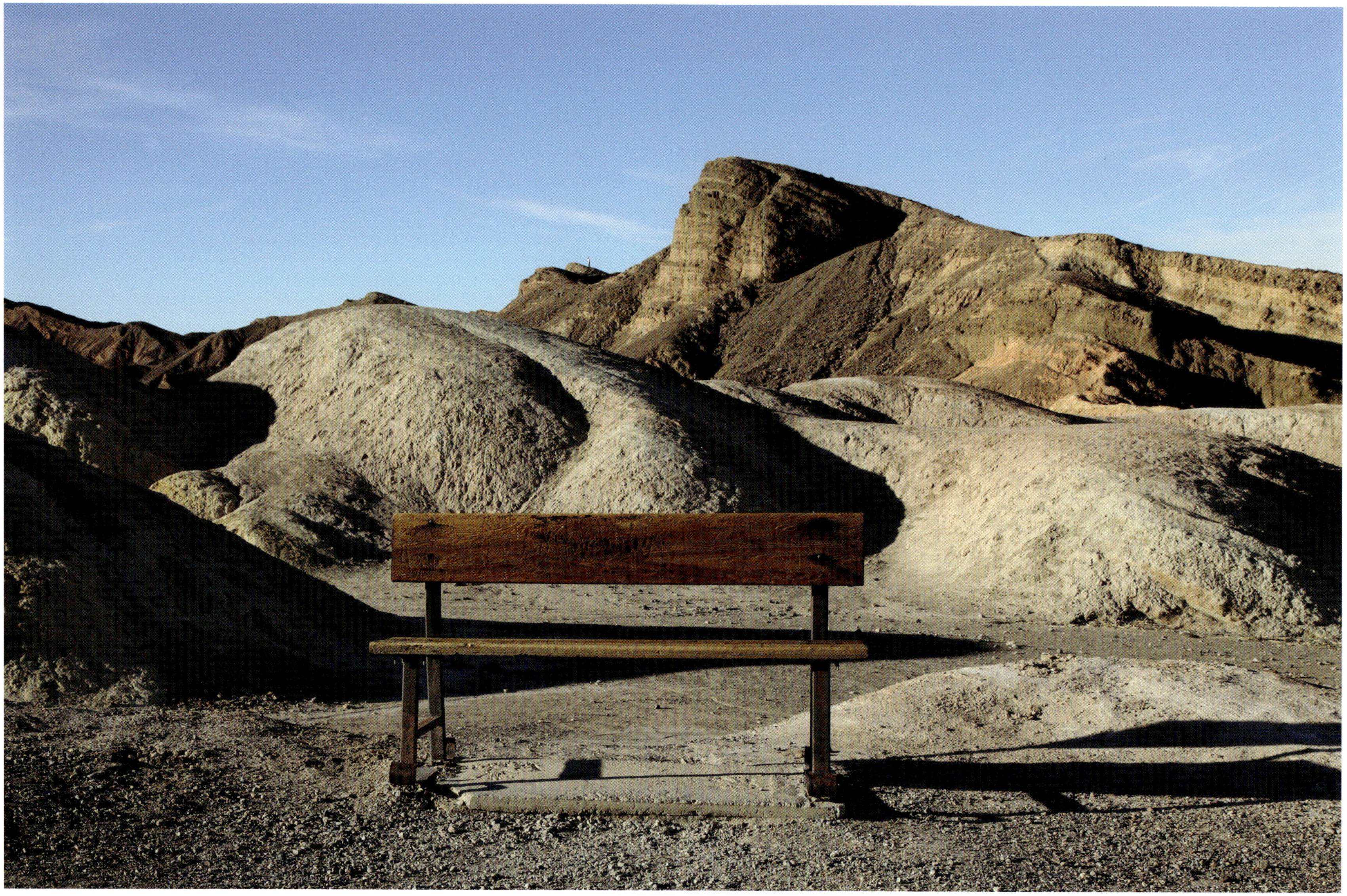

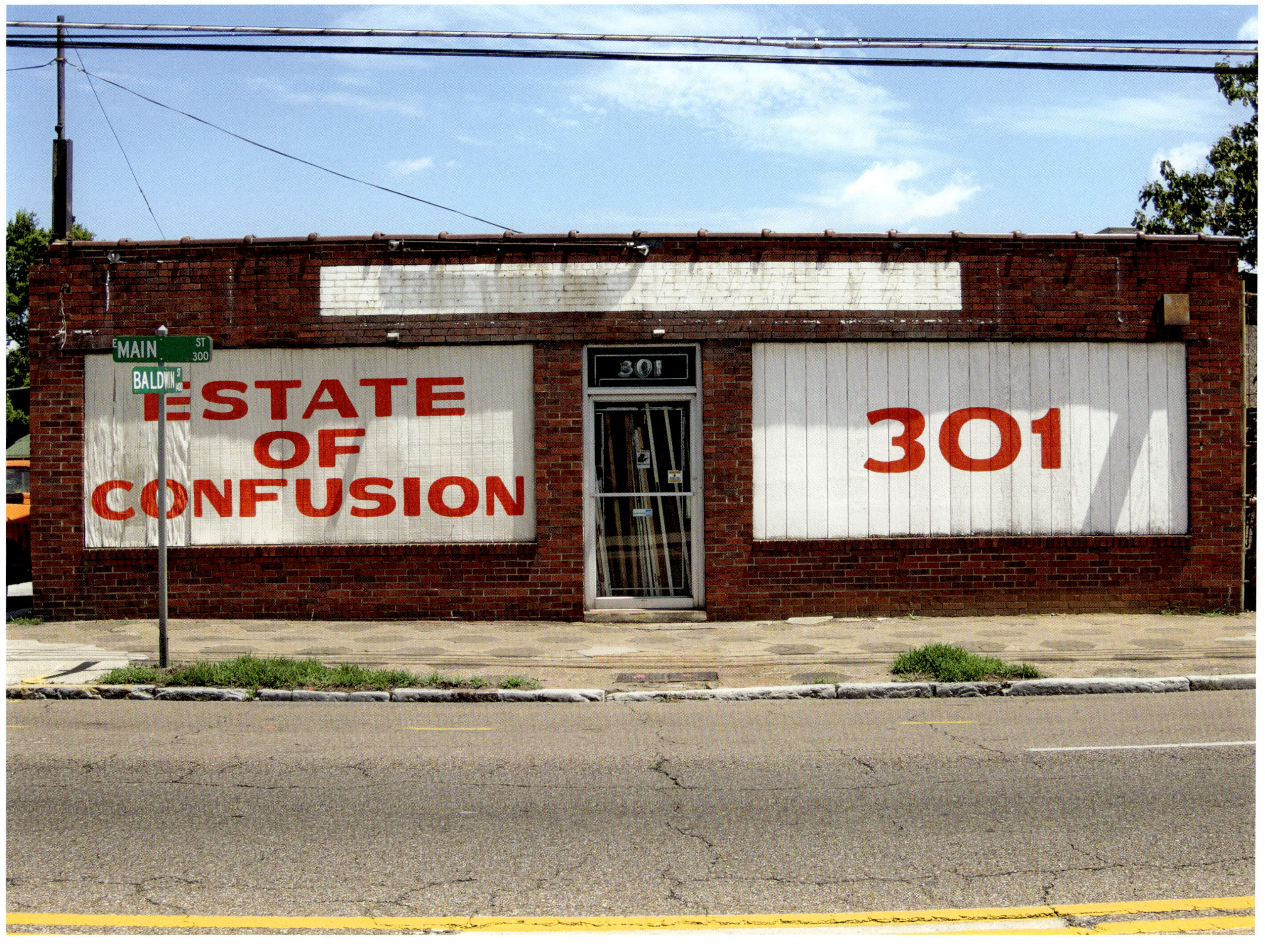
MAIN ST 300
BALDWIN
ESTATE OF CONFUSION
301
301

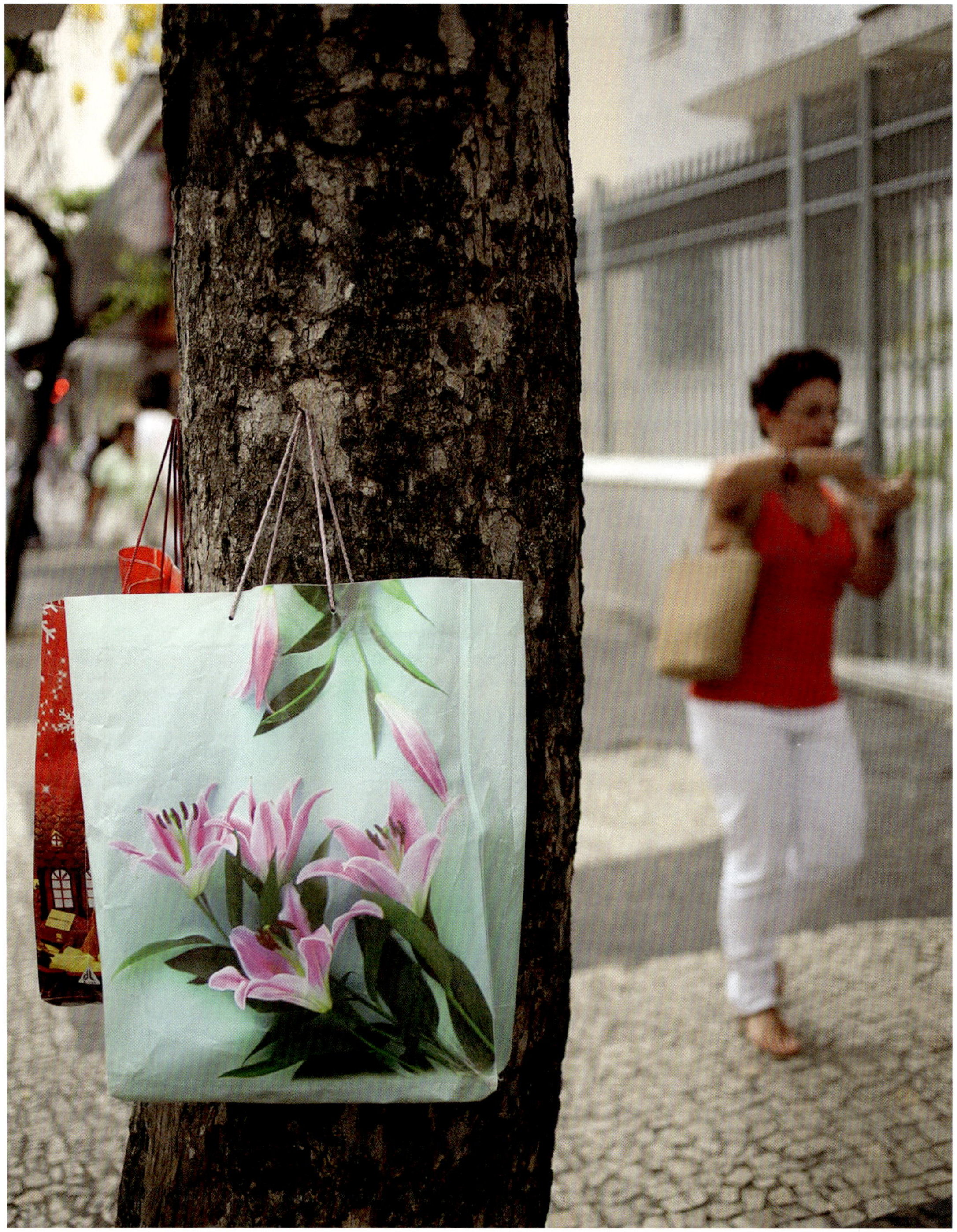

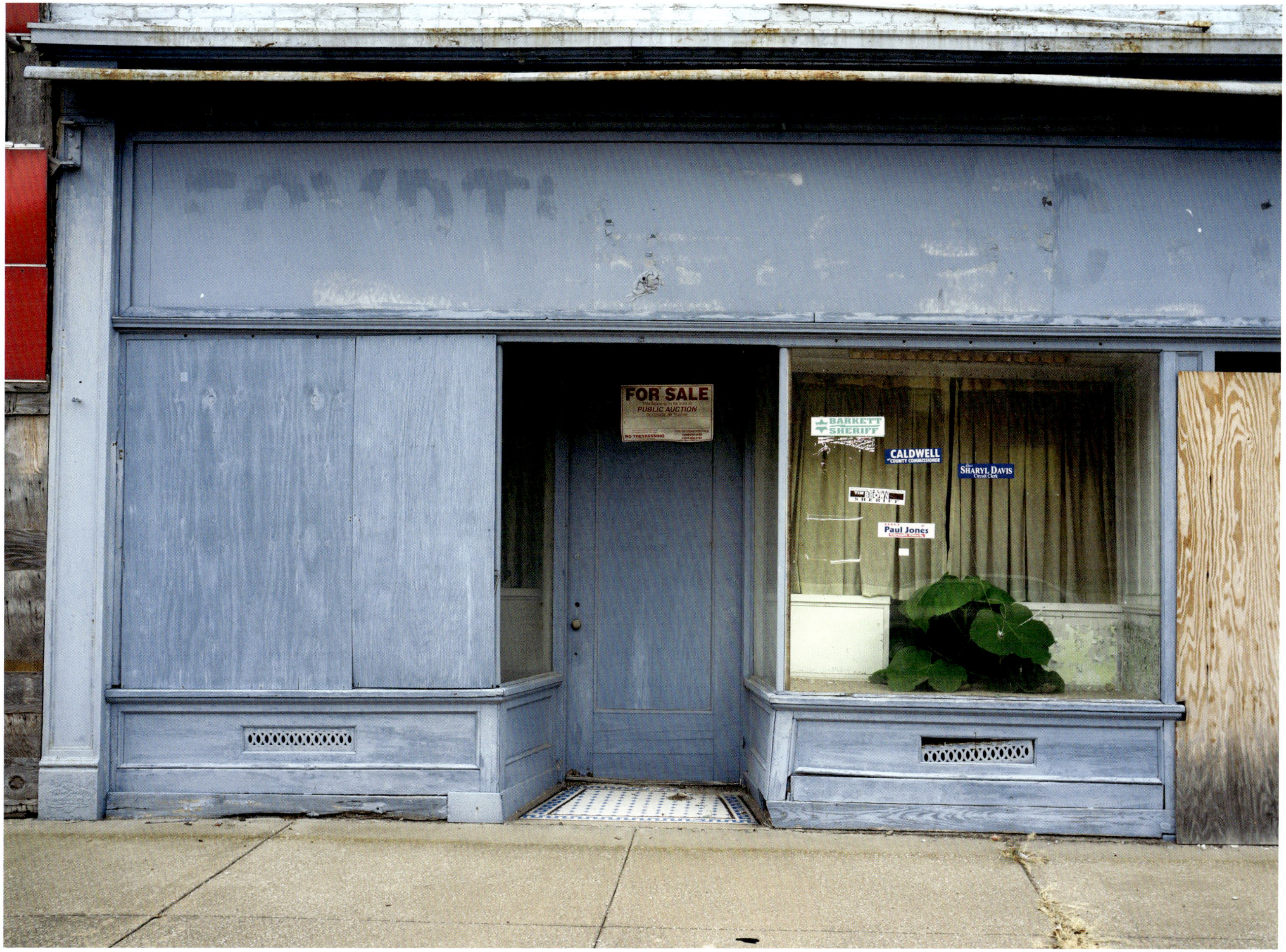

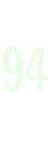

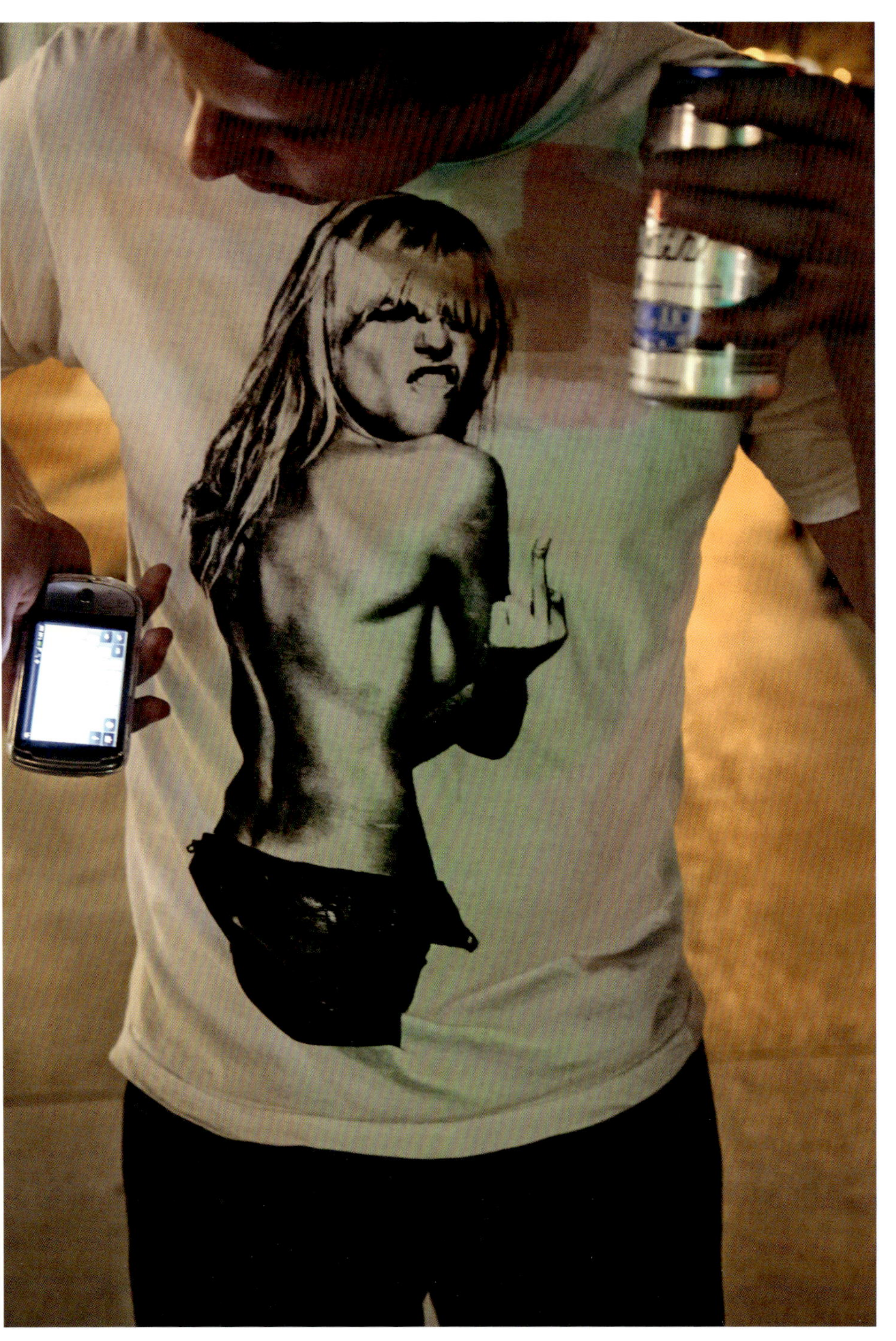

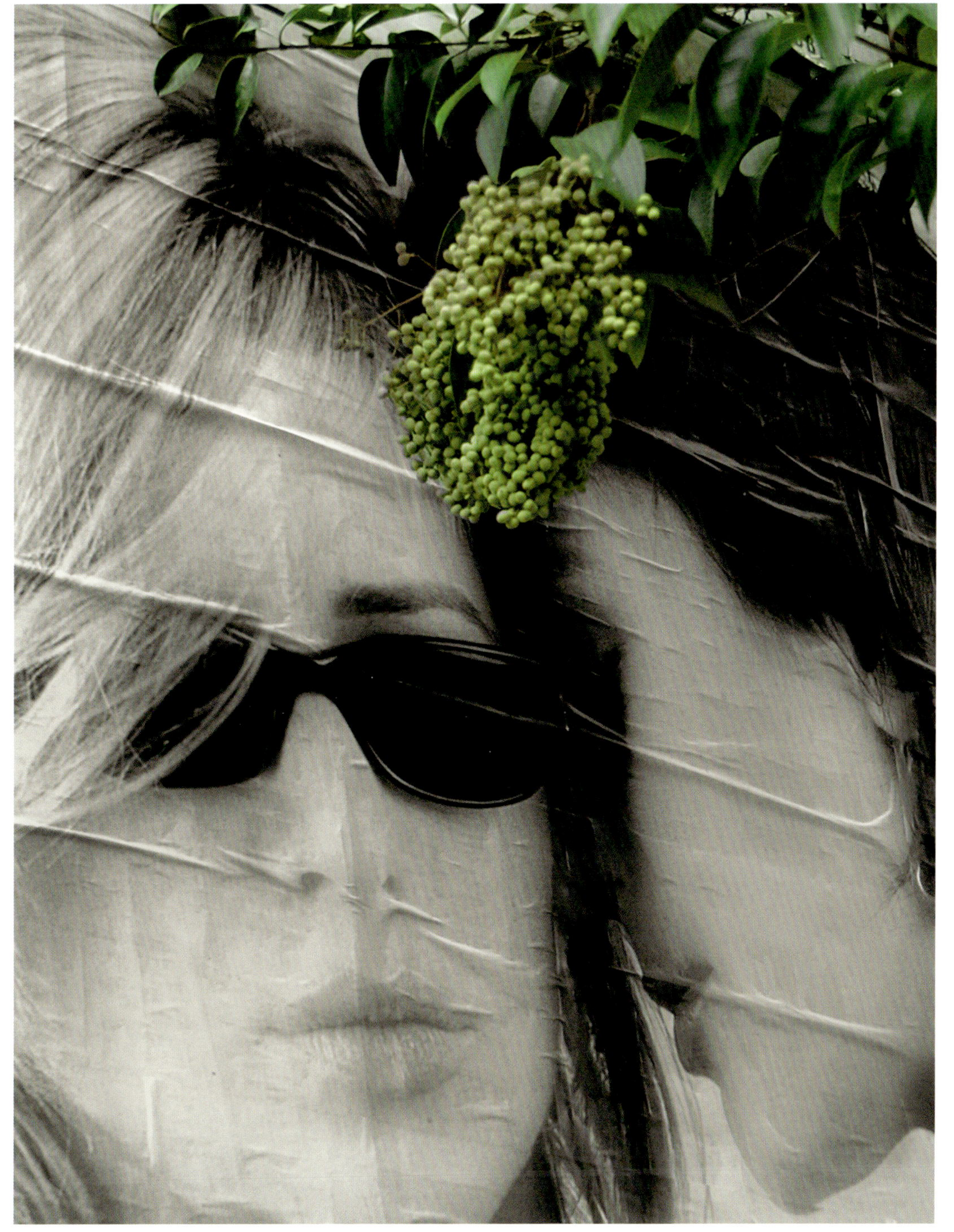

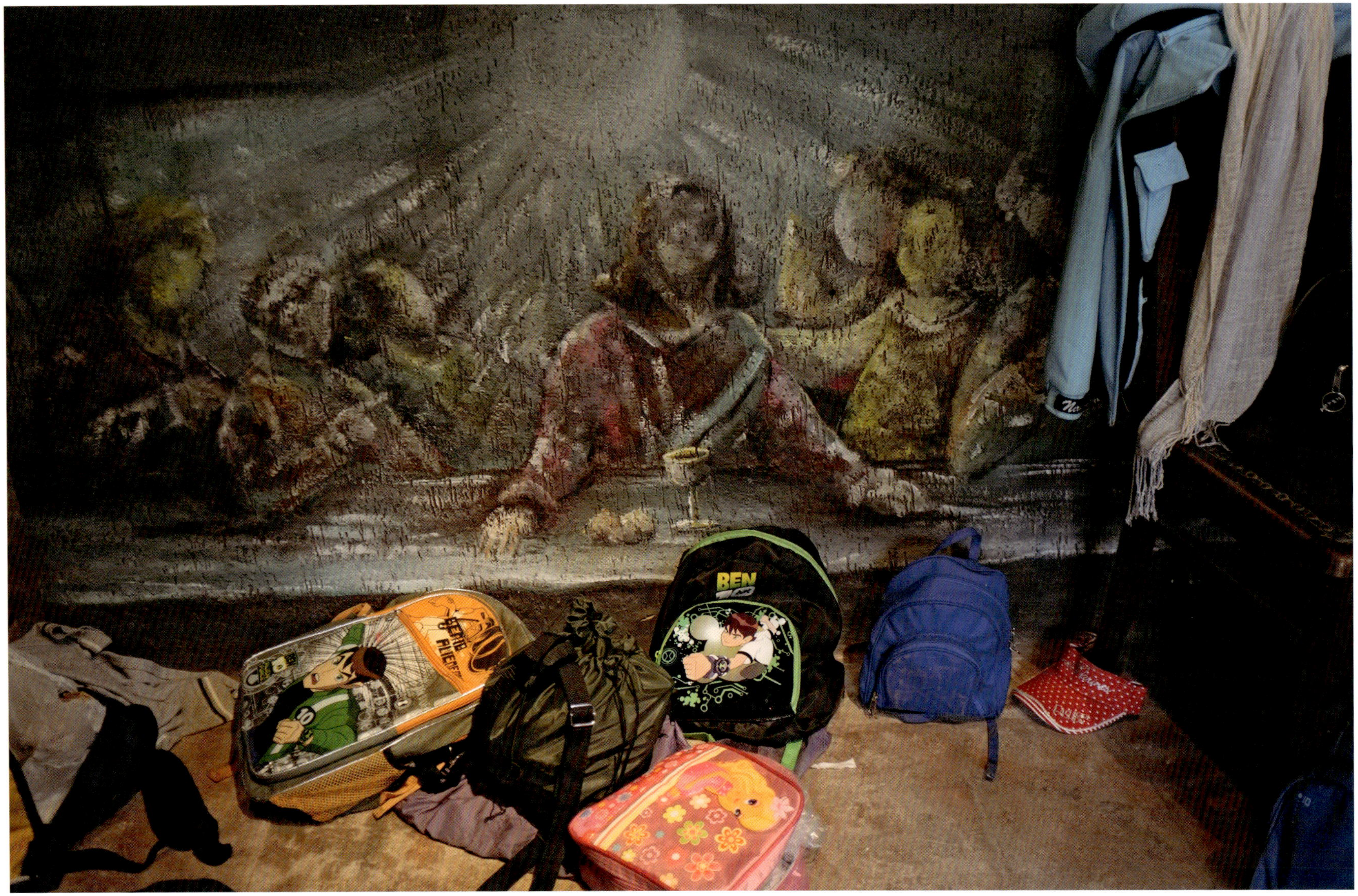

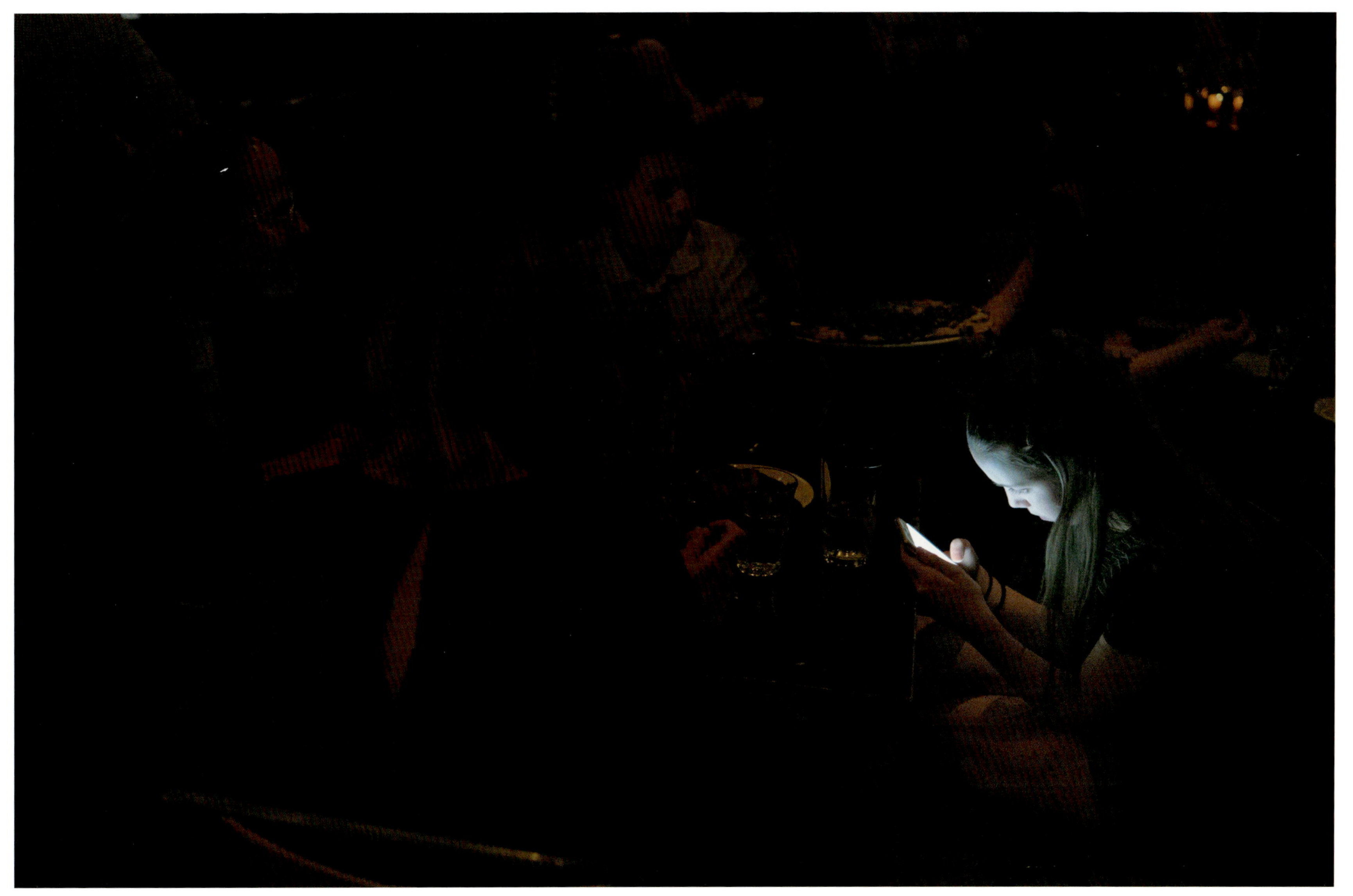

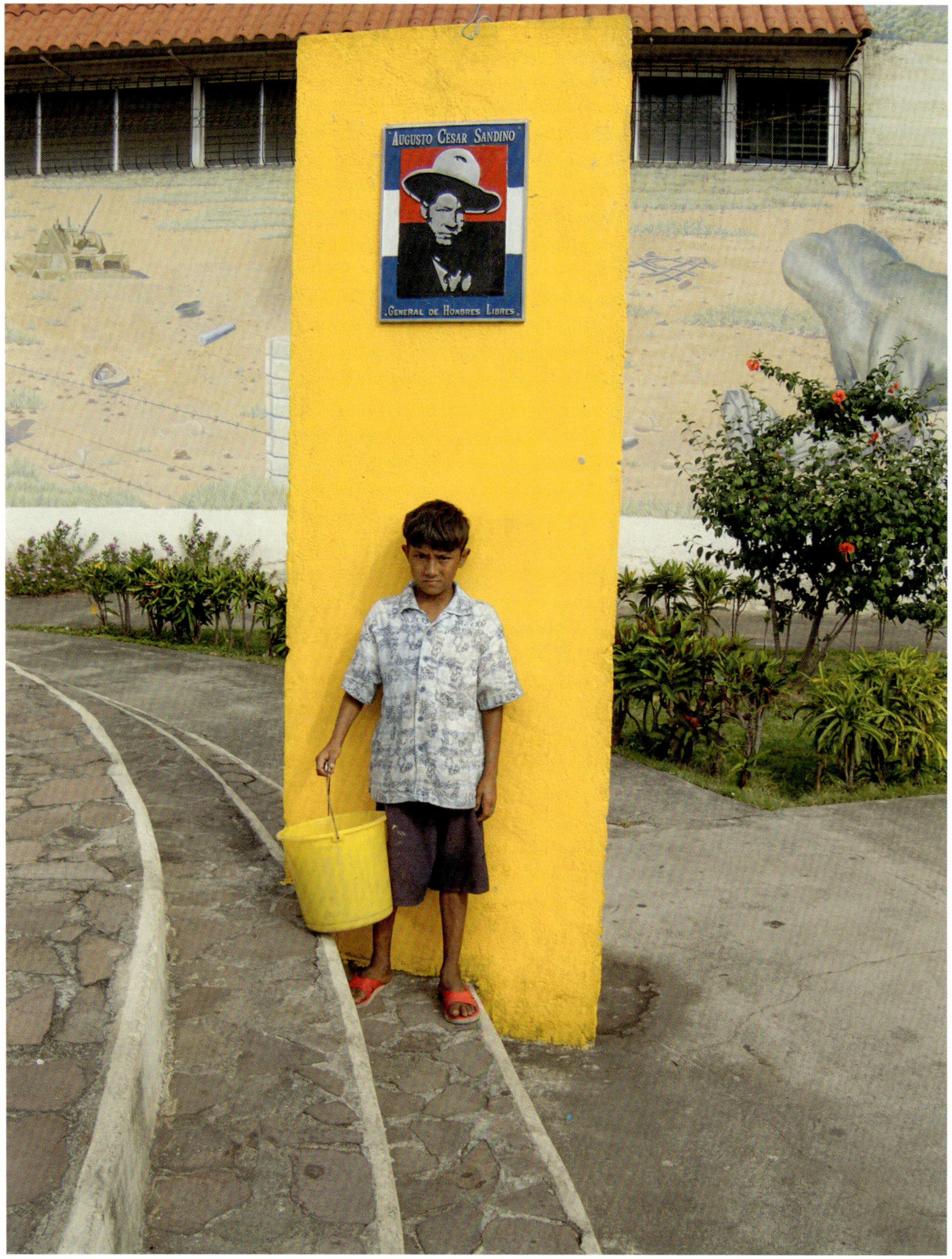

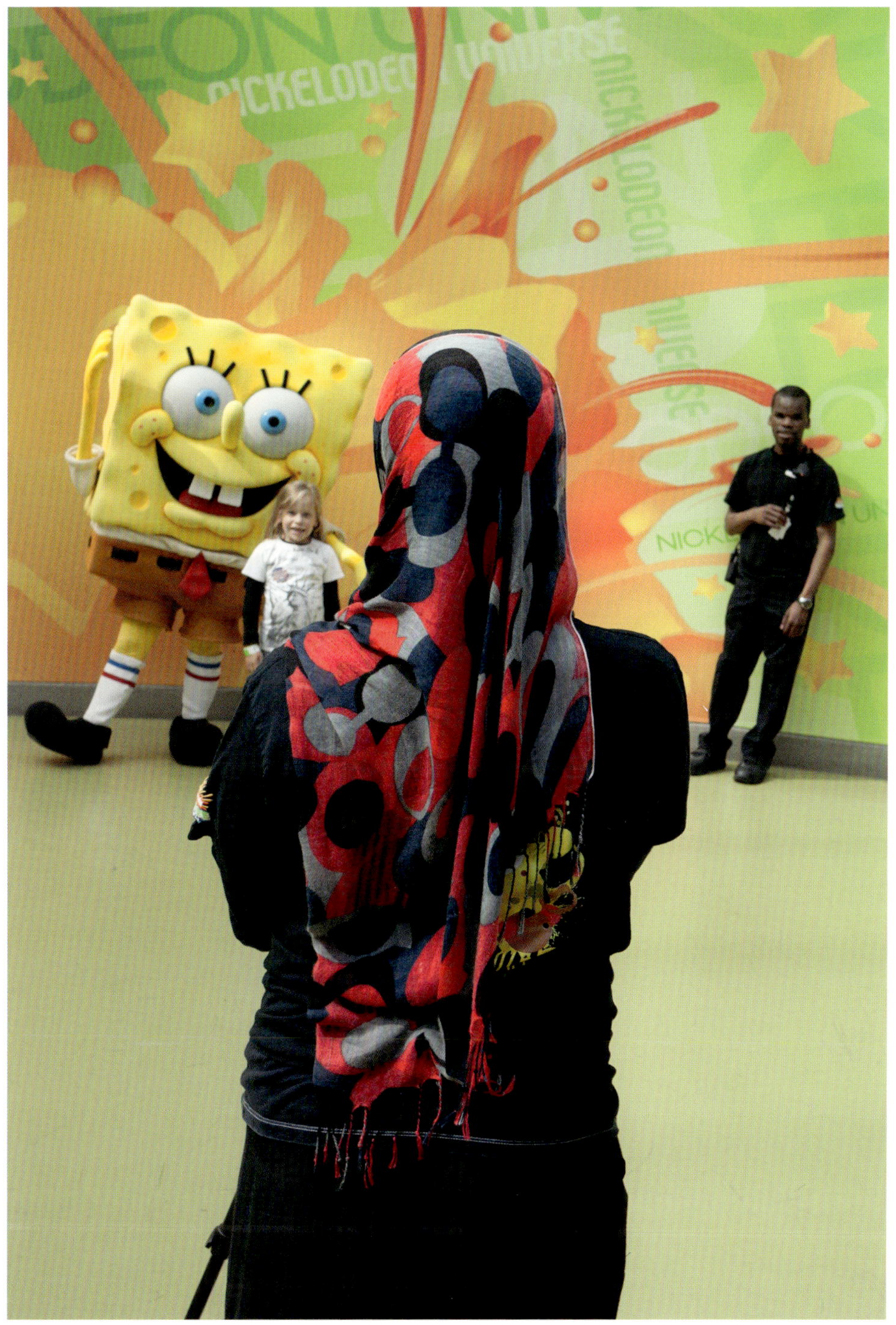
NICKELODEON

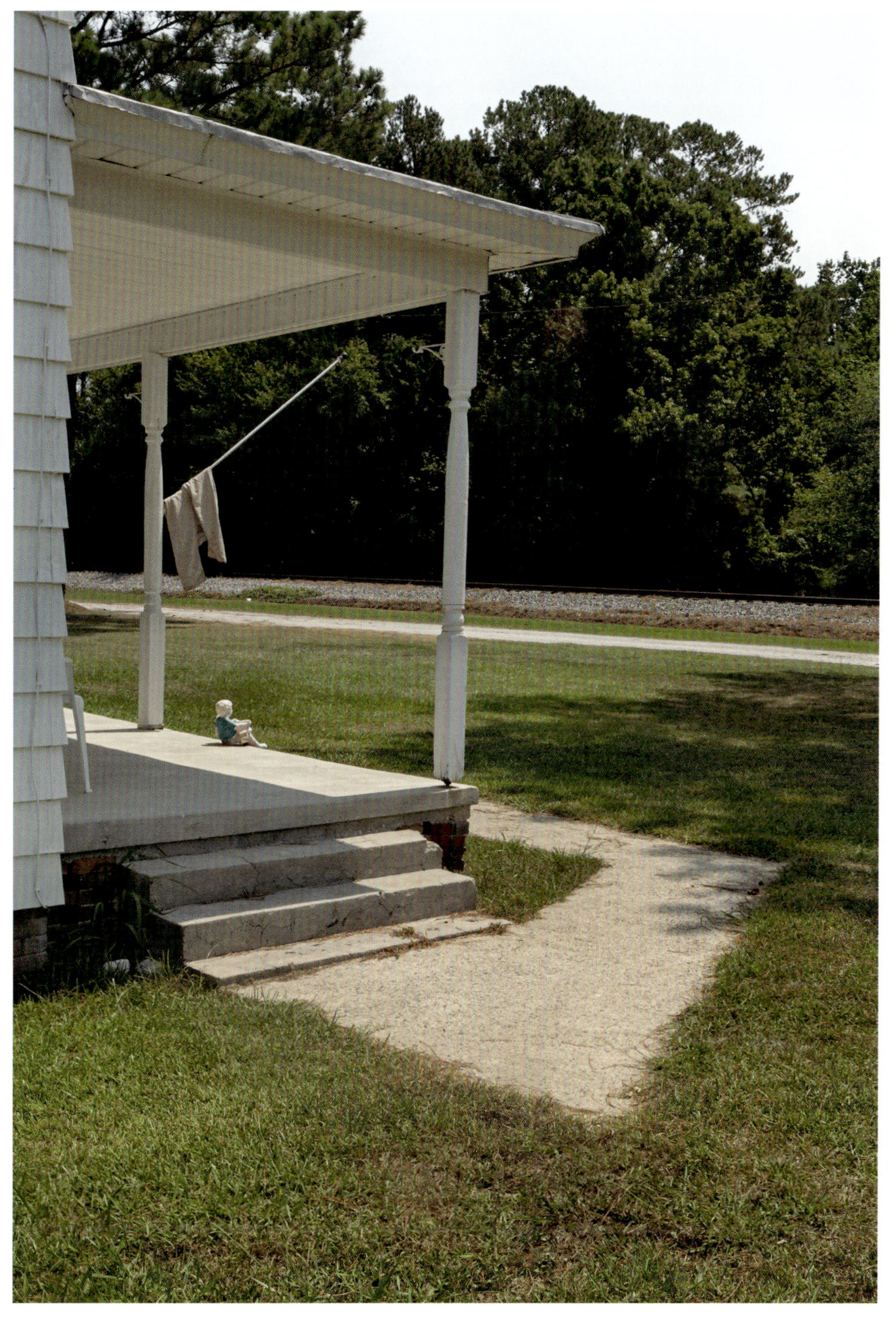

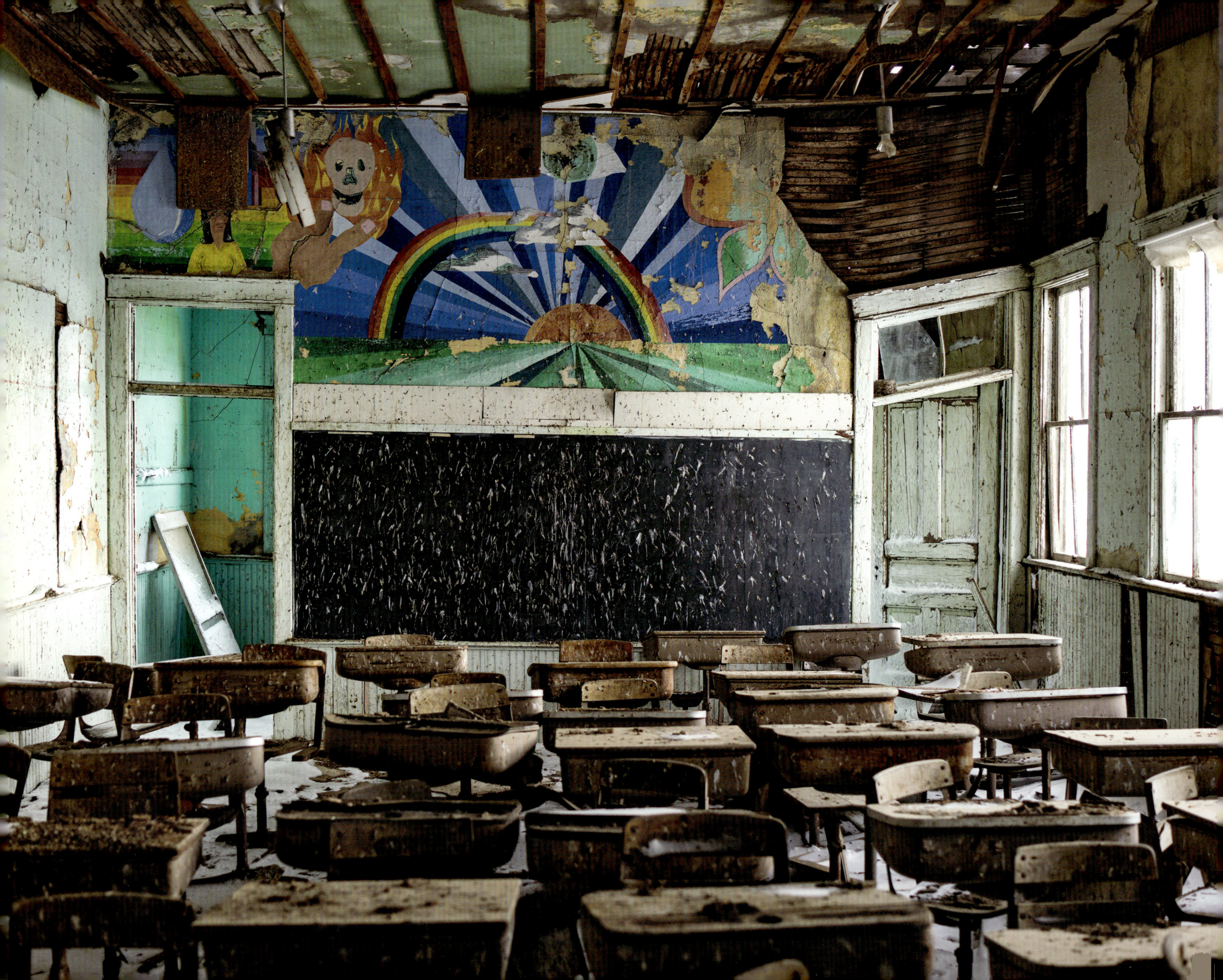

Umbrellas, Sewing Machines and Mirthless Frog Death

DAVID CAMPANY

Pick one of the photographs from this book. Any one. The one you like the most. Describe it. Put into words what you see, and what you think of what you see. The whole. The parts. The relations between the parts. The framing, the timing, the vantage point, the subject matter. The way the photographer's camera records, and transforms what it records, observing and shaping. The facts, the metaphors, the ironies. The sleight of hand and eye. Explain to yourself why you like it the most, if you can.

These are Charles H. Traub's taradiddles—plain and complex, straight shooting and evasive, and not altogether easy to describe. I think they are also profound in the way that photography seems uniquely predisposed to the profound: by being naturally and unapologetically light. That is, they are light about photography and light about the observable world. These images are also funny, and this presents an extra little twist to the challenge of description. *Analyzing a joke is like dissecting a frog: the frog dies and nobody laughs.* As they say. It's a joke about jokes. It fails to amuse and that is a special source of amusement. A joke at the expense of jokes. This has something to do with humor in photography generally, and with Traub's version of it in particular, for what amuses here is also bittersweet, startled, warped and woeful. Kindly consolation from a world awry. And at the risk of a little mirthless frog death, let us analyze it a little. These pictures can surely take it.

About photography there is always something a little surgical, a little dismembering. It's like an operating table. As Stephen Shore once noted, photography is an analytical medium. It studies what it pictures (or pictures what it studies), and this means that humor and analysis may coexist quite happily here, and by extension in the sensibility of the photographer. The set-up, the joke and its dissection come at the photographer, and then come at us, simultaneously. Suspended. Laid out. Laid bare.

There is always something a little surreal about photography too. That is a horribly abused adjective these days, so here's the source. The surrealists were thrilled and amused by Comte de Lautréamont's description from 1869 of a young boy being "as beautiful as the chance meeting on an operating table of a sewing-machine and an umbrella." They thrilled even more at the discovery that photography has such generous and easy access to chance encounter. To the stuff of life that you just cannot make up. The stuff that makes life, if not more livable, then at least thrilling and amusing from time to time.

What unites Traub's pictures here? They are all in one way or another about photography. They possibly even amount to a commentary upon photography as a phenomenon of daily life. Photography as something we do daily, and photographs as things we encounter daily, often by chance. To this extent at least, these are meta-photographs. And, when Traub is not including photographs within his frames, he's including frames within his frames, signs within his signs, representations within his representations. A hall of mirrors—monstrous, alluring and endearing.

This kind of self-awareness goes back all the way to the beginnings of photography. So many of the very earliest camera pictures were treatises on image making, on copying, doubling and reproduction. Indeed, the very earliest was a copy of a drawing. It was soon lost in the attempt to copy it in turn, and all we have to go on is a written account. As far as we know it wasn't funny but in its own way it must have been profound.

While the compulsion to make images of images is something of an origin story for photography, it is also an origin story for many photographers. Making emphatically reflexive images is something young photographers do to announce their intent and separate themselves from common snappers, or from their own temptation to snap commonly. In this way photographers underscore their position, amusing and thrilling to their own distanced measure. The first audience for any such photograph is usually the photographer. It's like practicing a joke in front of the mirror before telling friends.

There are other good reasons to include photographs within one's photographs. Chief among them is that it would be perverse not to.

“Photographs are,” as Susan Sontag famously put it, “perhaps the most mysterious of all the objects that make up, and thicken, the environment we recognize as ‘modern.’ ” That was in 1973. Since then photography has thickened the modern environment to the point of torpor, and maybe it has become a lot less mysterious in the process. Maybe not.

By 1973, Charles H. Traub had been serious and funny with a camera for a few years, and photographs had already found their way into some of his photographs. Being essentially restless, he has moved in all manner of directions in the intervening years, but something abides in his images of images. Perhaps he has now come full circle, accepting that one’s first intuitions about the medium will often remain the bedrock of a life’s picture making.

Getting to grips with a camera is not like learning the violin or the piano. You can pick up most of the technique in a very short space of time. A matter of weeks, or even days. It could hardly be simpler. And while it may take a lifetime to come to terms with what is possible with a camera, and what its implications are, that ease of access leaves a deep impression on most photographers. They know, or at least intuit, that something profound can be done with a camera almost immediately. That means mature work can be made very early. And in turn this complicates the idea of what it is for photographers to mature.

What work can photographers make after forty or fifty years that they couldn’t make in youth? Aside from self-portraits, it’s a difficult question to answer. We know what a late, great novel, or symphony, or suite of paintings can be, but such stature seems to elude photography, and when it is consciously reached for, the results are often excruciating. And so maybe, after decades of photography, what Charles H. Traub offers in his taradiddles is a renewal of humility. A good-natured coming to terms with the mere hill of beans.

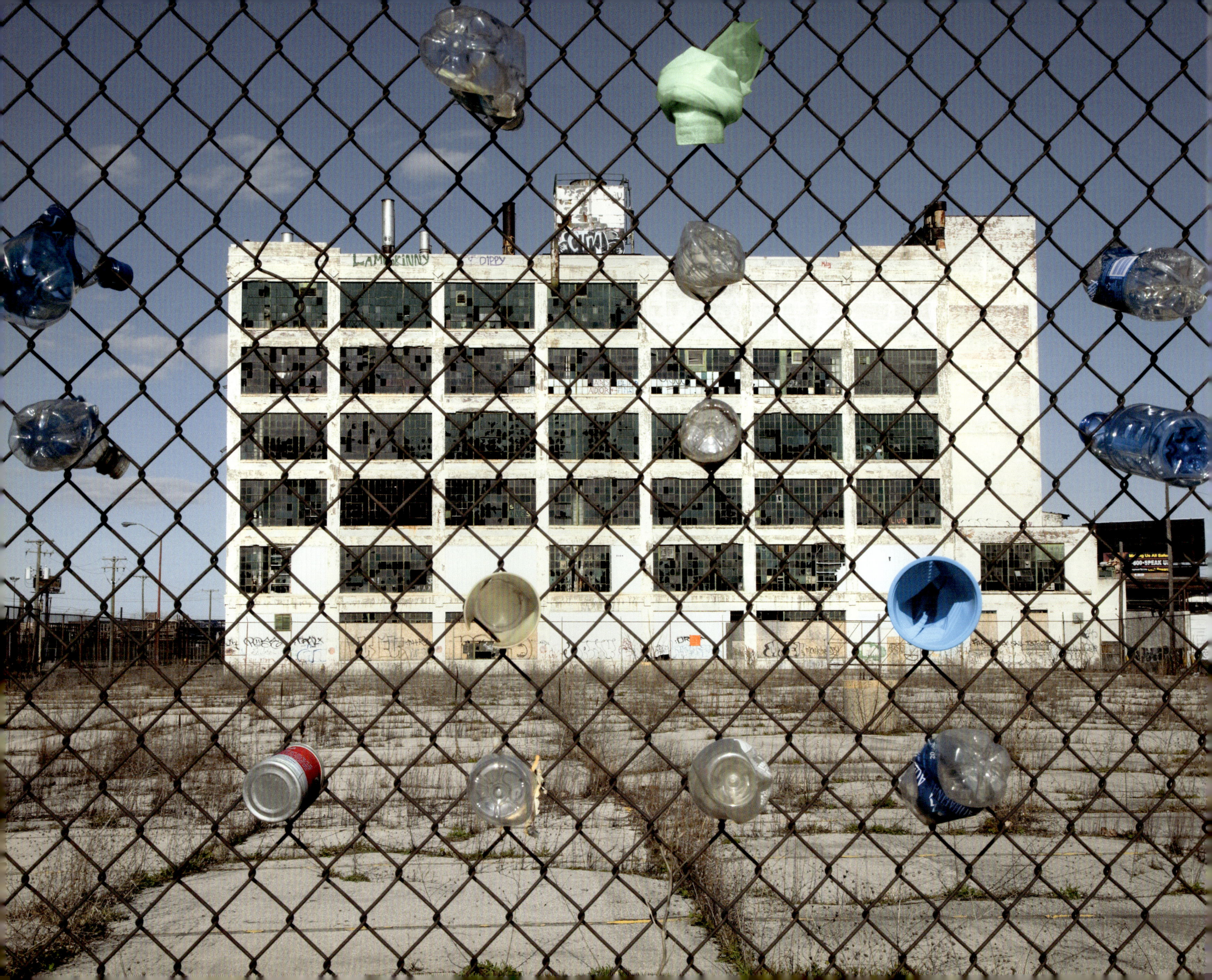

front cover: Monte Vista CO 2008
pg 1 Monte Vista CO 2008
pg 2 Tuscon AZ 2010
pg 3 Uncertain, USA 2007
pg 4 Todi, Italy 2017
pg 5 Assisi, Italy 2017
pg 6 Brooklyn, NY 2006
pg 7 New York City, NY 2003
pg 8 Verona, Italy 2004
pg 9 Ponca City, OK 2003
pg 10 Naples, Italy 2000
pg 11 New York City, NY 2003
pg 13 New York City, NY 2004
pg 14 Rio de Janeiro, Brazil 2006
pg 15 Bay of Kodor, Montenegro 2010
pg 16 Miami, FL 2003
pg 17 Padua, Italy 2004
pg 18 Cape Canaveral, FL 2007
pg 19 Uncertain, USA 2007
pg 20 Greenpoint, NY 2006
pg 21 Shanghai, China 2006
pg 22 Interstate 115, UT 2008
pg 23 Near El Paso, TX 2009
pg 24 Kansas City, MO 2009
pg 25 St. Petersburg, Russia 2003
pg 26 Padua, Italy 2004
pg 27 Rome, Italy 2007
pg 28 Bloomington, MN 2005

pg 29 Petropolis, Brazil 2005
pg 30 Santo Domingo,
Dominican Republic 2004
pg 31 New York City, NY 2001
pg 32 Detroit, MI 2009
pg 33 Cairo, IL 2011
pg 34 Uncertain, SC 2006
pg 35 Rome, Italy 2017
pg 36 New Orleans, LA 2007
pg 37 Albany, NY 2017
pg 38 Shanghai, China 2006
pg 39 Shanghai, China 2006
pg 40 Guthrie, OK 2003
pg 41 Route 44, SD 2007
pg 42 Rio de Janeiro, Brazil 2002
pg 43 Bloomington, MN 2010
pg 45 Bloomington, MN 2010
pg 46 New York City, NY 2017
pg 47 Wilmington, DE 2007
pg 48 Gettysburg, PA 2013
pg 49 Latrun, Israel 2000
pg 50 Rio de Janeiro, Brazil 2002
pg 51 Louisville, KY 2004
pg 52 NJ Turnpike, NJ 2007
pg 53 Niterói, Brazil 2006
pg 54 New York City, NY 2017
pg 55 Mt. Vernon, GA 2007
pg 56 Seaford, DE 2004

pg 57 Brooklyn, NY 2010
pg 58 Budapest, Hungary 2010
pg 59 Rapid City, SD 2007
pg 60 Monument Valley, UT 2008
pg 61 Fort Rice, ND 2016
pg 62 New York City, NY 2006
pg 63 Bloomington MN 2006
pg 64 Rio de Janeiro, Brazil 2006
pg 65 Delmarva Peninsula, USA 2004
pg 66 New York City, NY 2017
pg 67 Interstate 80, CO 2017
pg 68 Route 1, MS 2004
pg 69 Dubai, UAE 2011
pg 70 Meknes, Morrocco 2006
pg 71 Rio de Janeiro, Brazil 2008
pg 72 Pawling, NY 2003
pg 73 Tucson, AZ 2010
pg 74 New York City, NY 2017
pg 75 New York City, NY 2017
pg 76 Rio de Janeiro, Brazil 2005
pg 77 Zagreb, Croatia 2010
pg 78 Route 1, MS 2007
pg 79 New York City, NY 2007
pg 80 Petrovac, Montenegro 2010
pg 81 Four Corners, USA 2008
pg 82 Route 2, NE 2007
pg 83 Belize 2007
pg 84 New York City, NY 2011

pg 85 St. Petersburg, Russia 2003
pg 86 New York City, NY 2017
pg 87 Rio de Janeiro, Brazil 2006
pg 88 East Hampton, NY 2005
pg 89 Lone Pine, CA 2008
pg 90 Death Valley, CA 2009
pg 91 Chattanooga, TN 2006
pg 92 Lazise, Italy 2004
pg 93 Cairo, IL 2011
pg 94 Miami, FL 2009
pg 95 New York City, NY 2000
pg 96 Milan, Italy 2013
pg 97 Chicago, IL 2017
pg 98 Masaya, Nicaragua 2006
pg 99 Bloomington, MN 2010
pg 101 New Bern, NC 2007
opp. essay: Onida, SD
opp. where & when: Detroit, MI 2009
opp. acknowl: Meknes, Morocco 2006
last page: Gary, IN 2017
back cover: New Bern, NC 2007

For further information
about these images
please visit:
charlestraub.com/taradiddle/info

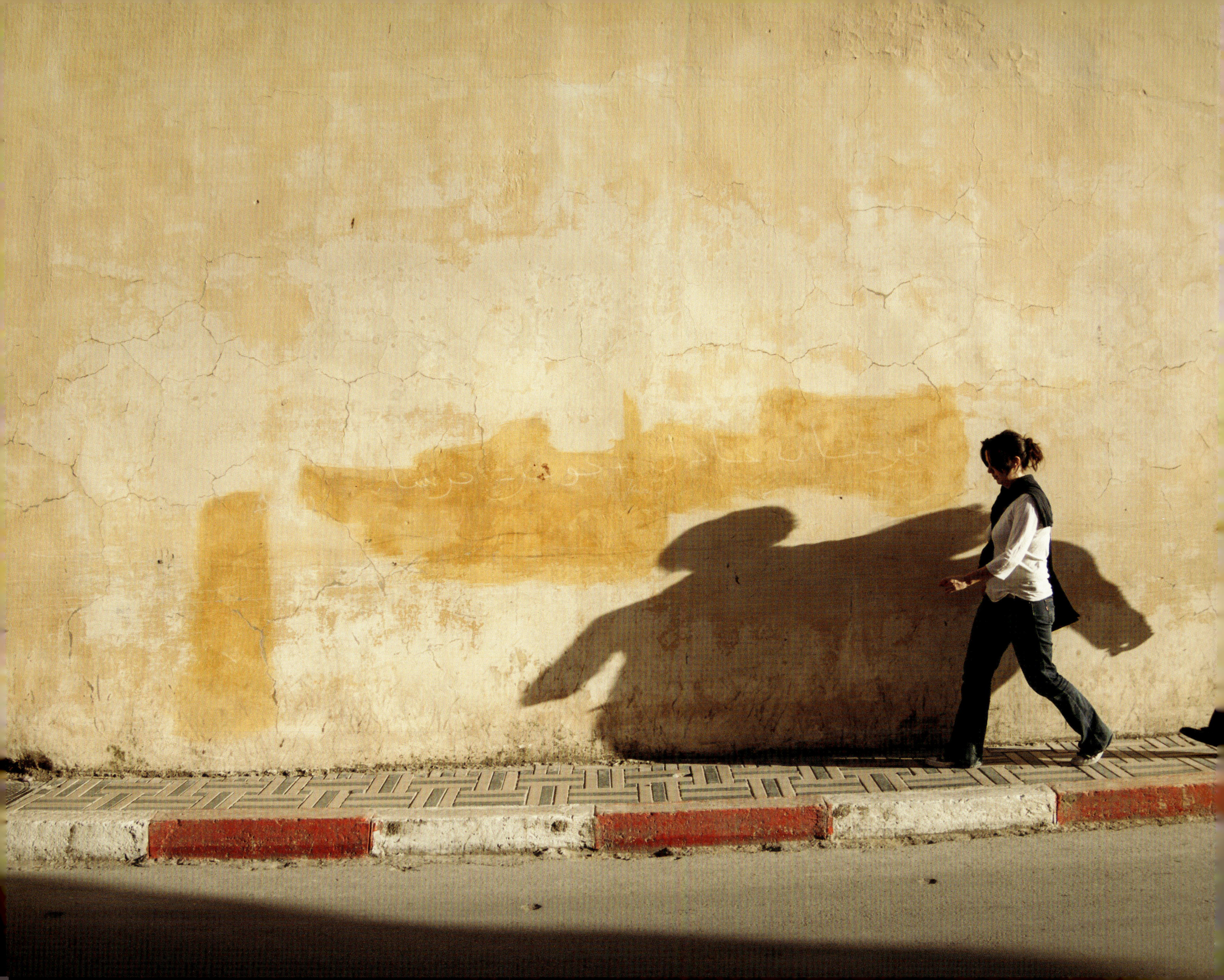

acknowledgements

These pictures were made on travels from 2002 to 2017. They were all observed in the real world and only when captured by my camera, as seen in a moment, did they become fabrications.

Matt Baum, Jonathan Lipkin and especially Kathy Shorr all helped enormously on those travels. They are all great photographers and great drivers. I am particularly grateful to Yoav Friedlander and Blake Ogden whose digital organization, post-production and printing brought these files to life. Deborah Hussey was and is always mindful of my texts. The design of this book is the creation of my friend David Schorr. In addition to being a remarkable designer, David is a great artist and an insightful editor—I dedicate this book to him. The School of Visual Arts and the MFA Photography, Video and Related Media program always supports my vision, and I am ever grateful. Lastly, I am greateful to David Campany whose writings has brought new context and meaning to these lies.

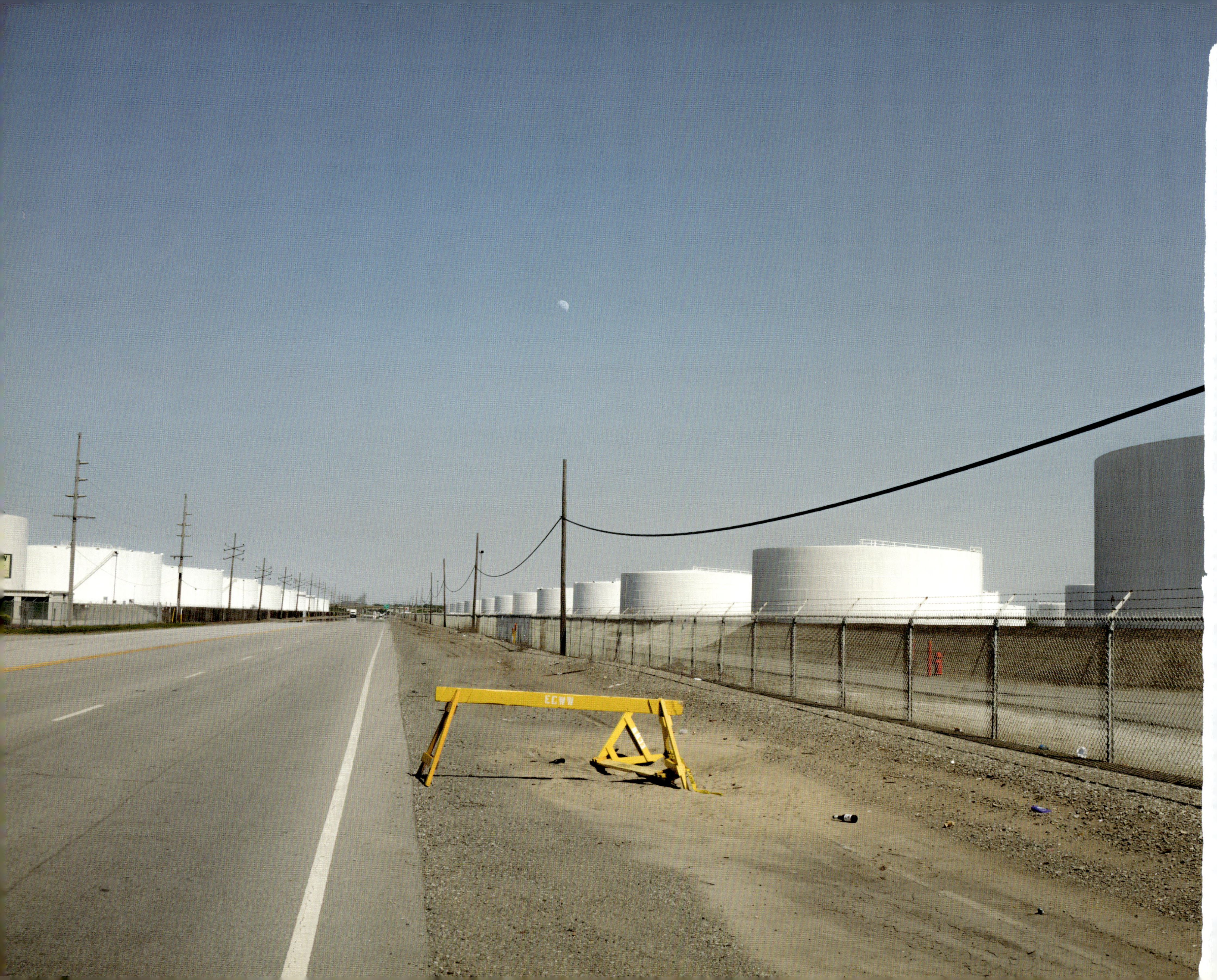
ECWW